Who Do the *Ngimurok* Say That They Are?

American Society of Missiology
Monograph Series

Series Editor, James R. Krabill

The ASM Monograph Series provides a forum for publishing quality dissertations and studies in the field of missiology. Collaborating with Pickwick Publications—a division of Wipf and Stock Publishers of Eugene, Oregon—the American Society of Missiology selects high quality dissertations and other monographic studies that offer research materials in mission studies for scholars, mission and church leaders, and the academic community at large. The ASM seeks scholarly work for publication in the series that throws light on issues confronting Christian world mission in its cultural, social, historical, biblical, and theological dimensions.

Missiology is an academic field that brings together scholars whose professional training ranges from doctoral-level preparation in areas such as Scripture, history and sociology of religions, anthropology, theology, international relations, interreligious interchange, mission history, inculturation, and church law. The American Society of Missiology, which sponsors this series, is an ecumenical body drawing members from Independent and Ecumenical Protestant, Catholic, Orthodox, and other traditions. Members of the ASM are united by their commitment to reflect on and do scholarly work relating to both mission history and the present-day mission of the church. The ASM Monograph Series aims to publish works of exceptional merit on specialized topics, with particular attention given to work by younger scholars, the dissemination and publication of which is difficult under the economic pressures of standard publishing models.

Persons seeking information about the ASM or the guidelines for having their dissertations considered for publication in the ASM Monograph Series should consult the Society's website—www.asmweb.org.

Members of the ASM Monograph Committe who approved this book are:

Robert Gallagher, Associate Professor of Intercultural Studies
    and Director of M.A. (Intercultural Studies),
        Wheaton College

Margaret Guider, O.S.F., Associate Professor of Missiology, Boston College

RECENTLY PUBLISHED IN THE ASM MONOGRAPH SERIES

Matthew Friedman, *Union with God in Christ: Early Christian and Wesleyan Spirituality as an Approach to Islamic Mysticism*

Megan Meyers, *Grazing and Growing in Mozambique: Developing Disciples through Contextualized Worship Arts*

Enoch Kim, *Receptor-Oriented Communication for Hui Muslims in China: With Special Reference to Church Planting*

Who Do the *Ngimurok* Say That They Are?

A Phenomenological Study of Turkana Traditional Religious Specialists in Turkana, Kenya

By Kevin Lines

American Society of Missiology Monograph
Series vol. 35

☙PICKWICK *Publications* · Eugene, Oregon

WHO DO THE NGIMUROK SAY THAT THEY ARE?
A Phenomenological Study of Turkana Traditional Religious Specialists in Turkana, Kenya

American Society of Missiology Monograph Series 35

Copyright © 2018 Kevin Lines. All rights reserved. Except for brief quotations in critical publications or reviews, no part of this book may be reproduced in any manner without prior written permission from the publisher. Write: Permissions, Wipf and Stock Publishers, 199 W. 8th Ave., Suite 3, Eugene, OR 97401.

Pickwick Publications
An Imprint of Wipf and Stock Publishers
199 W. 8th Ave., Suite 3
Eugene, OR 97401

www.wipfandstock.com

PAPERBACK ISBN: 978-1-4982-9802-5
HARDCOVER ISBN: 978-1-4982-9804-9
EBOOK ISBN: 978-1-4982-9803-2

Cataloguing-in-Publication data:

Names: Lines, Kevin.

Title: Who do the Ngimurok say that they are? : a phenomenological study of Turkana traditional religious specialists in Turkana, Kenya / Kevin Lines.

Description: Eugene, OR: Pickwick Publications, 2018 | Series: American Society of Missiology Monograph Series | Includes bibliographical references.

Identifiers: ISBN 978-1-4982-9802-5 (paperback) | ISBN 978-1-4982-9804-9 (hardcover) | ISBN 978-1-4982-9803-2 (ebook)

Subjects: LCSH: Turkana (African people)—Religion. | Kenya—Religion. | Experience (Religion).

Classification: LCC BL2480.T87 L45 2018 (print) | LCC BL2480.T87 (ebook)

Manufactured in the U.S.A.   04/04/18

Abstract

Who Do the *Ngimurok* Say That They Are?
A Phenomenological Study of Turkana Traditional Religious Specialists in Turkana, Kenya

This book is a missiological study of the phenomenon of traditional religious specialists in Turkana, Kenya, called *ngimurok*, and their relationship with Turkana Christians. Through an ethnographic-phenomenological approach, the study primarily provides a clearer understanding of the persistent and changing roles and practices of *ngimurok* in Turkana communities. It fills a void in the literature by offering a clear understanding of who the *ngimurok* are, defining what their roles are in Turkana communities, describing their rituals, and how they are connected to a persistent traditional religious understanding in Turkana. Seeking to avoid earlier colonial and social evolutionary descriptions, the study utilizes phenomenological self-defined descriptions provided by Turkana specialists themselves and those who consult with *ngimurok*. A complex view of *ngimurok* is presented through an analysis of 14 possible types of ritual specialists within the one category. Data is presented based on the researcher's lived experience in Turkana from 1999-2008, and an intensive research period in 2011, including 50 interviews, 33 with self-defined *ngimurok*, and a small sample survey of Turkana Christians. The study proposes an approach to religious specialists in Christian mission contexts that begins with phenomenological research as opposed to denunciation and demonization.

Contents

List of Tables and Figures | xi
Acknowledgments | xiii

1   Introduction to the Problem of *Ngimurok* | 1
    Introduction | 1
    A Research Problem | 5
    Outline of Book | 10
    Summary | 11

2   Research Objectives, Theories and Methodologies | 12
    Research Objectives and Research Questions | 13
    Theoretical Framework | 17
    Delimitations and Limitations of the Study | 36
    Research Methodology | 38
    Significance of the Study | 44

3   Definitions for the Study | 45
    Definition of Key Terms | 45
    Summary of Key Terms and Perspectives | 65

4   A Phenomenological Description of Turkana Religious Specialists | 66
    Introduction | 66
    Different types of *ngimurok* presented by the research participants | 74

Emuron of the Head who Dreams, the *Emuron* of God | 76

Emuron of Intestines and Sandals | 106

Emuron who Reads (Tobacco, Money) | 112

Akatuwan | 116

Summary of the Four Self-Identified Types of Ngimurok | 121

Malevolent Traditional Ritual Specialists | 125

Words used to Distinguish the Actions of the
Emuron, *Ekasuban*, and *Ekapilan* | 131

Other Traditional Ritual Specialists | 132

Three Additional Religious Specialists (Contested) | 133

Five Other Described Religious Specialists (Similar to *Ngimurok*) | 134

Other Descriptive Themes | 138

Other roles in the community | 148

Chapter Conclusion | 151

5 Specific Observed and Described Rituals and Ritual Objects of the *Ngimurok* | 154

Observed and Described Rituals | 154

Emuron Ritual Objects | 170

Conclusion of the Chapter | 173

6 What Turkana Ngimurok Say about Christians and What Turkana Christians say about Ngimurok: Ngimurok statements and a Turkana Christian Survey | 174

Ngimurok Statements about Christians | 175

A Turkana Christian Survey | 179

7 Conclusions: Toward a New Approach to Turkana Religious Specialists Today | 196

Overview of Accomplishments | 197

Evaluating the Research Objectives | 198

Further Missiological Implications | 207

Suggestions for Future Research | 209

Postscript | 211

Appendix A: Maps | 213
Appendix B: List of Interviews | 214
Appendix C: An *Emuron* Interview Model | 215
Appendix D: Rituals and Interviews Recorded on Video | 217
Appendix E: Photographs | 220
Appendix F: Glossary of Common Turkana Terms Related to *Ngimurok* Used in this Study | 226
Appendix G: Turkana Christian Survey Results
    G.A: A Sample Survey Response (two pages) | 230
    G.B: Complete Survey Responses | 232
    G.C: Graphs of Key Survey Responses | 249

Bibliography | 259

Tables and Figures

Table 1. Categories of Ngimurok Revealed From The Research | 76

Table 2. Confidence Levels of Turkana Christian Small Sample Survey | 180

Table 3. Gender of Survey Participants | 181

Table 4. Ages of Survey Participants | 181

Table 5. Clan (*Emachar*) Identification of Survey Participants | 181

Table 6. How Long Have You Been a Believer in Jesus Christ? | 183

Table 7. If a Church Leader, What is Your Position in the Church? | 183

Table 8. What Do You Think Are Reasons People Still Visit the *Ngimurok*? | 185

Table 9. Do You Personally Know Someone That Still Visits the *Ngimurok*? | 186

Table 10. Before You Were A Christian, How Many Times Did You Visit An *Emuron*? | 187

Table 11. After Becoming A Christian, How Many Times Did You Visit An *Emuron*? | 187

Table 12. What Are Good Things *Ngimurok* Have Done In Your Area In The Past And Now? | 188

Table 13. What Are Bad Things *Ngimurok* Have Done In Your Area In The Past And Now? | 189

Table 14. What Does Your Church Teach About The *Ngimurok*? | 189

Table 15. Where Do *Ngimurok* Power And Wisdom Come From? Turkana Christian Responses | 190

Table 16. From Your Understanding, What Are The Specific Practices That *Ngimurok* Do? | 192

Table 17. Is It Possible For A Pastor Or A Missionary To Be An *Emuron*? | 192

Table 18. Do You Know Any *Ngimurok* Who Are Followers of Jesus Who Still Do The Work Of An *Emuron*? | 193

Figure 1. Interdisciplinary Research Objectives | 16

Figure 2. What Do We Mean When We Classify Religions? | 21

Figure 3. Basic Sandal Throwing Configurations | 166

Figure 4. Extispicy Maps | 169

Figure 5. Separate Categories of Religious Specialists before the Introduction of Christianity (Priest 2012) | 202

Figure 6. The Category Shift after Christianity (Priest 2012) | 203

Figure 7. The Religious Specialist Category Shift in Turkana | 204

Acknowledgments

A project such as this cannot be accomplished without the help and support of many people. Foremost, I must thank the people of Turkana who have so many times welcomed me into their lives: The many church leaders who attended the Turkana Bible Training Institute who studied and prayed with me; The people of the villages of Kangirisae, Loupwala and Kaakimat who shared daily life with us; James Ibei Eipa who never gave up on me as I learned the Turkana language.

Many thanks to the missionaries who have supported us: Those we served alongside in Turkana: Bruens, Chapmans, Hams, Jaynes, Mordens, Pottenger, Westfalls; you will always be family. And those who served before us and helped to shape us: Rosses and Giles; someday I hope to be like you!

For those who have instilled in me a desire to study and learn both creatively and critically, I am forever indebted: Dr. Susan Higgins and Dr. Phil Kenneson at Milligan College; Dr. Charles R. Taber and Dr. Fred Norris at Emmanuel Christian Seminary; Dr. Eunice Irwin, Dr. Michael Rynkiewich, Dr. Steve Ybarrola and Dr. Terry Muck at Asbury Theological Seminary; every student I teach receives a small part of your wisdom.

I would especially like to thank the financial supporters of this project: Hill N Dale Christian Church in Lexington, KY and CMF International in Indianapolis, IN.

Finally, my family has been an ever-present joy and source of encouragement as I struggled through the difficulties of being far away during research and equally distant during my times of writing. Katy, you have carried me so often that I would surely be lost on my own by now. Patrick and Brian, I pray that you too will someday find the joy that comes from serving God with all your heart, soul *and* mind!

1

Introduction to the Problem of *Ngimurok*

INTRODUCTION

CHRISTIAN FAITH AMONG THE Turkana people of northwest Kenya is currently varied and intermingled with traditional Turkana religious practices. During my eight years of living among the Turkana people of northwest Kenya, my experience was that many people, both Christian and non-Christian, continued to be heavily influenced by traditional religious specialists called *ngimurok*.[1] While this influence seemed clear, numerous inconsistencies would present themselves, especially in light of Western missionaries and Turkana church leaders consistently teaching that *ngimurok* are dangerous, received their powers from the Evil One (*Ekipe*), Satan, and needed to be avoided. Yet, just as persistently, Turkana *ngimurok* continued to be sought out and consulted, even by many Christians, for a multitude of reasons: when there is an illness in the family, when animals become ill, when ancestors speak to the family through possession, when sacrifices and prayers are required for rain, before participating in a cattle raid, when animals are lost, when curses are cast, and at other times for various reasons. But in spite of these arguably benevolent roles *ngimurok* are known to play in the community, a tension

---

1. *Ngimurok* is the plural form of *emuron* (masc.) and *amuron* (fem.). These traditional religious specialists have been described in English as "witch-doctor," "diviner," "sacrifice-prophet," "priest," "healer" and "medicine man," among others. See the *Definition of Key Terms* below for a complete list of understandings. My position, as a researcher undertaking a phenomenological study of *ngimurok*, is to use the Turkana terms for these specialists. When clarification is needed, I have provided the reader a "Glossary of Common Turkana Terms Related to *Ngimurok*" in the Appendix.

2   Who Do the Ngimurok Say That They Are?

remains between the traditional roles of the *ngimurok* and the doctrines of the Christian churches in Turkana.[2]

One controversial example is found in the person of Nayoken,[3] an *emuron* with the ability to "read" tobacco leaves in the Kachala village near to where the Kalabata and Kerio rivers join. Church leaders from a nearby village would visit Nayoken's village for times of informal teaching and worship centered on Scripture and God's revelation of salvation through Jesus. Eventually an evangelistic event took place in Kachala, with nearly everyone accepting the message of Jesus together after four days of teaching, fellowship, the sharing of meals, and worship. Clear teaching was presented concerning the evils of *ngimurok*, with everyone mindful that Nayoken was himself an *emuron*. On the day when a decision was called for, there was little discussion; Nayoken and the other Turkana elders from the village decided to become Christians. Including the *emuron* Nayoken and the other elders, 130 people were baptized the week before Christmas, 2002, in the village of Kachala.

During regular Turkana church leader meetings and discussions I attended in 2003, Nayoken was mentioned numerous times. He was well known for his ability to answer people's questions by reading tobacco leaves. People would hire trucks in the town of Lodwar, the district capital, and travel the difficult four-hour, 110 kilometer, trip into the "bush" to ask questions of Nayoken and pay for his services. The church leaders did not think he should continue his *emuron* practices as a Christian and requested that I go with them to talk to him. Although old, Nayoken was a very strong man, both physically and intellectually, and thus was more intimidating than many *ngimurok* I have met. His response to the request to stop the *emuron* practices was simple: it was *Akuj*, the creator God, who gave him the ability to read tobacco leaves, and he saw no reason to stop using an ability that God had given him.

Even after repeated visits (some were concerning this issue, but most were for teaching and worship in the community), the issue was not resolved in the minds of the Turkana church leaders. To this day, Turkana church leaders do not know what to do with Nayoken. He supports the church, attends most worship services held in his village, and his family is

---

2. The larger church movements in Turkana that I am most familiar with, to which this statement applies, includes: Community Christian Church, the Catholic Church, AIC, RCEA, and the Full Gospel Churches of Kenya. These Christian doctrines concerning *ngimurok* were collected and summarized in chap. 6.

3. The names of *ngimurok* research participants and their locations have been changed to allow for anonymity. This is in accordance with agreements made at the times of the interviews and the ethical considerations outlined in chap. 2.

comprised of some very strong, faithful Christians; and although a leader in his community, his continued practice as an *emuron* is outwardly prohibited by the church and does not allow him to be recognized or trained as an official church leader.[4]

Reflecting on these difficulties, I began to notice other inconsistencies between Western missionaries' Christian profession of faith and the daily practices of Turkana Christians in the Turkana context. While Turkana Christians agreed in church that *ngimurok* were evil and to be avoided, it seemed that the *ngimurok* still played an influential positive role in many of the small rural communities where a majority of the people had become Christians. Paul Hiebert, Tite Tiénou and Daniel Shaw recognize this as a common occurrence throughout the world, wherever traditional religion is practiced: "people who become Christians continue to turn to shamans, diviners, medicine men, witch doctors and magicians to deal with their everyday problems of life."[5]

Many missiologists[6] follow Hiebert, Tiénou, and Shaw in describing this condition as "split-level Christianity": a form of Western Christianity adopted in non-Western contexts that focuses on the official teachings of the church but lacks the provision of answers to contextual problems, leading to simultaneously continued practice of folk beliefs, often hidden from the church leaders.[7] Hiebert, Shaw, and Tiénou suggest that while our first reaction to traditional religious practices that seem to contradict the gospel is a desire to "stamp them out," this would only lead to the practices being further hidden, making them even more difficult to address. The goal of missionaries and church leaders should not be to stamp out wrong practices, "but to transform churches into living communities where the gospel is heard and applied to all of life."[8] Christ has the power to transform and answer the questions raised by traditional religion, but the "answers must be rooted in a biblical, not an animistic, worldview."[9]

---

4. In fact, during my three days at Nayoken's home during my field research in 2011, in which he openly shared both his clients and practices with me, he repeatedly lauded me for being the one who brought the church to his area. In reality, it was the local Turkana church leaders who shared their faith in the area with my assistance. But the harmony in which he continues to hold both Christian faith and Turkana traditional ritual is a key issue for my research.

5. Hiebert, Tiénou, and Shaw, *Understanding Folk Religion*, 88.

6. More recently, see Moon, *African Proverbs*, 3; and Kraft, *Appropriate Christianity*, 60, although Kraft also credits the term "split-level Christianity" to Bulatao, *Split-Level Christianity*, 1966.

7. Hiebert, Tiénu, and Shaw, *Understanding Folk Religion*, 90–92.

8. Ibid., 92.

9. Ibid.

4   Who Do the Ngimurok Say That They Are?

From my years in Turkana as a missionary, and this subsequent research, my estimation is that Western missionaries and Turkana church leaders have tried to "stamp out" the role of the *ngimurok* in the lives of Turkana, but have been unsuccessful at either the stamping out or the equipping of the church to deal with the epistemological foundations that *ngimurok* symbolize in Turkana. Christian communities in Turkana have learned to relate to their traditional religion in patterns of "denunciation or of separateness" while "dialogue has been distinctively absent."[10] For Bediako, this was the pattern of mission in Africa, clearly defined when the Edinburgh 1910 missionary conference "concluded that African traditional religions... probably contained no preparation for Christianity."[11]

While there were certainly exceptions to this view,[12] religious theory at the end of the 19th century and beginning of the 20th century generally evaluated the religious traditions of Africa as the most primitive, least evolved, and furthest from the understandings of Christianity. Divination and spirit possession were summarily described by E. B. Tylor as a "savage theory... which has been for ages, and still remains, the dominant theory of disease and inspiration among the lower races."[13] Of course, Tylor was not so much interested in understanding the "savage lower races," as he was in tracing these primal practices "from grade to grade of civilization, breaking away piecemeal under the influence of new medical theories," in order to better understand enlightened "modern life."[14] As with most religious scholars during Tylor's era, the search was on to trace the evolution of religion from primitive animism to monotheism and onward toward an inevitable modern scientific humanism.

My experience has been that similar social evolutionary views persist in the church in regard to traditional religious understandings, especially among the mission initiated churches in Africa. Bediako explains the situation as one in which the church is marked by separateness rather than engagement with the culture:

> The Christian tradition as historically received through the missionary enterprise has, on the whole, been unable to sympathise

---

10. Bediako, *Christianity in Africa*, 69.

11. Ibid.

12. J. Stanley Friesen refutes Bediako's position on Edinburgh 1910 and points to the influence in 1910 of Henry Callaway's application of Fulfilment Theology to his meticulous examination of the Amazulu as a missionary as early as 1868, as a clear example, among others, who did see "animism" as a preparation for the gospel. But, Calloway's was certainly a minority view. See Friesen, *Missionary Responses*, 5, 146.

13. Tylor, *Religion in Primitive Culture*, 210.

14. Ibid., 211.

with or relate to the spiritual realities of the traditional worldview. It is not so much a case of an unwillingness to relate to these realities, as of not having learnt to do so.[15]

This research project is my contribution to the church in Turkana and the churches in East Africa of "learning to do so." That is, of viewing the traditional religion and the *ngimurok* as sincere and authentic ways of seeing and understanding that persist within Christian faith in Turkana and many parts of Africa; not as atavistic characteristics, but connected to the sincere epistemology of a people. As Andrew Walls contends, "What happens in African Christianity is intelligible only in the light of what has gone before in the African religious story."[16] If we seek to comprehend Turkana religious understandings through the *ngimurok*, we will also gain an understanding of Christianity in Turkana that is inevitably connected to and built upon a Turkana epistemology.

A RESEARCH PROBLEM

I recently received an email reply from an American missionary in Turkana regarding my research:

> Your research approach makes sense to me and I think it would be valuable to get all those concerned thinking more about how to deal with diviners[17] and their belief systems.
>
> You should know that I have declared war on diviners. I am urging everyone to bring me the names of diviners, small or big so we can have concentrated prayers for them to be saved. In the spiritual warfare class taught earlier this month [at the Turkana Bible Training Institute in Lodwar, Kenya,] we addressed diviners and acknowledged that several have said they work directly for Satan and do what he tells them. We addressed that many believers back slide and ask diviners for help when troubles come. The class, at least in word, said that it was wrong and acknowledged that the works of Satan and diviners are against God's plan and all offerings to diviners are to false gods. But how they live it out is still the real question. (July 2011)

---

15. Bediako, *Christianity in Africa*, 69.
16. Walls, *Cross-Cultural Process*, 120.
17. Most English speakers in Turkana use the term "diviners" for *ngimurok*. This follows Gulliver (*Preliminary Survey of the Turkana*), whose report was very influential in shaping the understandings of the first Catholic and Protestant missionaries to Turkana who arrived in the 1960s. Subsequent missionaries have followed this pattern, although many have never read Gulliver.

6   Who Do the Ngimurok Say That They Are?

This email highlights the fact that missionaries and church leaders in Turkana most often associate traditional Turkana *ngimurok* with satanic or demonic forces, evaluating all the work of Turkana diviners in a negative light. Indeed, this follows common evangelical missiological evaluations of traditional divination practices, that "divination is opposed to the very nature of God."[18]

Yet careful reading of other evangelical missiological writings, with which I am more sympathetic, reveal a nuanced approach that considers the assessing of motivations for seeking answers in divination a priority over demonization, and understanding the distinctions between manipulative divination and divination that occasionally appears in the biblical narrative that asserts God's control over a situation.[19] David Burnett goes so far as to suggest that some forms of divination misunderstood in the West might be biblical "spiritual gifts that have often been neglected" and "have become so meaningful in the global expansion of the Pentecostal and Charismatic movements."[20] This view is supported by those who point to a more ambivalent view of divination in the early church in the Bible, specifically in relation to casting lots, dream interpretations and even the Persian loan word for "magician," that appears to more accurately denote "a highly respected, learned and wise member of a priestly caste" than some form of demonization.[21]

Furthermore, my research reveals that the role of the *emuron* in Turkana is not entirely limited to religious practices as a separate function from everyday life, as most *ngimurok* are also seen as leaders in their communities. Some *ngimurok* have roles relating to the unity of the community and often provide leadership among the elders when adjudicating disputes in the community, especially in cases of continued drought or in regards to the proper implementation of rituals.[22] The *ngimurok* are links to both negative and positive communal knowledge, consistent with the "African perception of the connectedness among the dead, the community of the living, and the cosmic order."[23] While much of Turkana traditional religion is based on the fear of offending the ancestors and spirits (*ngikaram* and *ngipean*), the *ngimurok* are often seen as helpful, positive and unifying influences in regard to the everyday needs in the community, often providing protection

---

18. Van Rheenen, *Communicating Christ*, 192.
19. Hiebert, Tiénou, and Shaw, *Understanding Folk Religion*, 190–91.
20. Burnett, *World of the Spirits*, 120.
21. Klauck, *Magic and Paganism*, 15.
22. Barrett, *Sacrifice and Prophecy in Turkana Cosmology*, 109.
23. Magesa, *What is Not Sacred?*, 91.

Introduction to the Problem of Ngimurok

from the sources of fear in the world. Indeed, my research confirms both qualitatively and quantitatively that many Turkana Christians continue to turn to the *ngimurok* in times of need (Chapter 6).

A Lack of Clarity concerning Ngimurok

It is apparent that a lack of clarity has existed in understanding who the *ngimurok* are and what their influence and roles are in current Turkana communities. This lack of clarity through divergent views can be found in early explorer/military reports of those who were impressed with the strength of Turkana "witch-doctors";[24] early colonial anthropologist reports that affirmed the British subjugation and current insignificance of Turkana "diviners";[25] missionary reports and interactions with *ngimurok* as "witch doctors" that practice "ancient weird rites,"[26] with varied descriptions of the Turkana as "non-religious," to dualists, to practical pastoralists with no religious understanding in everyday life, to commonly referring to God, *Akuj*, in their daily conversations;[27] and more recent anthropological research in the region that notes the importance of *ngimurok* but are limited in their scope of contemporary roles and practices.[28]

With such a wide range of writings on Turkana religion and *ngimurok*, it is surprising that most recent studies relating to key issues for Turkana today, including food security,[29] water resources,[30] and cattle-raiding,[31] make no mention of the connections between these issues and the roles of the

24. White, "Notes on the Turkana Tribe"; Teleki in Hohnel, *Discovery of Lakes*.

25. Gulliver, *Preliminary Survey of the Turkana*; and Gulliver, *Central Nilo-Hamites*.

26. Anderson, *Team for Turkana*, 31.

27. Barrett, *Incarnating the Church*; Bruen, "*Akipeyos Nachamunet*"; Davis, "Church Growth"; Giles, "Folk Religion of the Turkana"; Jagt, *Symbolic Structures*; Tingle, "Relationship of Evangelism"; Grenham, *Unknown God*. Thomas Grenham's 2005 dissertation is especially frustrating in this regard. He does a magnificent job of tracing mission history, moving from inculturation to his new mission paradigm "interculturation," and providing biblical and theological support for interculturation, then claims that a Turkana Christian Christology of Jesus as the great *Emuron* is a perfect example. All that lacks is the foundational research into who the *ngimurok* actually are!

28. Best, *Culture and Language*; Lamphear, "Aspects of Turkana Leadership"; Sakumichi, "Coping with Illness"; Barrett, *Sacrifice and Prophecy in Turkana Cosmology*; Collins, "Turkana Patrol of 1918."

29. Leslie, *Turkana Herders*; Boogaard, "Food Insecurity"; Wawire, *Gender and the Social*; Homewood, *Ecology of African Pastoralist Societies*; Tagliaferri, "Impact of Nutrition"; Juma, "Turkana Livelihood Strategies."

30. DeLuca, "Fluid Intake."

31. Hendrickson, Armon, and Mearns, "Changing Nature of Conflict"; Gray et al., "Cattle Raiding"; McCabe, *Cattle Bring Us to Our Enemies*.

ngimurok. While ethnohistorical accounts of the Turkana place great importance on the *ngimurok* leading the resistance against the colonial powers during the first two decades of the 20th century,[32] and most accounts of *ngimurok* report one of their important roles as blessing those about to engage in cattle raiding and profiting significantly from the raids,[33] those seeking solutions to cattle raiding in the region almost exclusively take the anti-essentialist position of finding causality in external factors.[34] In spite of the apparent connections, an examination of the role of *ngimurok* in cattle raiding is missing in the many peace plans of the region.[35]

A Lack of Data Concerning Ngimurok

Much of what one finds written on Turkana religion in general and *ngimurok* specifically are merely reiterations of Gulliver's 1951 report and Barrett's 1998 dissertation. In my assessment, both of these studies are lacking in the research data needed to clearly explicate the persistent roles of Turkana *ngimurok*.

Gulliver's report notes that he spoke with only one Turkana *emuron* "at all well," only had a brief encounter with another, and admits to have only heard the names of six *ngimurok* during his research in 1948–9.[36] Yet,

32. Lamphear, "Aspects of Turkana Leadership"; Lamphear, *Scattering Time*; Collins, "Turkana Patrol of 1918."

33. Gulliver, *Preliminary Survey*; Barrett, *Sacrifice and Prophecy in Turkana Cosmology*.

34. Gray et al., "Cattle Raiding."

35. I have dealt extensively with this issue in an unpublished paper, "Is Turkana Cattle Raiding a Part of Turkana Ethnicity: An Anti-Anti-Essentialist View of Turkana *Ngingoroko*," in which I argue that often, the root causes of cattle raiding are identified by peace-seeking non-government organizations as directly related to 1) the scarcity of resources in the harsh arid environment and the ensuing poverty, and 2) the availability of automatic weapons (AK-47s). I argue that these external factors alone are insufficient in describing the root causes of Turkana cattle raiding. Internal ethno-religio factors, including the structure of a moral economy, the belief in divine ethnic election, and the role of traditional religious specialists (*ngimurok*) must also be examined as root causes for anyone seeking solutions to the problems of cattle raiding in the Northern Rift Valley.

36. Gulliver, *Preliminary Survey*, 240. John Lamphear confirms this lack of contact with *ngimurok*: "British administrators were perplexed to find that while 'witchcraft' was common, there seemed to be hardly any witch-doctors. A few cases were tried under the Witchcraft Ordinance, but punishments were relatively light and the British considered them only minor affairs. By the late 1940s many British officials serving in *Eturkan* were utterly unaware that the office of diviner existed at all. Even P. H. and Pamela Gulliver, the first professional scholars to study Turkana society, found the people hesitant to discuss magico-religious matters and gathered very little information on diviners" (Lamphear, *Scattering Time*, 249).

Gulliver provides eight pages of text on the hierarchy and types of *ngimurok*.[37] It is my belief that Gulliver's "hierarchy of diviners" came less out of his experience in Turkana and more from an expectation that there would be a hierarchy as described by others. For example, see Callaway,[38] or even Frazer's various classifications of magicians as kings, priests, those who controlled the weather, performed sacrifices, and expelled evil.[39] Following the biological sciences, classification and hierarchy was of the utmost importance in this period of history; "What Linnaeus had done for the botanical world was now being done for religion. The world of the sacred had to be mapped and its species, its 'classes of phenomena,' named and typed."[40]

Gulliver's conclusion was that the present day *ngimurok* play an insignificant role in Turkana life, and, most importantly to the colonial administration he worked for, "as things stand in Turkanaland, it is unlikely that diviners will be a source of trouble in the future anymore than they have been in the last two decades" because of the "efficient subjugation of the country."[41] While Gulliver's survey will stand the test of time as an impressive early ethnography of Turkana, his colonial concerns cloud its usefulness for understanding *ngimurok* today.

Barrett, who writes an entire chapter of his dissertation on *ngimurok*, dividing them into categories based on types of divination and following Gulliver's previous hierarchy, admits to relying heavily on his relationship with only one diviner, *Natuba*, in the Western part of Turkana.[42] Most of his other data came through his research assistant, *Ewalan*, who is not an *emuron*.[43] Indeed, Barrett's objective is to understand the meaning of sacrifice in Turkana, in which *ngimurok* play a significant part, but are not the focus of his study. His focus on *ngimurok* as the "sacrificer-prophets" provides a limited view of *ngimurok*, as even his own descriptions (following Gulliver) include *ngimurok* who are not involved in sacrifices.

Statement of the Problem

Thus, in the anthropological literature, missiological literature, religious studies literature, development studies literature and in the current situation of the church in Turkana, there is not a clear understanding of who

37. Gulliver, *Preliminary Survey*, 233–41.
38. Callaway, *Religious System*, 327.
39. Frazer *Golden Bough*.
40. Paden, *Religious Worlds*, 43.
41. Gulliver, *Preliminary Survey*, 241.
42. Barrett, *Sacrifice and Prophecy in Turkana Cosmology*, 16.
43. Ibid., 17

the *ngimurok* are, what their roles are in Turkana communities, what it is that they actually do, and how they are connected to a persistent traditional religious understanding and epistemology in Turkana. **This present study, through an ethnographic-phenomenological approach, primarily provides a clearer understanding of the persistent and changing roles and practices of *ngimurok* in Turkana communities.** Seeking to avoid earlier colonial and social evolutionary descriptions, I pursue self-defined descriptions provided by Turkana specialists themselves and those who consult with *ngimurok*. Seeking a clearer understanding through this research does not mean a simple explanation or conclusion will be provided. To the contrary, my current understanding after field research and analysis is that there are a complex range of various practitioners and practices in Turkana that are encompassed by the term *ngimurok*. Common religious studies categories of Shaman, Diviner, Witchdoctor, Witch, Priest, Healer, Prophet, Sorcerer, Magician, Ritual Specialist, et al, are each lacking in their ability to equate in parallel terms with the Turkana *emuron*. A Turkana *emuron* is best described in the category of *Emuron* in the local understanding long before being placed in a religious studies meta-category. I have sought here to describe and place *ngimurok* more articulately, more fully, more accurately, yet complexly, in the Turkana context than has previously been accomplished.

OUTLINE OF BOOK

In Chapter 1, the background of the study and my personal connection to the research is explained. The research problem is stated. Chapter 2 describes the research objectives and theoretical framework of the study within the interdisciplinary nature of the field of intercultural studies. My research methodologies are provided. Chapter 3 reviews the historical understandings of religion in Africa, and provides a review of the relevant literature covering studies of religious specialists and theories of understanding religious specialists in Africa. I also present the ways Turkana *ngimurok* have previously been understood in the literature. Other key terms for the study are defined. Chapter 4 provides an "exhaustive" description of the phenomenon of *ngimurok* in Turkana as revealed through my research participants and observations. Chapter 5 provides a description of rituals I was privileged to witness, along with other rituals of the *ngimurok* that were described to me by the *ngimurok*. This chapter also includes descriptions of the ritual objects that are regularly used by the *ngimurok*, especially the varieties of ochre and sticks. Chapter 6 begins with *ngimurok* descriptions of their relationship with Christians, then presents the findings of my survey of Turkana Christians regarding the *ngimurok*. This helps provide a snapshot of the current understandings of Turkana *ngimurok* found to be present among Turkana Christians. The data from this survey provides an opportunity to discuss the congruities and incongruities found in *ngimurok* self-descriptions and Turkana Christian descriptions of the *ngimurok*. Chapter 7 concludes the study with implications from the research for African religious studies, development issues in the region, and missiological issues for the church. The appendix includes maps, documentation of interviews, a glossary, photographs, an index of key oral stories and rituals recorded, complete survey data, the lineages of three ancestral *ngimurok* families, and selected interview transcripts in the Turkana language.

SUMMARY

For too long our tendency in churches, even in mission circles, has been to demonize the religious other, especially those seen as "primitive" religious practitioners. Instead of an approach of demonization, this research seeks to understand Turkana religious specialists from their own perspective. I humbly believe that Turkana Christians and Western missionaries would benefit from understanding the *ngimurok* through their own words; not as an attack on the validity of the roles of *ngimurok*, but in seeking to understand why the role of the *ngimurok* has persisted and continues to make sense in Turkana epistemology.

I have given years of my life for both this study and the church in Turkana because I do not see fruit in followers of Jesus in Turkana who merely seek to imitate the Western culture-bound faith of the missionaries who have shared the message of Jesus with them. Instead, my hope is that Christians in Turkana will learn to reflect upon what it means to be followers of Jesus as *Ngiturkana*, the people of *Turkan*, and that thoughtful connections will be made between the ways that God has spoken in continuity to the Turkana in the past and in the present.

This research does not seek to further romanticize the exotic nature of an African Traditional Religion, but to describe it through the words of those who continue to specialize in it. My hope is that this new data will provide fruit for the Christians and missionaries seeking to understand their own faith in the Turkana context, fruit for those who study African Traditional Religions as authentic contemporary ways of understanding, fruit for those who study the peoples of Eastern Africa, and fruit for those future descendants of Lokorijem, Lokedongan, and Lokerio seeking to understand their own identities who, in the near future, may no longer even speak the Turkana language.[44]

---

44. The ISO 639-3 code identifier for the Turkana language is tuv; see http://www-01.sil.org/iso639-3/documentation.asp?id=tuv.

2

Research Objectives, Theories, and Methodologies

INTERCULTURAL STUDIES IS AN interdisciplinary field that requires the intersection of Christian theology, religious studies, anthropology and history. The interdisciplinary nature of the field can create a complex theoretical web that supports and sustains intercultural studies research projects, occasionally to the detriment of the clarity of the research. The task of the intercultural studies researcher is to clarify the objectives of the research and describe the theories that sustain the research through this complex interdisciplinary matrix without losing sight of the primary goal of the research. While multiple tangential theories and objectives might be touched upon that are consistent with the field of intercultural studies, a focus must be selected for the purpose of the study.

In this chapter I state the specific research questions and objectives from three particular areas of study: religious studies phenomenology, interpretive anthropology, and Christian theology. After summarizing these objectives, the main theoretical framework for the study is described through each of these areas of study. Finally, I describe the methodologies employed, the limitations of the study and the ethical considerations.

While SIL and Ethnologue assign the Turkana language a hopeful "5: developing" on the EGIDS development and engagement scale and do not consider the language currently at risk for generational transmission disruption, I believe multiple external factors, including Kenyan government policies concerning the use of tribal languages in schools and global market pressures (including the recent discovery of oil in the region), will lead to increased levels of disruption in the generational transmission of the Turkana language. See http://www.ethnologue.com/cloud/tuv.

RESEARCH OBJECTIVES AND RESEARCH QUESTIONS

The primary goal of this study is to seek a clearer understanding of Turkana *ngimurok* through an ethnographic-phenomenological approach. While this phenomenological study is the priority, there are multiple research questions and objectives that the data from this phenomenological study ultimately seeks to answer and achieve. Since each of these research objectives is supported by a theoretical framework that fits the multidisciplinary nature of Intercultural Studies, the questions are grouped based on these categories.

Phenomenological Questions and Objectives (Primary)

The following phenomenological questions and objectives are the primary concern of this research project:

- How do Turkana *ngimurok* perceive and self-describe their roles in Turkana communities? How does this compare with other religious studies categories for religious specialists, specifically "shaman?"
- What are the specific practices of the *ngimurok*?
- Where and how do *ngimurok* receive the knowledge of these practices? Are they learned from other *ngimurok*, received from a spiritual realm, transmitted through the *ngimurok*, or learned in some other way?
- Are there different types of *ngimurok*, or a hierarchy of *ngimurok* as suggested by previous researchers?

In this project, phenomenology seeks to achieve the following research objectives:

1. To articulate an exhaustive, non-evaluative, bracketed, interpretive understanding of Turkana *ngimurok*.
2. To evaluate prior descriptions of Turkana *ngimurok* in the literature.

Anthropological Questions and Objectives (Secondary)

- Are Turkana *ngimurok* best described interpretively through theories of social function, social healing, dramaturgy or theatre, problem solving, displaying the epistemology of a people or in other ways?
- Turkana social structure has been described as acephalous. How do Turkana *ngimurok* leadership roles fit into an acephalous structure?

- What are the problems *ngimurok* are asked to solve in Turkana communities?
- What practices and other means do *ngimurok* use to solve these problems?
- Other than consultation and divination, what rituals do *ngimurok* participate in or lead in the community?
- Are there connections between *ngimurok* roles and practices in community and an interpretive understanding of Turkana epistemology?
- What is the prevalence of Turkana Christian reliance on the *ngimurok*?
- Are the roles of the *ngimurok* changing as there is more contact with outside influences? Are Christian communities displaying parallel roles and functions as the *ngimurok* in Turkana communities?
- Why do Turkana Christians continue to visit and consult *ngimurok*?

The exploration of these anthropological questions seeks to achieve the following research objectives within the scope of this study:

1. To describe the ways that Turkana *ngimurok* are a persistent, integral part of Turkana identity, religious understanding and foundational epistemology.
2. To produce quantitative and qualitative evidence of the persistence of *emuron* consultation from among self-ascribed Christians in Turkana.

THEOLOGICAL QUESTIONS AND OBJECTIVES (TERTIARY)

Refer to the theoretical framework below for a more complete rationale of these questions and objectives. Although important for the missiological aspects of this research, the acquisition of data through the phenomenological study is primary. These questions are to be investigated later:

- Are there areas of continuity between Christianity and Turkana Traditional Religion as understood through the *ngimurok*?
- Can Jesus be seen as the fulfillment of Turkana law/tradition (*etal*) and prophetic revelation through the *ngimurok*?
- The church often suggests that *ngimurok* are "in league with Satan." Does an ethnographic-phenomenological study of Turkana *ngimurok* reinforce a path of discontinuity or suggest greater continuity between traditional Turkana religious understanding and a contextual Turkana Christian understanding?

- How does an epistemology that incorporates *ngimurok* creatively incorporate and accept a Christian faith epistemology?
- Can Jesus as the "Great *Emuron*" be a valid christological understanding?

These theologically oriented questions seek to achieve the following tertiary research objectives following this study:

1. To test the reemerging ecumenical mission understanding of fulfilment theology with Turkana traditional religion and *ngimurok* as a test case.
2. To look for ways that *ngimurok* may have been or may continue to be part of *missio Dei*.
3. To consider contextual christological implications of the roles and practices of *ngimurok*.
4. To seek opportunities for learning about ourselves and our own theology from *ngimurok* understandings.

A Summary of Research Objectives

To summarize, the overarching goal of this project is to provide an interpretive ethnographic-phenomenological description of Turkana *ngimurok* that is based on relationships and conversations with multiple *ngimurok*.

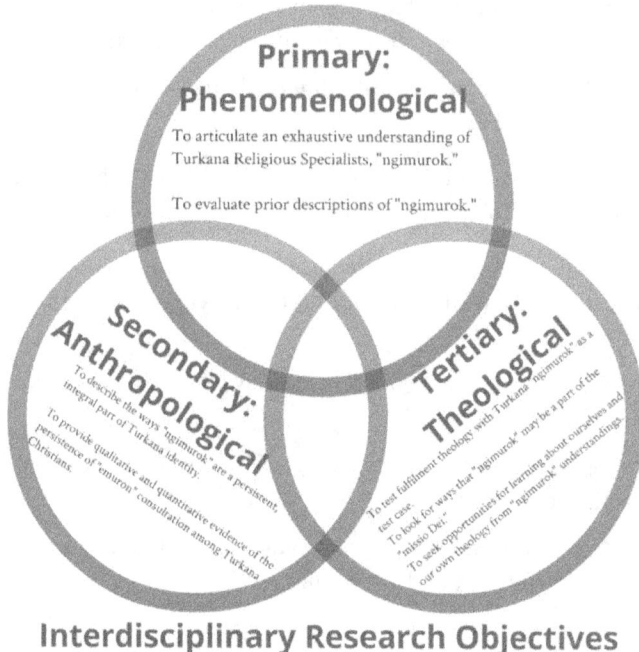

Figure 1. Interdisciplinary Research Objectives

For religious studies, the data from this research will offer greater understanding of the variety of African traditional religions still being practiced today and will be useful in evaluating previous descriptions of traditional religious specialists and Turkana religion.

Anthropologically, this new description should help in greater understanding of what it means to be "Turkana" today, the ways that Christianity and globalization are impacting the continued practice of traditional religion, and the ways that traditional religion continues to persist in Christian communities and shape indigenous understandings of Christianity.

Theologically, this description of *ngimurok* should provide Turkana and other East African Christians with more phenomenological data that is necessary for sympathetic and critical understandings of the roles and activities of traditional religious specialists. This data could provide the first step in further critical contextualization of local practices. It could also lead to a more dialogical and open relationship with traditional religion and specialists, alleviating split-level concerns in the church and demonization of the religious other.

THEORETICAL FRAMEWORK

The multi-disciplinary research objectives of this project have emerged from a similarly multi-disciplinary theoretical framework. Religious studies provide this research with a **phenomenological** theoretical perspective alongside **comparative theology**. Anthropology has provided **interpretive** and **symbolic** theories that support this research. Theories on the **anthropology of religion** and **anthropology of Christianity** have influenced and expanded my framework. Theologically, this research is buttressed by the theories of *missio Dei*, **fulfillment theology** (in post-colonial iterations), and theories of **contextual theology**. Theories of mission that have more recently shaped this framework include **giftive mission** and **ontic expansion**. Source material and the specific contributions to this study for each of these theories are outlined below.

Phenomenology

In *Religious Worlds: The Comparative Study of Religion*, William Paden outlines a number of responses and explanations Christians have had in regard to other religions:

1. The evil origin explanation, first as "demonstrative of humanity's fallen nature," and second "that other religions were specifically directed by demons or by Satan."[1]

2. Theories of historical diffusion: this purported "that everything truly religious in religious history was in fact historically derived from the original monotheism of the biblical patriarchs, whereas everything false in other religions was a degeneration from that once pure source."[2] This approach enabled Christians to "take credit" for any respected qualities of other religions. A variety of explanations grew out of this approach, including degeneration theories, plagiarism theories, euhemerism theories (the gods are idealizations of great historical figures; used polemically in the early Christian era), and prior contact theories.

3. Other religions were seen as allegories of Christian truth. That is, the gods of any religion provide us with some sort of lesson that can be learned about the one true God. This was especially popular in classical Christian explanations of Greek mythology.[3]

---

1. Paden, *Religious Worlds*, 17–18.
2. Ibid., 18–19.
3. Ibid., 22.

4. Through objective demonstrations, Christians would attempt to prove the superiority of Christianity in comparison to the inferiority of other religions.

5. What Paden calls the "doctrine of *Logos* conveyed the idea that the divine is present in the whole of creation and that every human innately bears the image of God."[4]

Responses to Turkana traditional religion by Western Christian missionaries and Turkana Christians have often fallen into two or three of these categories of Christian response. Most prevalent is the idea that Turkana traditional religion has evil origins and is directed by Satan and demons. Often, the "non-evil" parts of Turkana Traditional Religion (and this is highly subjective) were used as allegory or teaching points for Christian truth.[5] Occasionally, miraculous events would point to the superiority of Christianity.

Seeking to understand Turkana *ngimurok* from their own perspective while attempting to not initially evaluate their belief system will provide the data required for later evaluative exercises. Phenomenology of religion provides a perspective of studying the phenomena (or appearances) of religions sympathetically, on their own terms, and even "value-free".[6] The goal of a phenomenological approach is "the development of insight into the essential structures and meanings of religious experience."[7] For my study, this includes a non-evaluative study of the phenomena of *ngimurok*. The theory would suggest that this data would provide insight into Turkana understandings of the world unknown to Western perspectives.

Comparative Theology

Terry Muck describes a theology of religions as "the theological position we take regarding other religions," whereas comparative theology is the "process of doing theology in the context of other religions, with an emphasis on contextualization and engagement with the world."[8] A current

---

4. Ibid., 25.

5. See especially Bruen, "*Akipeyos Nachamunet*," where a traditional goat roast for reconciliation, *akipeyos nachamunet*, is considered as a model for contextualizing Christian Eucharist; also, an early work by Barrett (*Incarnating the Church in Turkana*), in which he offered "incarnational" ceremonies and rituals for the church based closely on Turkana traditional religious rituals and ceremonies.

6. Barua, *Phenomenology of Religion*, 48.

7. Ibid., 47.

8. Quotes taken from personal class notes, MW775 Christian Witness and Other Faiths, "Comparative Theology," September 23, 2009.

survey of comparative theologies would reveal a wide continuum of positions. On one end of the continuum we find the likes of Wilfred Cantwell Smith (1981), who proposes the formulation of a world theology as a single, perennial theological option that is not specific to any one World Religion. At the other end of the continuum we find William Dyrness (1990) and other evangelicals contemplating a global Christian theology that seems to exclude the truth claims of other religions.[9]

In the theoretical basis for my research, I approach comparative theology from a position somewhere in the middle of these two ends of the continuum, pieced together from Muck's definition and the introduction of Keith Ward's, *Religion and Revelation: A Theology of Revelation in the World's Religions* (1994). For the theologian engaged in comparative theology, the first step should be "studying the religious phenomenon of the world before moving on to say what the characteristics of revelation are and what sort of certainty is obtainable in religion."[10] While this may seem like an impossible task, Ward insists, "the time has come when it is positively misleading to consider religious traditions in isolation;" for even as Christians, we "cannot properly understand the mode of Divine revelation within Christianity unless [we] can set it in the context of human religious activity in general."[11]

For Christians, comparative theology should be the important first stage of inquiry and understanding when developing a contextual theology. In *Constructing Local Theologies*, Robert Schreiter believes that in order "to develop an adequate local theology, one must listen to the religious responses already present in the culture."[12] Popular theology is grounded in the realities of everyday life and is intertwined with the needs and concerns of local people, offering the much-desired power that official religion often lacks. What Schreiter calls "popular religion" is also similar to what Hiebert and others call folk religion. It is already present upon the arrival of a world religion or an official religion, and will most likely remain, often hidden, to deal with the existential needs and problems of the people that the official religion does not address.

To truly understand the people of a specific contextual reality one must study and seek understanding of the local religion. Uncovering the popular religion is the comparative theologian's task that can partially unravel the mystery of who people are, as traditional religion is often undifferentiated from the identity and everyday lives of a people. One of the positive results

---

9. Ott and Netland, *Globalizing Theology*.
10. Ward, *Religion and Revelation*, 36.
11. Ibid., 37.
12. Schreiter, *Constructing Local Theologies*, 123.

of comparative theology has been the ability to better understand the needs of a people and their methods for retaining identity through times of difficulty or oppression, or even the homogenizing effects of globalization.[13] Thus, comparative theology is a process in which the theologian is seeking to understand the local context through the lens of the local context. For the Christian comparative theologian, this local understanding is then applied in the development of a contextual Christian theology.

In this brief introduction of comparative theology, one might suppose we are talking about the same thing as "critical contextualization,"[14] or more recently, "missional theology."[15] But I believe they are different on a number of counts. First, contextualization is a process that looks at a specific form in a local context and then asks the question, "Can this form be adapted for Christian use?" Comparative theology moves beyond this in asking, "Can the current contextual religious understanding not only be considered as compatible with Christian understanding, but also instructive for deepening the Christian understanding?" This is not a process that is only concerned with fitting Christian faith into context, but is concerned with bringing the context into the Christian faith. I see this difference as a difference in starting points: while contextualization begins with the one true faith (from the perspective of the Christian), comparative theology starts with the contextual epistemological understandings of religion.

Such a comparative theological position informs the theoretical framework of the current research by making it imperative to begin with an examination of the belief system and epistemological understandings of the *ngimurok*. For myself, this is not done at the exclusion or relativization of Christian faith. Even if the eventual goal of such a study is a greater Turkana understanding of Jesus as "Lord" from within the contextual epistemology, a "devout scholar," such as myself, should initially be more deeply concerned with Turkana *ngimurok* religious understanding on its own than evaluation based on my Christian faith.[16]

---

13. Ibid., 134
14. Hiebert, "Critical Contextualization."
15. Hiebert and Tiénou, "Missional Theology."
16. There will be those, like Robin Horton, who will doubt the authenticity and legitimacy of such research by a "devout scholar" of religion in Africa because of belief in "the allegedly invariant theistic features of religion" (Horton, *Patterns of Thought*, 168). It may also be, as E. E. Evans-Pritchard suggests, "As far as a study of religion as a factor in social life is concerned, it may make little difference whether the anthropologist is a theist or an atheist, since in either case he [sic] can only take into account what he can observe. But if either attempts to go further than this, each must pursue a different path. The non-believer seeks for some theory . . . which will explain the illusion; the believer seeks rather to understand the manner in which a people conceives of a reality and

Comparative Religion and Comparative Theology of African Traditional Religions

As mentioned in the introduction, Bediako claims that Western mission-initiated churches in Africa have "been unable to sympathise with or relate to the spiritual realities of the traditional worldview." He concludes that more recently, "it is not so much a case of an unwillingness to relate to these realities, as of not having learnt to do so."[17] I believe that part of the "learning to do so" can be accomplished through the application of comparative theology and dialogue with traditional religion in ways that religious studies scholars have dialogued with World Religions for more than a century.

Because of the continued dominance of classifications of religion from the lowest, primitive, compact and simple in Africa to the highest, evolved, differentiated and complex in the World Religions of Asia and Europe, many of the theories and methods used by scholars to study the World Religions, especially those that assume there is something to learn from those religions, have not been applied to the religious traditions

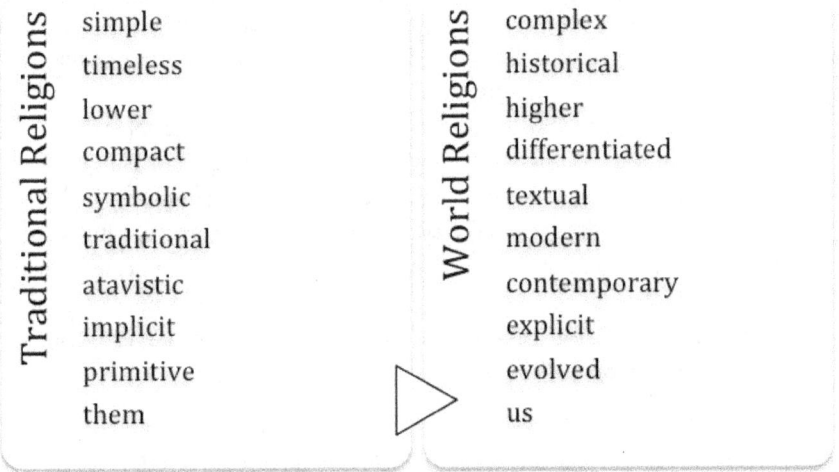

Figure 2. What Do We Mean When We Classify Religions

their relations to it" (Evans-Pritchard, *Theories of Primitive Religion*, 121). My goal is for the data of my research to be considered authentic and legitimate as far as the theories of comparative theology and social anthropology would evaluate the data. While my missiological applications and conclusion will certainly be further fodder for Horton et al., I will attempt to carry out my research without either "invariant theism" or atheism, seeking instead the understandings of the *ngimurok*.

17. Bediako, *Christianity in Africa*, 69.

of Africa. Recent introductions to both interreligious dialogue and the study of World Religions have emphasized the need to evaluate our inherited biases against traditional religions and begin reappraising them as legitimate contemporary belief systems.

Peter Feldmeier notes that while Mircea Eliade, more than fifty years ago, "battled ignorance and bias to insist on including native traditions" in the study of religion, the overwhelming view was that traditional religions "were simply too small, idiosyncratic, and numerous to contribute to the wider world of knowledge."[18] Feldmeier continues on with his thesis that now, more than ever, because of increasing concern of ecological crises, traditional religions in which harmony with the earth are more important than "anthropocentrism", "listening to native wisdom and its posture toward nature may be the only way to ensure the future of humankind."[19] While some may evaluate this as a romantic vision, I am at least encouraged that a book devoted to Christianity in interreligious dialogue includes a chapter on "indigenous traditions" alongside Judaism, Hinduism, Buddhism and Islam.

Even more recently, Irving Hexham has traced the religious studies bias against African traditional religions in chapter 2, "A Biased Canon" of his *Understanding World Religions* text (2011). Hexham's survey of religious studies texts from the 1960s to present reveals that "there can be no doubt that textbooks dealing with African religions suffer from a racist heritage."[20] It appears that a common understanding of African traditions is that they are basic practices that are seen everywhere. Citing Ninian Smart,[21] Hexham points to Smart's unintended conveyance "that African ritual sacrifices are really not worth serious consideration because they simply duplicate things that happen more interestingly elsewhere."[22] Hexham does a masterful job of revealing the religious studies bias against African traditional religions and encourages more diligence:

> From these comments it seems safe to conclude that if the reality of African religion contradicts some pet theories current in religious studies departments, it is because those theories are flawed in their very essence. The problem, simply stated, is

18. Feldmeier, *Encounters in Faith*, 219.
19. Ibid., 220.
20. Hexham, *Understanding World Religions*, 32.
21. Smart's six-hundred-page text, *The World's Religions*, contains fifteen pages on the "classical African religions." Hexham only slightly exaggerates when stating that Smart includes only six pages covering African religions.
22. Hexham, *Understanding World Religions*, 36.

that Durkheim, Otto, van der Leeuw, and Eliade were armchair theorists. They analyzed written texts. But to study African religions meaningfully we must move beyond the text to the life experience of living people.[23]

Hopefully, Hexham's text will receive wide readership and encourage a new generation of religious scholars, anthropologists and missiologists to approach religious traditions in Africa with the same respect and dialogue that they approach other written-text based religions. That is the approach of this research project.

Symbolic and Interpretive Anthropology

The theoretical framework of this book is also built upon interpretive and symbolic theories for understanding groups of people, and more specifically, for understanding "religion" and *ngimurok* in Turkana. Claude Lévi-Strauss (1908–2009) began to describe "culture" as systems of symbols that functioned in much the same way as a language. Lévi-Strauss was particularly interested in the way varieties of languages, kinship patterns and myths could be studied to reveal more universal deep structures. His theory was that people unconsciously impose "forms upon content" and,

> if these forms are fundamentally the same for all minds—ancient and modern, primitive and civilized (as the study of the symbolic function, expressed in language, so strikingly indicates)—it is necessary and sufficient to grasp the unconscious structure underlying each institution and custom.[24]

This system of symbolic interpretation is considered a structuralist theoretical approach to understanding culture and religion. While his ideas concerning the importance of symbols revealing meaning in culture continues to be significant to symbolic and interpretive anthropologists today, his idea that there is a universal structure revealed in these symbols seems "merely quaint, an academic curiosity" that is not based on the realities of ethnography.[25] For Geertz, Levi-Strauss was not interested in understanding people, but "Man," in a more philosophical than anthropological manner.[26]

Following in a symbolic approach, but not in structuralist theories, were anthropologists Victor Turner (1920–1983), Mary Douglas (1921–2007) and Clifford Geertz (1926–2006). Turner's theoretical focus was on

23. Ibid., 58–59.
24. Lévi-Strauss, *Structural Anthropology*, 21.
25. Geertz, *Interpretation of Cultures*, 359.
26. Ibid., 356–57.

the ways that symbols are shaped by society, and specifically, the ways that ritual symbols provide deep meaning to communities in context. In recent years (especially in the E. Stanley Jones School of World Mission at Asbury Theological Seminary and other missiological studies), the focus has been on Turner's ritual process theory incorporating liminality and *Communitas* as a method for transformation and Christian discipleship.[27] More foundational to my research is Turner's concept that the symbols of a specific context reach to the deepest epistemological understandings of that context. These are deep symbols that go "to the root of each person's being and finds in that root something profoundly communal and shared."[28]

Clifford Geertz, critical of structuralism, elevated the importance of interpretation in understanding the symbols of culture. His definitions of culture and religion, and his hermeneutical understanding of ethnography, have made significant theoretical and methodological impacts on myself, the researcher, and this research endeavor. Geertz' definition of culture was an expansion of Max Weber's understanding of culture as an "infinite causal web" which an investigator attempts to penetrate, but is "obviously bound by the norms of our thought."[29] Geertz explains:

> The concept of culture I espouse, and whose utility the essays below attempt to demonstrate, is essentially a semiotic one. Believing, with Max Weber, that man [sic] is an animal suspended in webs of significance he himself [sic] has spun, I take culture to be those webs, and the analysis of it to be therefore not an experimental science in search of law but an interpretive one in search of meaning. It is explication I am after, construing social expressions on their surface enigmatical.[30]

27. Turner, *Ritual Process*; Zahniser, *Symbol and Ceremony*.
28. Turner, *Ritual Process*, 138.
29. Weber, *Max Weber on the Methodology*, 84.
30. Geertz, *Interpretation of Cultures*, 5. This understanding of culture as "webs of significance" in relation to *ngimurok* in Turkana recalls Evans-Pritchard's 1937 description of the interconnectedness of belief, "witch-doctors," and identity among the Azande:

"Azande do not consider what their world would be like without witch-doctors any more than we consider what it would be like without physicians. Since there is witchcraft, there are naturally witch-doctors. There is no incentive to agnosticism. All their beliefs hang together, and were a Zande to give up faith in witch-doctorhood he would have to surrender equally his belief in witchcraft and oracles . . . In this web of belief every strand depends upon every other strand, and a Zande cannot get out of its meshes because this is the only world he knows. The web is not an external structure in which he is enclosed. It is the texture of his thought and he cannot think that his thought is wrong. Nevertheless, his beliefs are not absolutely set but are variable and fluctuating to allow for different situations and to permit empirical observations and even doubts."

Here we find key elements to interpretive anthropological theory: people create "webs of significance" in community; analyzing culture requires an interpretive search for meaning within those webs; interpretive explanation of particular "webs" is sought above the search for universals.

Of further importance to my research, Geertz provides a definition for religion within his "webs of significance" understanding of culture and a two-stage process for the anthropological study of religion. First, religion is, according to Geertz:

> ... a system of symbols which acts to establish powerful, pervasive, and long-lasting moods and motivations in men [sic] by formulating conceptions of a general order of existence and clothing these conceptions with such an aura of factuality that the moods and motivations seem uniquely realistic.[31]

It is the careful study of these important "symbols" that is primary for the researcher before further analysis of social structural systems can be made. Geertz explains this anthropological study of religion as "a two-stage operation":

> first, an analysis of the system of meanings embodied in the symbols which make up religion proper, and, second, the relating of these systems to social-structural and psychological processes. My dissatisfaction with so much of contemporary social anthropological work in religion is not that it concerns itself with the second stage, but that it neglects the first, and in so doing takes for granted what most needs to be elucidated.[32]

Geertz complains that too many studies attempt to investigate the role of traditional religion in "political succession," "kinship obligations," "agricultural practices," or "social control," to name a few, with only "the most general, common-sense view of what ancestor worship, animal sacrifice, spirit worship, divination, or initiation rites are as religious patterns."[33] Geertz' understanding of religion and culture demands that we first carefully analyze the symbolic structure of religion before an attempt is made to interpret the connections between the religion and other social structures.

The implications of Geertz' assessment here can be applied to many previous missiological and current developmental studies in Turkana. These studies begin with a very general understanding of traditional religion,

---

(Evans-Pritchard, *Witchcraft*, 194–95).
31. Geertz, *Interpretation of Cultures*, 90.
32. Ibid., 125.
33. Ibid.

divination or the religious practitioner, *emuron*, often based on previous outdated colonial research, and quickly move to missiological implications, or completely fail to connect the symbolic structures of Turkana religion with current environmental or conflict issues.[34] This current study, based on interpretive and symbolic anthropological theory, seeks primarily to significantly understand the symbolic religious structure in Turkana, specifically in relation to the *ngimurok*, before moving to secondary developmental or missiological implications.

Anthropology of Religion

Recent texts on the anthropology of religion rely heavily on interpretive and symbolic anthropology. In defining an anthropological approach to the study of religion, Michael Lambek suggests:

> Good anthropology understands that religious worlds are real, vivid, and significant to those who construct and inhabit them and it tries, as artfully as it can, to render those realities for others, in their sensory richness, philosophic depth, emotional range, and moral complexity. In acknowledging the value and power of such worlds, but also their variety and competition, anthropology must understand them as so many means for acting, asking, shaping, and thinking, rather than as a set of fixed answers whose validity either can be independently assessed (objectivism) or must be accepted as such (relativism).[35]

In addition, Lambek points out that the anthropological approach needs to include "arguments that are variously holistic, universalistic, ethnographic, comparative, contextual, historical, dialogical, and critical."[36] This leaves us with a very complex, all-encompassing view of an anthropology of religion.

What anthropologists have identified as "religion" ranges from very formalized universal systems of belief, as world religions demonstrate, to very particular systems of belief among peoples who have no such word as "religion" in their vocabulary, as many traditional religions demonstrate. Escaping general categorizations of religious practices around the world,

---

34. The only two notable exceptions are van der Jagt, *Symbolic Structures*, and Barrett, *Sacrifice and Prophecy in Turkana Cosmology*. Van der Jagt explicitly seeks to explore Turkana symbolic understandings of *Akuj* and *Ekipe* ("God" and "Evil One"), and Barrett explores Turkana symbolic understandings of sacrifice. Still, both of these studies rely heavily on former descriptions of *ngimurok* as their basis for their explanation of symbolic understandings.

35. Lambek, *Reader in the Anthropology*, 5.

36. Ibid., 2.

more recent studies have described a commonly occurring complex mixture of both universal and particular religious understandings as "webs of significance," or even as "jumble," that is unique to each context.[37]

A significant understanding from recent anthropology of religion literature that theoretically informs this research is that all "religions" are complex systems that are connected to local contexts. While a world religion may share the same myths, symbols, revelations and belief systems worldwide, the anthropological study of the world religions in local communities has revealed a more complex situation: that universality, localization, synchronization (what Christians normally refer to negatively as syncretism), and traditional religions are "more complex and differentiated than would be supposed."[38] Anthropological studies of religion display that, in spite of the homogenizing effects of colonization, the spread of world religions and globalization, these processes "have in turn generated a host of new kinds of local innovation and differentiation, and religious pluralism."[39]

It is in this complex web of understanding, within the processes of colonization, conversion to world religions and globalization that I will be seeking understanding of Turkana *ngimurok*. This entails placing the *ngimurok* within a contemporary Turkana symbolic structure instead of seeking a "traditional" invention that has not changed over time. This also entails understanding Turkana "religion" not merely as an external category of identity, but as connected to the core understandings of what it means to be human in a particular context, specifically Turkana.

Anthropology of Christianity

The new, and surprisingly late, manifestation of the Anthropology of Christianity is really not new at all. In many ways, its origins can be found in the studies of Durkheim, Mauss and Weber, who included Christian religious understandings in their studies. But most anthropological and ethnographic study of religion since has been focused on "the supposed elementary forms of the religious life" with assumption "that by examining what was prior to and other than our own society, we would uncover simultaneously . . . what was universal . . . and what was distinctive about both the worlds of both the examined and the examiners."[40] Because anthropology emerged

---

37. Geertz, "Shifting Aims, Moving Targets," 15.
38. Winzeler, *Anthropology and Religion*, 261.
39. Whitehouse, *Religion, Anthropology*, 5.
40. Cannell, *Anthropology of Christianity*, 8.

from a Christian context, Christianity was not "other" and "was, generally, considered the least urgent object of study."[41]

It was assumed that Christianity was known, familiar, and therefore, not interesting for anthropological study. When anthropologists studied religion in locations where significant numbers of people had converted religiously to Christianity, the existence of Christianity was often overlooked in their studies. Today, the emergence of an Anthropology of Christianity seeks to recognize the authenticity and particularities of Christianities around the world, and has even begun to legitimate Christian perspectives in anthropology.[42]

The anthropological study of Christianity today makes two central arguments against previous dominant assumptions about Christianity, articulated by Fenella Cannell:

> It is not sufficient to assume that we know in advance what Christian experience is—even when popular practice appears to be most highly conformist to the standards of the church concerned; second, that it is unhelpful to treat Christianity as simply a secondary phenomenon of underlying political or economic change.[43]

Anthropological studies of Christianity today seek "to see the experiences of Christianity, in all their diversity, complexity, and singularity, for what they are."[44]

Research that seeks to understand Turkana *ngimurok* must not avoid the contemporary complexities of Christianity intermingled with "traditional" practices. The anthropology of Christianity suggests that one might even find *ngimurok* who claim faith in Jesus Christ, continue to relate to the ancestors, and practice divination techniques learned from their fathers. If there are aspects of Christianity in the lives of the *ngimurok* today, this is not something to be avoided, but explored.

Missio Dei

Theologically, the theoretical framework of this research is built upon a concept of the *missio Dei*. The *missio Dei* is a missiological metanarrative recognizing that *missions* are the particular activities of the church and missionaries, while *mission* "is not primarily an activity of the church, but an

41. Ibid.
42. Howell, "Repugnant Cultural Other."
43. Cannell, *Anthropology of Christianity*, 29.
44. Ibid., 45.

attribute of God."[45] Simply stated, God has a mission in the world, and it is God's mission, this *missio Dei*, that we work within.

Finding its roots in the Trinitarian theology of Karl Barth (1932), the Willingen International Missionary Council (1952), and the writings of Karl Hartenstein (1933), the *missio Dei* perspective "was clearly articulated in and widely popularized by George Vicedom's book *The Mission of God: An Introduction to a Theology of Mission* (1965)."[46] Since then, this concept has led to some controversy, as interpretations began to describe the *missio Dei* as not only larger than the mission of the church, but excluding the mission of the church, especially as expressed in Johannes Hoekendijk's *Church Inside Out* (1966), contrary to the intentions of both Barth and Hartenstein.[47]

Nevertheless, the *missio Dei* concept can still help us understand our place in God's mission. It is in the nature of God to be missionary. From the beginning, God was reaching out to humankind to be in relationship. As early as the calling of Abraham we can see God's plan to reach all people: "And by your offspring, shall all the nations of the earth gain blessing for themselves, because you have obeyed my voice."[48] We are inherently a missionary people because our God is a missionary God.

The implication of *missio Dei* for this study is the theory that God is at work among the Turkana accomplishing God's mission within the Turkana epistemological framework. *Missio Dei* suggests the possibility that God has been working through the positive roles the *ngimurok* and others have played in Turkana communities to accomplish God's purposes. This possibility, therefore, requires closer examination of the roles and practices of the *ngimurok*.

Fulfilment Theology

A major theme at the Edinburgh 1910 Missionary Conference was an examination of the way elements of other religions could be regarded as "preparation" for Christianity. In the survey sent out to missionaries as research for the Report of Commission IV, "The Missionary Message in Relation to Non-Christian Religions," two questions revealed this theme:

---

45. Bosch, *Transforming Mission*, 390.
46. Van Engen, *Mission On the Way*, 151.
47. Bosch, *Transforming Mission*, 392. For a more complete history of the term *missio Dei*, I have found the following summaries helpful: Bosch, *Transforming Mission*, 389–93; Van Engen, *Mission On the Way*, 150–56; see also Rosin, *Examination of the Origin*, and as an implicit theme of Newbigin, *Open Secret*.
48. Gen 22:18, NRSV.

> What attitude should the Christian preacher take towards the religion of the people among whom he [sic] labours?
>
> What are the elements in the said religion or religions which present points of contact with Christianity and may be regarded as preparation for it?[49]

Throughout the report, positive assessments were made of certain aspects of the non-Christian faiths. Indeed, "the report held to the view that Christianity was the fulfilment of these other religions, though they were not seen as preparations for Christianity in the same way that the Old Testament was; rather, they were on a par with Hellenism" and were seen to contain "seeds of truth."[50]

Even among those respondents from the context of "animism," most felt "that there is a 'modicum of truth' to be found therein."[51] Consistent with Bediako's assessment, Hedges notes there were few at Edinburgh who saw animism as a preparation for Christianity, but that nearly all saw points of contact between animism and Christianity, even if only through analogies.[52] These reports underline the fact that "fulfilment theology" was a driving force of Edinburgh 1910.

Fulfilment theology[53] has been traced biblically to an interpretation of Matthew 5.17, " . . . I have come not to abolish, but to fulfill," which understands Jesus as the fulfilment not only of the Jewish religious tradition but of any religious tradition. Numerous other biblical passages are cited in support of Jesus being the fulfilment of any religious tradition.[54]

Support for this position is also seen in the writings of a number of the church fathers, most notably Justin Martyr (103–165), who taught that Greek philosophy, like the Jewish law, could serve as a teacher, pointing to Jesus. Justin formed the idea, based on scripture, that the *spermatikos logos*, "seed of the Word" (that is, Christ) was available to all people and present,

---

49. Hedges, *Preparation and Fulfilment*, 243.
50. Ibid., 245.
51. Ibid., 249.
52. Bediako, *Christianity in Africa*, 69; Hedges, *Preparation and Fulfilment*, 249.

53. It should be noted that the "fulfilment theology" described in this section is that which primarily came out of Britain in the late nineteenth and early twentieth centuries. I intentionally use the British spelling to differentiate from other concepts of fulfillment, such as Knitter's "fulfillment model." Fulfilment theology is in no way related, in my estimation, to what some Evangelical missiologists now refer to as an eschatological "theology of fulfillment" based primarily on Matt 24:19, that expects the return of Jesus when the gospel has been preached to all nations.

54. In addition to Matt 5:17, citations often include: Gal 3:24; Acts 10:34–35, 13:23, 14:16–17, 17:22–23; and John 1:9.

in part, in the philosophies of all people.[55] Following Justin Martyr, Eusebius of Caesarea (263–339) wrote his *praeparatio evangelica*, "Preparation for the Gospel," claiming that God has worked among all people, leaving a testimony within their own understandings that prepares them to receive the message of Jesus Christ.

Leading up to Edinburgh 1910, British fulfilment theology is seen to have come through various theologians with historical factors contributing to its growth. The historical factors cited by Hedges include the rise of the British Empire; increased contact and knowledge of non-Christian religions; increased British missionary activity around the world (through which much of the knowledge of the religions came); and a gradual shift in the 1870s, beginning in India, to a positive attitude toward non-Christian religions.[56] In addition to these historical factors, the rise in popularity of 19th century social evolutionary theory greatly affected the understanding of the world's religions. It was commonly understood that religion evolved from the "lower-level" non-Christian religions toward Christianity.[57] Just as British society at the turn of the 20th century was seen as the highest evolved form of humanity, Christianity was likewise the highest evolved form of religious understanding through the special revelation of Jesus.[58] For many, fulfilment theology meant that Christianity was the natural progression of where all the religions were heading.

Significant contributions to the growing fulfilment theory included F D Maurice's, *The Religions of the World and their Relations to Christianity* (1847), Rowland Williams', *Dialogue on the Knowledge of the Supreme Lord* (1856), Monier Monier-Williams' *Modern India and the Indians* (1879), Friedrich Max Muller's *Natural Religion* (1889), and John Farquar's *The Crown of Hinduism* (1915). Although these writers did not completely agree with each other concerning the truth of non-Christian religions, all viewed them positively as either preparation for Christ or as containing the seed of the Gospel.[59]

As the world wars of the 20th century dissolved much of the optimism of social evolutionary theory, it became apparent that there were

---

55. Hedges, *Preparation and Fulfilment*, 21, cites Justin Martyr, *Apology* 1.46 and 2.10, 13. Other earlier church fathers referenced in support of fulfilment theology include Clement of Alexandria and Origen of Alexandria.

56. Hedges, *Preparation and Fulfilment*, 24–25.

57. Ibid., 31.

58. Ibid., 101.

59. An excellent summary of the literature leading up to Farquar can be found in the beginning of Eric Sharpe's 1965 dissertation, *Not to Destroy but to Fulfil: The Contribution of J.N. Farquhar to Protestant Missionary Thought in India before 1914*.

significant problems with the fulfilment theology present at Edinburgh 1910. These problems included connections to British colonialism that were being challenged around the world, a connection to social evolutionary theory, and a tendency towards viewing other religious systems as not true or complete in their own context. As Karl Heim stated after World War I at Jerusalem 1928, "Since the war we cannot say any longer to the non-Christians: Become Christians because Christianity brought to the nations of the West their historic greatness, their superior civilization, their advanced political institutions."[60] Theologically, there was a growing understanding that Christianity should be viewed more in discontinuity with the non-Christian religions than in continuity. This view was brought to the forefront at Tambaram 1938 in Hendrick Kraemer's *The Christian Message in a Non-Christian World* published as a study guide for the conference. Kraemer clearly stated that the revelation of Jesus can only be seen as discontinuity with all other religions:

> In the illuminating light of the revelation of Christ, which lays bare the moving and grand but at the same time distressing and desperate reality of human religious life, as reflected in the various religions, all 'similarities' and points of contact become dissimilarities.[61]

For evangelicals, Kraemer's text marks the end of an evangelical understanding of fulfilment theology, although "the idea of a radical positive assessment of world religions without relinquishing the supremacy of Christianity found new expression in . . . inclusivism."[62]

As theology of religions began to follow a more standard paradigm of pluralist, exclusivist and inclusivist positions, fulfilment theology came to be understood in the inclusivist category.[63] Paul Knitter traces a development of a "fulfillment model" approach to non-Christian religions beginning with scripture and the church fathers. Surprisingly, Knitter omits

---

60. Quoted in Kärkkäinen, *Introduction to the Theology of Religions*, 154.

61. Kraemer, *Christian Message*, 136.

62. Tennent, *Christianity at the Religious Roundtable*, 19–20. Upon reading Kraemer I was struck by how positively he viewed other religions, and the possibilities that "new incarnations and adaptations of Christianity" around the world "are natural and legitimate" (Kraemer, *Christian Message*, 313). Kraemer strongly disagrees that traditional religion in Africa could be *praeparatio evangelica* or that God's revelation is seen in non-Christian cultures (this is akin to "romantic love-making" for Kraemer! [340]) (338). Yet, he "cordially agrees with the desire to adopt a constructive and creative relation towards the reality of indigenous life as the material in which Christianity needs must become incarnated" (Kraemer, *Christian Message*, 338).

63. Race, *Christians and Religious Pluralism*, 44, 52–55.

British fulfilment theology and does not include any of the authors or works listed above as adding to his fulfillment model, choosing to jump from the church fathers to Karl Rahner, whom he describes as "a pioneer in exploring uncharted religious terrain."[64]

Veli-Matti Kärkkäinen more carefully links British Protestant fulfilment theology and the fulfillment theology growing in the Catholic Church to the growing "open-minded attitudes toward other religions" in historical religious studies.[65] Karl Rahner extended these ideas even further in the Catholic Church, suggesting that the Spirit of God is at work in all peoples of the world in such a way that a non-Christian religion contains "supernatural elements arising out of grace which is given to men [sic] as a gratuitous gift on account of Christ;" leading Rahner to conclude, "for this reason, a non-Christian religion can be recognized as a lawful religion without thereby denying the error and depravity contained in it."[66] Rahner was influential in the Vatican II council in which the Catholic Church clearly affirmed the understanding that "whatever goodness or truth is found among them, it is considered by the Church as a preparation for the Gospel."[67]

Knitter provides a non-technical description of what a fulfillment model for engaging with other religions means, placing the utmost importance on the role of the Holy Spirit today:

> Given these nonnegotiable convictions about Jesus, those Christians who follow the Fulfillment Model are open to finding in other religions truths about God and humanity that they have not received in Jesus. Still they cannot imagine agreeing to anything that would contradict what they have learned in Jesus. The Spirit may have more to say than what was said in Jesus; but the Spirit could never oppose Jesus.[68]

This is a position that seeks to reconcile the universal *missio Dei* with the revealed particularity of salvation through Jesus Christ, and which I find compelling.

While I must admit that evil exists in the world and that discernment is needed to take a closer look at "the demonstrated capacity of evil to co-opt a religion (including Christianity, of course) and to bend it to its

---

64. Knitter, *Introducing Theologies of Religions*, 68. Knitter's "fulfillment" focus is clearly displayed in the theological changes in the Catholic Church leading up to Vatican II and *Lumen Gentium*.

65. Kärkkäinen, *Introduction to the Theology of Religions*, 103–4.

66. Rahner, "Christianity and the Non-Christian Religions," 293.

67. Vatican II, *Lumen Gentium*, 16.

68. Knitter, *Introducing Theologies of Religions*, 103.

own ideological ends"[69] and that, as a Christian, I hold firmly to the non-negotiable conviction that Jesus is Lord, my evaluation of other religions is more positive than most standard evangelical exclusivist positions.[70] I see evangelicals leaning in this direction, with acceptance of Don Richardson's "redemptive analogies" concept, in which spiritual truths are seen in local customs as "the secret entryway" for the message of Jesus,[71] but this does not move far enough. I expect to see God working through other religions, not only as preparation for the Gospel, but as truth from which even I, as someone from a different context and epistemology, can learn about God. As I seek to understand the *ngimurok*, missiologically, I am expecting to find, not merely redemptive analogies, but the possibility of encountering God actively at work in Turkana epistemology. This understanding leads directly into adjacent parts of my theoretical framework, the concepts of giftive mission and ontic expansion.

Giftive Mission

In seeking new metaphors for Christian witness in their text *Christianity Encountering World Religions*, Terry Muck and Frances Adeney present the metaphor of "giftive mission" as a new possibility for interacting with adherents of other faiths.[72] Through a biblical and cultural examination of gift giving, Muck and Adeney provide a contemporary model for mission that centers on the reciprocal grace-filled possibilities of giving the story of Jesus as a gift, in context. Giftive mission moves away from witness based on coercion, fear, competition, marketing and one-way transactions, toward witness based on meeting needs, hope, relationship and two-way giving/receiving.[73] This is a powerful metaphor that allows Christians to freely seek the ways that God is already at work in a specific context as they share the story of Jesus. We learn from others in our mission. We have gifts to offer them and they have gifts to offer us.

The missiological implications of my phenomenological study of *ngimurok* are framed by this model of giftive mission. As Christians tell the story of Jesus in Turkana, what do the *ngimurok* offer in return? Are we willing to listen to them before evaluating?

---

69. Taber, "Contextualization," 34.

70. A few current evangelicals who openly hold to inclusivist/fulfillment model views include Clark Pinnock and John Sanders.

71. Richardson, *Eternity in Their Hearts*, 10.

72. Muck and Adeney, *Christianity Encountering World Religions*, 353–77.

73. Ibid., 273.

Ontic Expansion

As a theoretical extension of fulfilment theology and giftive mission, the concept of "ontic expansion" is also part of my theoretical model for research. Ontic expansion implies that the unchanging truth of God will be more fully revealed as Christians giftively share their contextual perspectives of God and scripture with each other.

In much the same way that Stephen Bevans states, "only as the church enters into serious dialogue with every culture can it be a witness to the 'Pleroma' that is Jesus Christ,"[74] Timothy Tennent, in his chapter on African Christology, suggests that as the Good News of Jesus has been translated into a multitude of particular realities, "we gain more and more insights into the beauty and reality of Jesus Christ;" a phenomenon described by Tennent as the "ontic expansion of God in Jesus Christ."[75] Tennent clearly states that this ontic expansion does not change the ontological nature of either God or Christ, but instead refers to "how our own understanding and insight into the full nature and work of God in and through Jesus Christ is continually expanding as more and more people groups come to the feet of Jesus."[76]

As I have sought to build on Tennent's theory[77] elsewhere in its relationship not only to *theological* reflection from the Majority World, but also to hermeneutical frameworks that could provide insight to our own western exegetical interpretive blind-spots,[78] the concept of the "ontic expansion of God in Christ" is also a theory that applies to the current research. If there are positive ways that God has used Turkana *ngimurok* in their communities, and some of the *ngimurok* have accepted faith in Jesus, how can the truth of God, from a *ngimurok* perspective expand our own understandings of God?

A similar understanding is found in the "broken-light" metaphor expanded by W. H. T. Gairdener, following Edinburgh 1910, when he reflected on the possibilities of learning from other religions: "the conviction has grown that their 'confused cloud-world' will be found to be 'shot through

---

74. Bevans, *Models of Contextual Theology*, 15.

75. Tennent, *Theology in the Context of World Christianity*, 111. Also, Tennent, "Challenge of Churchless Christianity," 174–75; and Tennent, *Invitation to World Missions*, 89.

76. Tennent, *Theology in the Context of World Christianity*, 111.

77. While the phrase "ontic expansion" may be particular to Tennent in this usage and meaning, Tennent credits others for the concept, including Jonathan Edwards. See Tennent, *Invitation to World Missions*, 89. For the phrase "it takes a whole world to understand a whole Christ," see Tennent, "Challenge of Churchless Christianity," 174; a phrase originally published by Cragg, *Call of the Minaret*, 183.

78. See Lines, "Exegetical and Extispicic Readings."

with broken lights of a hidden sun.'" This led Gairdner to further assert that "Christianity, the religion of the light of the World, can ignore no lights however 'broken'—it must take them all into account, absorb all into its central glow."[79] Gairdner further describes this discovery of "broken-lights" which may also be the "discovery of facets" of Christianity's

> own truth, forgotten or half-forgotten –perhaps even never perceived at all save by the most prophetic of her sons. Thus, 'by going into all the world' Christ's Church may discover all the light that is in Christ, and become, like her Head, as it is His will she should become, —Lux Mundi.[80]

The application of ontic expansion in my research suggests that I expect to find truth about God that may not fit a Western Christian paradigm, and that I need not attempt to fit it into a Western theological paradigm.

DELIMITATIONS AND LIMITATIONS OF THE STUDY

This research does not attempt a definitive systematic description of Turkana traditional religion, but primarily seeks to understand and place the religious specialist *ngimurok* in their context today in Turkana. As a phenomenological study, the research is intentionally limited to the phenomenon of traditional religious specialists in Turkana. Understanding the *ngimurok* is only a fraction of understanding the people and epistemology of Turkana, but it is a window of understanding that has often been neglected. These understandings will secondarily be applied to both missiological and developmental concerns in the region.

Specifically, interviews with *ngimurok* were limited to the central southeastern sections of Turkana county along the northern Kerio and eastern Turkwel rivers. Visiting with and interviewing a single *emuron* often took multiple days. The Turkana Christian Survey (Chapter 6) was primarily limited to respondents from the mission-initiated Kenyan denomination Community Christian Church, the denomination I worked alongside of while serving as a missionary from 1999–2008. This church denomination is often the only church in the most remote parts of Turkana. The final field research time was limited by the availability of funds, but took place over a period of 3 months (October-December 2011).

Other obvious limitations come from the fact that I am not Turkana. Although I have the advantage of nearly a decade of experience in Turkana and the ability to speak the Turkana language fluently, I will never be able

---

79. Gairdner, quoted in Hedges, *Preparation and Fulfilment*, 245.
80. Gairdner, quoted in Hedges, *Preparation and Fulfilment*, 246.

to view the world completely as a Turkana insider. Even as I sought to allow the *ngimurok* to self-describe themselves, any understanding of their descriptions are, in the end, my interpretation. I do not want to add another Western invention of Africa to the literature or blindly apply a Western paradigm of religion onto the Turkana. Although these were my intentions, my postmodern tendencies say that I have no other option but to interpret the Turkana through my own epistemological lens.

Phenomenology as Precursor to a Contextualization Study

The well-defined critical contextualization process that initiated with Paul Hiebert more than 20 years ago has been a useful tool in the missiology toolbox for many years. But there is a growing understanding that this well-defined process is a tool that a researcher cannot use alone. If my research project were to be part of a formal contextualization process, it would only be located in the initial phenomenological step of the process, which is often the most neglected part.[81] The rest of that well-defined process would be best left to the church in Turkana to decide if the process was needed or if there was a better way to understand the Christian relationship to the *ngimurok*.

One of the key questions in my mind concerning critical contextualization is, who controls the interpretation of the biblical material when deciding the "biblical" acceptability of a cultural practice? Another concern is the idea (not part of Hiebert's intent) that once the process has taken place, then a phenomenon has been "contextualized" and the issue is no longer up for discussion. Even Hiebert warned, "contextualization must be an ongoing process in the life of the church."[82]

A few missiologists are suggesting it is time to move beyond the critical contextualization model. I was surprised recently to read an article by R. Daniel Shaw suggesting the need for a new model:

> A contextualized biblical theology reflects God's intention for the people of a particular time and place and enables those involved (both insiders and outsiders) to be transformed more fully into the image of God. At this point, cognitive studies become highly significant for contemporary mission: we must value the "receptional apparatus" God has created. Human beings everywhere were created by God with a mind-brain for processing, through language and psychosocial awareness, all manner of human experience, including new transculturated conceptualizations. It is necessary to move beyond contextualization, as previously

81. Hiebert, Tiénou, and Shaw, *Understanding Folk Religion*, 369.
82. Ibid., 387.

conceived, to recognize God's presence in the midst of people everywhere and to recognition of the ways that presence enables people to 'know God.'[83]

In the ways that Shaw describes here, this study of the *ngimurok* in Turkana seeks to recognize the presence of God in Turkana, for the possibility of transformation of both insiders and outsiders through understandings of *ngimurok*.

RESEARCH METHODOLOGY

The Phenomenological Method

The non-evaluative data I seek concerning Turkana *ngimurok* will eventually be evaluated, but as I have presented in the research problem, the data does not yet exist for clear understandings and evaluations. This essential phenomenological non-evaluative characteristic is historically described as "epoché," by Husserl (1913), and more often today as "bracketing."[84] The ideas are the same, that researchers attempt to temporarily suspend or lay aside their presuppositions and convictions in order to understand other convictions, religious systems, or even "worlds," from the other's perspective.[85] That is the primary goal of this research in understanding Turkana *ngimurok*. But bracketing convictions is not the end in itself. It is a primary, yet temporary, suspension, not meant to abandon "evaluation as an important part of religious studies."[86]

In the social sciences, another key characteristic of phenomenological approaches is that the subjects of study, whom Jonathan Smith prefers to call "the research participants," provide their own interpretations of their experiences to the researcher.[87] In my research I make interpretations of Turkana *ngimurok* based on their own interpretations provided to me. In this sense, the phenomenological researcher "is engaged in a double hermeneutic because the researcher is trying to make sense of the participant trying to make sense of what is happening to them."[88]

Clark Moustakas provides an outline of nine core principles, processes and methods for human science phenomenological research.[89] My sum-

---

83. Shaw, "Beyond Contextualization," 212.
84. Muck and Adeney, *Christianity Encountering World Religions*, 249–62.
85. Paden, *Religious Worlds*, 64–65.
86. Muck, *How to Study Religion*, 96.
87. Smith, Flowers, and Larkin, *Interpretative Phenomenological Analysis*, 3.
88. Ibid.
89. Moustakas, *Phenomenological Research Methods*, 58–59.

mary of these core facets that will help guide my research methodology includes:

1. A focus on the appearance of things "just as they are given."
2. A concern with wholeness and viewing phenomena from multiple perspectives "until a unified vision of the essences" is achieved.
3. Seeking meaning from phenomena through "intuition and reflection on conscious acts of experience."
4. A commitment to descriptions of experiences, not explanation or analysis. These descriptions should "retain the original texture of things."
5. Questions that account for personal involvement and interest of the researcher. The researcher should be connected with the phenomenon.
6. Subject and object are integrated by the researcher in a way that makes "the objective subjective and the subjective objective."
7. While the research is intersubjective (as in 6. above), every perception can only begin with the researcher's own understanding.
8. "The data of experience, my own thinking, intuiting, reflecting, and judging are regarded as the primary evidences of scientific investigation."
9. The research question must remain the clear focus of the entire investigation and guide the research methods.

A phenomenological approach to understanding the *ngimurok* best fits the current situation and need for greater clarity concerning Turkana *ngimurok*. It is an approach that seeks to initially be non-evaluative, yet inherently recognizes and expects that the researcher is intimately involved with the phenomena being studied. It is also an approach that seeks to prioritize the self-interpretations of the study participants. While the findings of any study, any text, will ultimately be the interpretation of the researcher, an interpretive phenomenological approach requires the interpretation to be based on sustained reflection on the self-interpretations of the participants; in this case, the *ngimurok* and their clients.

Ethnography

While interpretive phenomenological methods have grown mainly out of religious studies and, more recently, the fields of psychology and education, anthropology offers ethnography as its own similar method of enquiry.

Ethnographic fieldwork is "the alpha and omega of social anthropology" that seeks a holistic "artisanal approach to social research." Geertz has colloquially described the method as one of talking to people, "largely free-form, in a one thing leads to another and everything leads to everything else manner, in the vernacular and for extended periods of time, all the while observing, from very close up, how they behave."[90] Utilizing techniques from this mostly qualitative method of research has greatly aided my efforts to understand the *ngimurok*.

As I previously described, a secondary research objective in studying *ngimurok* is to alleviate the separateness and denunciation, and even demonization, that occurs in Turkana that, in my estimation, is not based on adequate research, but instead on anecdotal stereotypes and older incomplete research. I seek to foster a more dialogical and open relationship with traditional religion and specialists in Turkana, alleviating split-level concerns in the church and demonization of the religious other. This is one of the possible outcomes of ethnographic research.

Stereotypes are unavoidable and ambivalently work to "create order in an otherwise excruciatingly complicated social universe," to "justify privileges and differences in access to a society's resources" and are "crucial in defining the boundaries of one's own group."[91] But Eriksen also notes, "stereotypes need not be true, and they do not necessarily give good descriptions of what people actually do."[92] Through ethnography, I seek to test these stereotypes; to test whether the "dichotomization" of the us-them relationship between Turkana Christians and Western missionaries against *ngimurok* could transition to a we-you "complementarization" of discourse and interaction described by Eriksen.[93]

Ethnographic method encourages participation in the "whole continuum" of communication Hortense Powdermaker has described as varying "from spontaneous to planned, from superficial to deep, from subjective to objective areas of interest, from purely verbal to more subtle and emotional expression."[94] Furthermore, ethnographic method discourages me from seeking to create a reified Turkana traditional religious cosmology based on other Western or World Religion cosmologies. Instead of finding universals in traditional religion or African divination systems, I seek ways in which the particularity of Turkana *ngimurok* "reveal the enduring natural

---

90. Geertz, *Available Light*, 93.
91. Eriksen, *Ethnicity and Nationalism*, 25.
92. Ibid.
93. Ibid., 28–29.
94. Powdermaker, *Stranger and Friend*, 287.

processes that underlie them."[95] Instead of building universal systems, ethnography seeks to articulate the complexities of a subject's identity through their own categories and theories. It is an attempt at Clifford Geertz's "trick . . . to figure out what the devil they think they are up to," not what we think they are up to through our own theological categories or particular positive and negative presuppositions.[96]

Summary of Methodology

Various ethnographic methods are available that seek understanding through the subject's own perceptions, their own eyes, their own words, and their own actions. These include **participant observation, formal and informal interviews, life-history interviews, sharing meals, mapping** and **proxemics** exercises, and **attending events (rituals) important to the community**. I have utilized these techniques in this and in previous studies, and am indebted primarily to these methods as explained in Crane and Angrosino (1992), Spradley and McCurdy (2005), Bernard (2006) and Wolcott (2008).

An integrated phenomenological and ethnographic method of qualitative research required spending time in conversation and observation with Turkana *ngimurok*. I accomplished this initially through previous relationships with *ngimurok* and then utilized previous research on the location of *ngimurok* to visit with others. My research assistant in Turkana, James Ibei Eipa, was also able to use many of his familial relationships to locate the homes of *ngimurok*. While I compiled a list of key questions in the form of a survey, I was not able to follow a formal interview model, relying instead on mostly narrative visits with the *ngimurok* that were more acceptable in the context (see Appendix C for the original interview model). These "ethnosemantic" interviews were informal with an attempt on my part to direct the conversation in order to discover answers to my key questions.[97] I was able to record the audio of almost all the interviews (Appendix B), and record video of multiple interviews and rituals (Appendix D), with permission. I was also able to capture numerous photographs during my research (Appendix E).

In multiple areas visited, a survey was given to Turkana Christians in an attempt to qualitatively understand Turkana Christian perspectives of the *ngimurok* and in an attempt to obtain quantitative data regarding the continued Christian use of ngimurok services. A sample survey can

95. Geertz, *Interpretation of Cultures*, 44.
96. Geertz, "From the Native's Point of View," 58.
97. Crane and Angrosino, *Field Projects in Anthropology*, 121–35; Spradley and McCurdy, *Cultural Experience*, 35.

be found in Appendix G. These surveys were administered in both written and oral forms, by myself and my research assistant. Although my initial goal was to receive back at least 100 surveys, my assistant and I were only able to receive 71 completed surveys from respondents from various Christian churches.

My Turkana research assistant, James Ibei Eipa, was hired and travelled with me to assist in the interviews, surveys and transcriptions. We travelled to each of the *ngimurok* areas as time permitted, based on the map of *ngimurok* locations from previous research. Most of the time we slept outside at the homes of the *ngimurok* as we visited with them. A Toyota Landcruiser was rented from Lodwar. We also found it helpful to hire another assistant who aided in the cooking, cleaning and keeping watch over our vehicle and belongings on the numerous occasions when we found the only path to reach an *emuron* home was on foot. Although I did visit with American missionaries in Turkana, my former role as a field team leader and the desire of the missionaries for extended visits was a distraction to my limited research time; thus, I limited my time spent in the homes of the missionaries, preferring instead to stay at the homes of both Turkana friends and the homes of the *ngimurok*.

Ethical Considerations

There is precedence of government "witch-hunting" in Turkana history that make the *ngimurok* nervous when it comes to sharing information that could provide the government with a means for identifying and locating *ngimurok*. It is my intention that the locations of *ngimurok* and any identifying information available to me will be kept confidential. I have kept all my notes, recordings (audio and visual), and maps confidential.

At the same time, I followed all the laws of Kenya regarding research. I intentionally operated within the ethical standards and procedures described in a legal document from the Ministry of National Development and Planning in Kenya which deals with research in Kenya. The following ethical standards were observed:[98]

1. I carried a letter from Asbury Theological Seminary for identification and to confirm the purpose of my research. A copy was given to those who requested.

---

98. Many of these standards were formed in consultation with Dr. Michael Lolwerikoi.

2. I made available the purpose of the research being conducted to all who asked, carrying a copy of the research proposal for those who wished to read.

3. I explained the reasons why the Turkana people, church leaders, development agencies, local and international mission partners could benefit from the research and its contributions.

4. Every participant was given an opportunity to hear the explanation of the research and to agree verbally to participate.

5. Participation in this research was voluntary. Any participant was free to participate or withdraw from this research at any time.

6. I assured the confidentiality of the information of every participant.

7. I gave all participants my contact information, in case they have any questions about my research. I also left my contact information with key leaders and missionaries for those who wanted to contact me.

8. Coding has been used to identify the participants in my research field notes, and names have be changed in the final book.

9. All collected data is stored in a secure locked box and/or encrypted on a hard drive.

Data Analysis

Phenomenological data analysis techniques were used in this study. Similar to the analysis of ethnographic data, proponents of phenomenological analysis suggest "analyzing data for significant statements, meaning units, textural and structural description, and description of the 'essence.'"[99] These emerging themes are then organized into "super-ordinate" themes from individual interviews and then in comparison with all interviews.[100] These clusters of themes and meanings are then constructed into an exhaustive description of the phenomenon, including "textural descriptions, structural descriptions and an integration of textures and structures into the meanings and essences of the phenomenon."[101] Thus, the structure of the phenomenological description in chapter 4 is guided by the themes that emerged directly from the data (interviews, observations, videos) and not from any external structures devised to explain and categorize African Traditional Religions or Traditional Religious Specialists.

99. Creswell, *Qualitative Inquiry*, 79.
100. Smith, Flowers, and Larkin, *Interpretative Phenomenological Analysis*, 91–107.
101. Moustakas, *Phenomenological Research Methods*, 118–19.

After an exhaustive description of the phenomenon *emuron* is provided, this data and subsequent description is then reflected back though the research questions and theoretical framework of the research. Careful comparison of the description of *ngimurok* rising out of this research with previous descriptions of the *ngimurok* is also made. Finally, missiological implications and areas for future research are discussed.

SIGNIFICANCE OF THE STUDY

This study primarily intends to fill the void of data concerning *ngimurok* in Turkana with data provided by the *ngimurok* themselves. This should provide significant resources for future religious, anthropological and missiological studies. Should they choose to do so, it would also provide the Turkana church with data useful for moving toward the construction of a more contextual Turkana theology. Hopefully, the exploration of *ngimurok* will also refine or expand my own understanding of the way God works in the world.

In addition, the 104 pages of Turkana language transcription, three ancestral *ngimurok* lineages and the descriptions of *ngimurok* rituals, will provide data for future generations of Turkana who will be seeking their own identity as *Ngiturkana* after the Turkana language has begun to pass away. Indeed, some of the motivations of the *ngimurok* to share so openly with me during this research were related to their visions of descendants who will no longer understand the voices of their fathers in their dreams; that somehow in my recording of their words, their descendants would still be able to hear their voices.

3

Definitions for the Study

THIS CHAPTER EXPLORES THE literature and key terms surrounding traditional African religious understandings in general, and specifically in the Nilotic context of Turkana. These understandings helped to inform the research and represent a move toward more contextually specific local definitions and terminology. This is an intentional move away from older generalized definitions in the field of African religious studies.

DEFINITION OF KEY TERMS

"Primal" Religion Terminology

Especially in light of the colonial relationship Western countries have had and often continue to have with Africa, an audit of frequently used terms will help to be as accurate and specific in the research as possible. Religion that is typically found among rural peoples is often referred to as "popular" (Schreiter), "folk" (Hiebert) or "primal" (Turner). Many religious studies scholars are moving away from usage of the term "primal," as it has negative connotations based on an erroneous concept of religious evolution with primal as the basic form. Some now prefer "indigenous" as opposed to "traditional," or "primal."

African Traditional Religion has been described in many ways. Often the terms "primitive," "traditional," "animism," "folk," and "popular" are used to describe the forms of religion found among many peoples in Africa. But, the reality is that these are all terms frequently used in an attempt to broadly categorize all religious forms and understandings that do not fit into the category of world religions.

Tite Tiénou, missiologist and academic dean at Trinity Evangelical Divinity School offers his perspective on use of the word "primitive" when describing religion in his article titled, "The Invention of the 'Primitive' and Stereotypes in Mission." Tiénou provides a much-needed non-Western viewpoint, reminding us of the stereotypes and Western arrogance implicit in many of the social sciences, including anthropology, religious studies and missiology. While initially describing an "ideal" form, Tiénou points out that "primitive" soon became the term used by anthropologists to mean the "antithesis of highly evolved European society."[1] Even today, missionaries and theologians continue to be influenced by this same evolutionary social theory. The difficulty that arises when anthropologists and missionaries try to find a single word that can encompass all religions outside of the major world religions is that any one word becomes a "general category which resembles 'stereotypes.'"[2] While Tiénou admits that most stereotypes are born from truth and sincere observation, he implores us to remember their dangers: "nevertheless, stereotypes become oppressive when they are used by a powerful group to define a weaker group so as to justify certain behavior patterns of the people in power or to enlist support for a cause."[3]

We need to heed Tiénou's call and watch for signs of ethnocentrism in our mission strategies and language. We are partners in God's mission to the world, which "is too serious an endeavor for us to spoil it by our recourse to stereotypes in order to justify our involvement in it."[4] Seeking to understand Turkana religious specialists will not be possible if we study from a position of intellectual and religious superiority or, if "before we come into contact with the people we intend to study, we have resolved in our mind that their difference from us constitutes their essence and identity."[5] Tiénou concludes that, "since the 'primitive' was an erroneous construct, its influence can only be detrimental to the cause of mission."[6]

In a similar fashion, yet more thoroughly articulated, Alan Kuper, in his updated book, *The Reinvention of Primitive Society: Transformations of a Myth*, provides an historical critique that argues that the concept of "primitive society" came out of European ethnocentrism in which European philosophy, science and religion were the highest evolved forms and primitive society was the first ideal from which all others evolved. As an

1. Tiénou, "Invention of the 'Primitive,'" 296.
2. Ibid., 299.
3. Ibid., 300.
4. Ibid., 301.
5. Ibid., 298.
6. Ibid., 295.

anthropologist, Kuper argues that this ideal society never existed except in the minds of those who created it. Kuper is thankful that "this branch of anthropology seems to have parted company from the mainstream," and that "anthropology can no longer be defined as the study of primitive societies" because "primitive society is universally recognized to be a fiction."[7] We live in a world in which it is commonly recognized that all societies, cultures and religions are fluid, and even more so now in the waves of globalization. What had been considered "primal" exists today alongside the "modern" and the two cannot simply be seen in terms of strict linear progression.

Keith Ward, retired Professor of Divinity at the University of Oxford, explains the difficulty in suggesting that we can find in the contemporary practice of traditional religion the very first forms of religion:

> Present-day tribal religions may differ in many ways from the early faiths of humanity. They have, after all, existed for longer than most world religions and may have undergone many changes in that time.[8]

Ward goes on to cite the frustrations of Evans-Pritchard with those who want to deduce the origins of all human religion by examining present day primal religions. Especially difficult for Evans-Pritchard were the theories of Spencer and Tylor, and even Durkheim on the origin of religion. All of these theories tended to negate the authenticity of all religion by "relegat[ing] such beliefs to the realm of the primitive and superstitious."[9]

Especially in the situation of increasing globalization, in which Christianity as a truly world religion is interacting with other religious traditions all over the globe, let us not continue our research in the old gutters of social Darwinism and ethnocentrism, where one form of religion is merely the next progression or development of another; likewise, let us not think that Majority World Christianity is now only destined to follow in the patterns of Western Christianity. As sociologist Paul Freston, suggests:

> If the West is not paradigmatic for the whole world with a time-lag, then an epistemological equalization of the whole globe and some degree of worldwide empirical knowledge are vital. Of course, global religious trends have to be interpreted in terms of the major tendencies of globalization, but are not in a 'delayed reaction' paradigm.[10]

---

7. Kuper, *Reinvention of Primitive Society*, 223.
8. Ward, *Religion and Revelation*, 58.
9. Ibid., 59.
10. Quoted in Kalu and Low, *Interpreting Contemporary Christianity*, 25.

It is only when we come to our research with a view toward "epistemological equalization" that we can begin to see the truly local, indigenous religious realities around the world *on their own terms*. This "epistemological equalization" will not only lead to an increasing authenticity of Christian contextual theologies, but could also allow us to be more inclusive in our evaluation of the truth claims presented in authentic inter-faith discussions.[11]

"Traditional" Religions

In this study, religious understandings in the local Turkana context will be termed "traditional." Everywhere in the world, traditions persist, even as creatively destructive globalized economic forces appear to rule the day. Yet traditions are often not ancient; old traditions are contested, adapted, renewed; new traditions emerge. The "traditional" can be very problematic if we think we are talking about something that has existed on its own for centuries or millennia. Traditions are only accepted or created by living people who collectively choose to recognize them. This "collective choice" helps explain why examining traditions "frequently reveals significant features about the people who maintain them."[12]

Thus, traditional religion is here understood as a belief system growing out of the collective choice of a group that is based on a collective understanding of a metanarrative and/or a mythic understanding of unique descent. This is one reason "traditional religion" is often linked with theories of ethnicity and identity: that African traditional religions are ethnic religions, in which "beliefs are largely identified with a specific ethnic group and cater for the needs of that group."[13] This is consistent with Eriksen's note that identity requires "we-hood," including "a shared language or religion."[14]

Anthony D. Smith further explains this traditional religious understanding as a pattern for ethnic survival based on "the myth of ethnic election."[15] This understanding places people in the ethnicity under certain moral obligations. Following the traditions and remaining pure achieves righteousness in the community. For Smith, this is described as a *communal-demotic* pattern of ethnic survival that

> attaches the myth directly to the people in their sacred land. In these cases the community has usually been conquered and is

---

11. Ibid., 16.
12. Knighton, *Vitality of Karamojong Religion*, 3.
13. Wijsen, *Seeds of Conflict*, 81.
14. Eriksen, *Ethnicity and Nationalism*, 67.
15. Smith, "Chosen Peoples," 189.

struggling to preserve its former rights and way of life, claiming that its members are the original inhabitants and their culture is in the vernacular.[16]

Wijsen relates a similar idea when he states:

> Many ethnic groups believe that they are 'the only people' and other ethnic groups are non-people. Not infrequently there is a religious myth underpinning the superiority complex. The Maasai cattle raiding the Kikuyu is justified by a myth that all cattle were given to the Maasai by God and belong to them.[17]

The Turkana are similar to the Maasai in this way, for the one true creator God, *Akuj*, has given all the domesticated animals to the Turkana.

"African" Traditional Religion(s)

In the seminal text for understanding African Traditional Religion, E. Bolaji Idowu describes the difficulties associated with attempts to define and reify traditional religion in Africa. Not the least of these difficulties is the immense size of the continent and the diversity that abounds in the geography, climate, languages and people. It has become far too common for researchers to make broad generalizations concerning Africa. While Idowu considers the worst researchers and experts on Africa to be those who have never actually *been* to Africa; the next are those who convey the "misleading impression that having visited Tanzania or Ghana or lived for a few days in Kano, they have not only seen and known the whole of Africa but have also become authorities on her overall nature—physical, moral, spiritual, and economic."[18] The multitude of languages and the lack of written histories add to this difficulty of attempting a clear understanding of an African Traditional Religion, if there is such a singular form. A further difficulty includes the painful history of colonialism that in many places in Africa makes it nearly impossible "to say precisely what are the aboriginal cultures and beliefs."[19] Idowu speaks here of "colonial indoctrination" that in some circumstances has caused Africans to "despise whole-heartedly their own native cultures and religious values, and ultimately abandoning them and

---

16. Smith in Hutchinson 1996:195
17. Wijsen, *Seeds of Conflict*, 122.
18. Idowu, *African Traditional Religion*, 78.
19. Ibid., 79.

forgetting their basic tenets and practices."[20] This is what some have called the worst form of colonization, the "colonization of the mind."[21]

Elizabeth Isichei brings together many of the difficulties Westerners have faced in attempting to study and understand African Traditional Religion in more recent years. In the recent past, African theologians have tended to react to "missionaries who rejected traditional religion as demonic" by looking for areas of compatibility between African Traditional Religion and Christianity.[22] African theologians, such as John Mbiti, began to consider African Traditional Religion to be the unwritten Old Testament for African Christians. Yet, theologian Okot p'Bitek became an early critic of this Christian view and response to African Traditional Religion, claiming that a "Christian interpretation of traditional religions distorted them."[23]

While Isichei asserts that in relation to the anthropological and religious study of traditional religion the "Judeo-Christian spectacles have long since been discarded," I would argue that many who study in the field of missiology still continue to read Christianity back into traditional religion in ways that over simplify African Traditional Religion.[24] This has often happened in the well-intentioned quest to find significant "redemptive analogies" in every context.[25] While we should certainly expect to find God's footprints wherever we go,[26] we must be careful to not too quickly gloss over the complexity of traditional religion.

Like Idowu, Isichei also cautions against endeavoring for overarching statements concerning African Traditional Religion. "There are both continuities and differences in this vast body of ethnic religions, and there are exceptions to every statement. In a very real sense, no such thing as 'African Traditional Religion' exists."[27] To say that there is a singular concept or understanding of "African Traditional Religion" reifies something that is uniquely experienced by every ethnicity in Africa and is part of particular ethnic identities. Traditional religion is not an easily comprehensible or articulated code

---

20. Ibid., 80.

21. Some point to Steve Biko's early writings on the South African situation as the beginning of the understanding of "the colonization of the mind." See Biko, "Towards True Humanity in South Africa." More recent discussions in missiology on the "colonization of the mind" have centered on the meaning of conversion. For an excellent article with this approach, see Stanley, "Conversion to Christianity," 315–31.

22. Isichei, *Religious Traditions of Africa*, 8.

23. Ibid., 9.

24. Ibid.

25. Richardson, *Eternity in Their Hearts*.

26. Norris, "God and the Gods," 55.

27. Isichei, *Religious Traditions of Africa*, 9.

of doctrines and practices. Each ethnic group has their own understanding of traditional religion as part of who they are, with unique mythologies, teachings, and practices. Even at the local level, these are not codified or static, but can vary by family or even individual practitioner.

Even our Western understandings of "belief" and religion have been called into question "as Eurocentric," for more important among many Africans than belief is access to power, participation, and knowledge. Certainly any study of traditional religion in Africa must begin with an attempt to understand the *particular* expressions of faith from within the context. Isichei suggests that ethnographers have done the most insightful studies of traditional religions in Africa in recent years. Yet, even the likes of Victor Turner and Mary Douglas admit that their studies "have often produced a picture that members of the society they studied would not have recognized, and to which most of them have no access anyway."[28]

Unlike Isichei, there are many who still hold value in considering African Traditional Religion as a singular entity with essential beliefs that encompass all of Africa. Laurenti Magesa suggests that the variety of particular expressions found in African Traditional Religion should "not be taken to mean a diversity of fundamental belief," but should instead be understood "much like the varieties of expression we find in any major religion," such as the denominations and sects found within Christianity.[29] This further serves to support Magesa's position that African Traditional Religion should likewise be considered a major world religion. Citing the earlier writings of E. E. Pritchard as support for his position, Magesa suggests that the dichotomy of revealed religion against natural religion only reveals an arrogance and ethnocentrism in the study of religion instead of anything "very insightful or helpful" in the study of religion.[30]

Because of Magesa's position, he is more willing to attempt an overarching view of African Traditional Religion based on an ethical perspective of full life.[31] This view does not attempt a Western systematic theology, but is inherently "synthetic and expository" in nature.[32] The four main components of his view of African Traditional Religion comprise: 1)

---

28. Ibid., 10.

29. Magesa, *African Religion*, 15–17. Magesa suggests these others offer similar views of a singular African Traditional Religion: Taylor, *Primal Vision*; and Mbiti, *African Religions and Philosophy*. Although Mbiti's work is titled "Religions," Magesa claims that, in his work, Mbiti posits that there is only one philosophy, not philosophies, that underlies all African religious expressions.

30. Magesa here quotes Evans-Pritchard, *Theories of Primitive Religion*, 2–3.

31. Magesa, *African Religion*, 77.

32. Ibid., 32.

identifying with the life force, which includes ancestral communion, birth, naming of children, initiation, and social groups such as age-sets;[33] 2) transmitting the life force, which includes marriage and kinship, children, sexual relations, taboos, and maturity through death into the ancestral power;[34] 3) identifying the enemies of life force, including wrongdoing, affliction, and evil;[35] and 4) restoring the life force, including the practical means of dealing with affliction and evil through powers, sacrifices, protective and curative medicine, reconciliation rites, and diagnosing the sources of affliction by means of divination.[36]

I offer the general views of Magesa, Isichei and Idowu concerning African Traditional Religion here as an aid for helping me understand ways that I can best proceed in attempting to understand Turkana "religion." While I am not yet convinced that there is something called African Traditional Religion in the singular, I find Magesa's framework for understanding compelling. Upon further study and reflection, we might find that Magesa's framework is not so much an accurate description of African Traditional Religion, but is actually a relational framework for an understanding of religion in general.

My own perspective on African Traditional Religion (ATR) has been shaped by these authors, and others; yet, because of my research in Africa, I am not compelled to believe there is such a thing as ATR in the singular. Africa is far too complex for the existence of only one religious understanding. It may be that general statements can be made concerning ATRs, just as general statements can be made about many other religions in describing their commonalities, but for the sake of seeking to understand the cosmologies and grand narratives of specific groups of people in Africa, the broad brush strokes must be set aside. Each group has a peculiar and particular religious understanding about the world and how one is to best live in response to that understanding. Thus, my research perspective is that there is not one African Traditional Religion, but that there are African Traditional Religions.

Turkana

"Turkana" is the English name for the people, language and land of northwest Kenya. Turkana call themselves *ngitunga*, "people" or *Ngiturkan*, "the Turkana," literally, "the cave dwellers." They call their language *angajep a*

33. Ibid., 77–114.
34. Ibid., 115–60.
35. Ibid., 161–92.
36. Ibid., 193–244.

ngitunga, "the tongue of people" or *Ngaturkana*. The land is designated *akwap*, "land," and is located in the political region identified as Turkana County in the northern Kenyan Rift Valley. In many ways, the Turkana are similar to the Nuer of Sudan, as extensively documented by Evans-Pritchard: characterized as pastoralists, patrilineal, monotheistic, and nomadic or semi-nomadic.[37] Some differences from the Nuer are documented by P.H. Gulliver and Anthony Barrett, including an acephalous structure, which I contend is more accurately described as polycephalous, with the elders of each family and village working together to make decisions for the community, a focus on smaller livestock, and almost no agricultural production. From my own research I would also add that the Turkana rely heavily on crosscutting identity markers that provide stability and unity to the community. These crosscutting identity markers include a dual system of moiety in which all people, animals and objects are either *emorut*, "mountains" or *irisait*, "leopards;" a system of family brands, *ngimacharin*, or clans, with specific traditions and ritual practices, including actual symbolic brands used on the animals;[38] an age set system based on male initiation; and age grades. Polygyny is commonly practiced, but marriage is required to be exogamous, with mates selected from outside both the brand of one's father and mother's father. A bride wealth of many animals is exchanged from the groom's family to the bride's family. Upon marriage, a woman leaves the clan of her father and, through the *akinyonyo* ritual, is assimilated into the clan of her husband.

There are approximately 900,000 Turkana living in NW Kenya and across the borders of Uganda, Sudan and Ethiopia. The 1999 official Kenya census figure for Turkana ethnicity was 450,860, which was considered by many in Turkana to be too low. The 2009 Kenya census figure originally came back as 988,952, placing Turkana as the 10th largest ethnicity in Kenya. This figure was deemed inaccurate (too high) by the Kenyan government and was officially removed from the census until the Kenyan High Court in February 2012 ruled that the government accept the 2009 census figures.

John Lamphear has made the best attempts at chronicling Turkana history in the recent past (1976, 1992, 1993). His research theorizes that the Turkana were aggressively expansionist in the middle of the nineteenth century, after dividing from the Karimojong people in the Ugandan highlands.

---

37. For Evans-Pritchard's full work, see *The Nuer*.

38. Barrett has identified at least twenty-four of these brands in his book *Turkana Iconography*, in which he attempts to list the major traditions of each brand. This text has had mixed reviews among the Turkana, due largely to the fluidity of changing brand traditions.

In expansion, Turkana identity was fluid enough to assimilate numerous smaller groups into the Turkana ethnicity. A more monolithic closed-set identity was formed by the beginning of the twentieth century when co-ordinated opposition to the British was required for survival (1993). This history has not been contested by other historians or linguists and has been confirmed and retold by Turkana scholars Pauline Lokuruka and Michael Lokuruka (2006).

Turkana Traditional Religion

In describing Turkana Traditional Religion in the particular, I am attempting to describe it as it is practiced and understood now, whether interfered with by colonialism or changed through interaction with others in Kenya or not. I also attempt to describe the religion based on Turkana terms and understandings, without my own personal evaluations. Certainly my description is selected and seen through my own lens of understanding, but I do so with an attempt to withhold personal evaluation.

As is often noted concerning traditional religions, there is not a clear boundary drawn between the sacred and the profane in Turkana society. In this regard, Turkana Traditional Religion is undifferentiated from Turkana social structure or epistemological reality—the religion and the culture are one. The Turkana are pastoralists whose lives are shaped by the extreme climate in which they live. Each day one must seek to find the blessings of life—water, food, spouses, children—in a manner that appeases the ancestral spirits and is in harmony with the relational peace of the community. Properly following the traditions in daily life will certainly lead to blessing. Blessings are understood to be an increase in wealth, whether livestock, children, spouses, or even food. It is only through proper relationships with God, *Akuj*, and the ancestors, proper protection from evil, and participation in the moral economy of the community that one can be blessed.

Essentially, Turkana believe in the reality of a supreme being called *Akuj*. Not much is known about *Akuj*, other than the fact that he alone created the world, lives somewhere above us in the sky, and is in control of the blessings of life. There is also a belief in the existence of ancestors, *ngipean* or *ngikaram*; yet these are normally seen to be malevolent, requiring sacrifices to be appeased. When angered or troubled, the ancestors will possess people in the family in order to verbally communicate with the family. There is also the recognition of "The Ancestor," *Ekipe*, who is seen as much more active in the everyday lives of people than is *Akuj*, yet only in negative ways. There is much concern over protecting one's family and oneself from the evil of the *Ekipe*. Turkana Christians and missionaries equate the *Ekipe* with the biblical character of the devil or Satan, and it is a real possibility that Christian interpretations of *Ekipe* have in turn influenced Turkana traditional religious categories. Turkana religious specialists, *ngimurok*, act as intermediaries between living people and ancestors and *Akuj*, and also help with problem solving in communities.

Beyond this, I prefer to not further delimit Turkana Traditional Religion as a well-defined system of belief. It is not a code and I am unwilling to codify it. One can easily find inconsistencies among various Turkana explications regarding *Akuj*, *ngikaram*, *ngipean*, or *Ekipe*. My position is similar to Robin Horton's, in that we must be careful to not place our own categories and understandings of religion arising out of our own cosmologies onto the traditional religions of Africa.[39] A well-defined cosmology of the spirits, ancestors, *Akuj*, and *Ekipe* might not be very important or necessary for the Turkana mythos. We should be reminded that our own Western Christian popular understandings of spirits, ghosts, angels and demons varies widely, even among Christians after nearly two thousand years of written church doctrine. Why should we expect to find systematic popular understandings of a cosmology among others?

Ngimurok and other religious specialists

Turkana: *emuron (m.s.); amuron (f.s.); ngimurok (p.)*

As in most African traditional religions, traditional religious specialists[40] in Turkana are present and play an active role in almost every community event. In my experience and as understood by others in Turkana, *ngimurok* help to identify both the source of evil, sickness or other problems that present themselves, and the solution or specific cure or sacrifice that needs to take place in order to restore abundant life in the family and the community. Within Turkana Traditional Religion there are various types of religious specialists, differentiated by the *emuron*'s source of revelation. According to Barrett, but not confirmed in my experience, the "true diviners," also known as the *ngimurok a Akuj*, "diviners of God," are the most respected of the *ngimurok* because they receive revelations directly from *Akuj*, normally through dreams.[41] These "true diviners" follow in the

---

39. Horton, *Patterns of Thought*, 161.

40. In this study I use "traditional religious specialist" as a general category that includes what have variously been described as a shaman, diviner, prophet, priest, healer, witch-doctor, witch, sorcerer, and Turkana *emuron* in the anthropological and religious studies literature.

41. Barrett, *Sacrifice and Prophecy in Turkana Cosmology*, 112

pattern of the most famous Turkana *ngimurok*, Lokerio and Lokorijem.[42] Lokorijem regularly received dreams from *Akuj* informing him of the location of the British Army during early twentieth century colonial struggles, Lokerio is said to have used the power and knowledge of God to divide Lake Turkana so that warriors could walk across the lake to steal camels.[43] These *ngimurok a Akuj* can be found throughout Turkana, each in their own territory, alongside specialized *ngimurok* who have received specific abilities to read tea leaves, tobacco, intestines, shoes, stones and string. The general understanding in the literature is that *ngimurok* are the people that *Akuj* speaks to in dreams; they are also the ones who can communicate with the ancestors to discern what sort of animal sacrifice is needed to restore peace, or the ones who know a remedy for a child's illness, or who can properly bless the families at a wedding.

Because of the positive impact many *ngimurok* have on their communities, I have occasionally argued for usage of the English word "priests" in translation. The Turkana translation of the Bible, *Abibilia: Ngakiro Naajokak*,[44] uses *emuron* for "priest" in both the Old Testament and New Testament. Sometimes specialists who regularly receive dreams are only called *ekerujait*, or a "dreamer." These would be similar to a "prophet." There are also hidden evil specialists, *ngikapilak* and *ngikasubak* who specialize in pronouncing very strong curses, but these are not normally included in the term *emuron*. The most evil specialists have a separate designation, *ekapilan*, and are known for their use of dead animals and human body parts for their practices. I have never heard anyone other than missionaries or church leaders who use the term *emuron* when referring to an *ekapilan*.

From these descriptions of Turkana *ngimurok*, one might notice the possibility of a major difference in Turkana cosmology from most other African Traditional Religions and Folk Religions. The *ngimurok* in each area receive direct revelations from *Akuj*, who is still directly active and concerned with the created world. These *ngimurok* do not speak or receive messages through an intermediary god, spirit or ancestor. This is unlike most of the examples presented in Michael Kirwen's well-known dialogue with the Luo diviner, Kiana, in which, as seems common to most descriptions of African Traditional Religions, the one high creator God is distant, separate

---

42. Ibid., 106

43. This "dividing of the lake" myth attributed to Lokerio, was the most common story told by my research participants concerning Lokerio. It can also be found in Barrett, *Sacrifice and Prophecy*, 144–45; and as related by Lamphear, "Aspects of Becoming Turkana," 96.

44. Nairobi: Kenya Bible Society, 2001

and not accessible. In the case of the Luo, the diviners pray to, and through, *Iryoba* and *Nyamhanga*, the sun and the moon.[45]

There are no such spirit intermediaries in Turkana; furthermore, possession by a spirit or ancestor is not necessary for Turkana prophetic work, and is unheard of by those with whom I have conversed in regards to Turkana *ngimurok*. While ancestor possessions are common in Turkana, they normally occur among younger people at the home, so that the ancestor can communicate its message to those in the home. The *emuron* would then be consulted as to what should be done. *Ngimurok* are not identified as people who are normally possessed.

While the *ngimurok* fit within Magesa's components of identifying evil and restoring the life force and may be seen as the most important aspect of Turkana Religion, there are also important clan[46] rituals in Turkana that represent the acknowledgement and transitions of life force. The most important rituals are the birth rituals (*akidoun*), male and female initiation rituals (*asapan* and *akinyonyo*), marriage rituals (*akuuta*), annual blessing sacrifices (*apiaret a awi*), and death rituals (*akinuuk*). The elders of the clan, both men and women, oversee each of these rituals. The elders also oversee the community wide wedding rituals, but an *emuron* normally plays a role in blessing the marriage.

As identified in the research problem, the literature is varied in its description of Turkana *ngimurok*. No clear understanding of their role in Turkana has existed. The above description is pieced together from personal experience, stories shared in Turkana and archival research. Chapter four of this book will provide a complete description of Turkana *ngimurok* differentiated as various types of religious specialists using various methods for receiving knowledge and providing solutions to problems in the community.

Divination and Diviner

"Divination" and "diviner" are the English terms most frequently used to translate the Turkana phenomenon of *emuron*. This follows Gulliver[47] and all others since Gulliver. In direct opposition, it is the intention of this researcher to not use the term "diviner," but to instead use vernacular Turkana

45. Kirwen, *Missionary and the Diviner*, 16.

46. The Turkana word for clan is *emachar*, literally "brand." One's clan is closely associated with the brands on the animals belonging to the clan. In addition, each male member of the clan has a special "bull name," which is used among men and at certain ceremonies and dances. Both the "clan" and the "bull name" reveal a strong connection in Turkana between identity and domestic animals and are further examples of cross-cutting identity markers.

47. Gulliver, *Preliminary Survey*.

terminology for the traditional religious specialists who participated in this research. A brief sampling of the many uses and understandings of both "divination" and "diviner" will reveal general meanings that are applied broadly in religious studies, anthropological and missiological literature. Recent researchers are more interested in local understandings of religious specialists and their particularities rather than broad, general categories.[48]

Definitions of divination range broadly. Anthropologist Victor Turner (1920–1983) generally defines divination as any means used for "bringing into the open what is hidden or unknown" to aid in solving problems.[49] Missiologist Gailyn Van Rheenen defines divination as a two-stage process; the first is the seeking of the source of a common problem. The second is seeking "to determine an appropriate human response based on the knowledge gained during the initial stage of divination."[50] John Mbiti provides an even broader definition for diviners "as agents of unveiling mysteries of human life" that function from the medical to the priestly.[51] While acknowledging the use of "mediums, oracles, being possessed, divination objects, common sense, intuitive knowledge and insight, hypnotism and other secret knowledge," Mbiti does not downplay the intellectual abilities of diviners to "keep their ears and eyes open to what is happening in their communities so that they have a store of working knowledge which they use in their divination."[52] From these broad definitions, it would be easy to include Western medical doctors, psychologists, psychiatrists, and even clergy in the category of "diviner."

One difficulty with "diviner" definitions is that source material containing local understandings of divination in Africa is still scarce. Mbiti notes, "with few exceptions, African systems of divination have not been carefully studied, though diviners and divination are found in almost every community."[53] Because of this great diversity and lack of local studies, Mbiti was unwilling to "solve" the "puzzling problems" of divination, willing only to state generally that "a certain amount of communication goes on between diviners and non-human powers (whether living or otherwise or both)."[54]

---

48. Waller, "Kidongoi's Kin"; Fratkin, *African Pastoralist Symbols*; Curry, *Perspectives for a New Millennium*.
49. Turner, *The Forest of Symbols*, 29.
50. Van Rheenen, *Communicating Christ*, 170.
51. Mbiti, *African Religions*, 172.
52. Ibid.
53. Ibid., 173.
54. Ibid., 174.

He concludes, "whatever it is, divination is another area which adds to the complexity of Africa concepts and experiences of the universe."[55]

Anthropologist Philip M. Peek explores African divination systems as those that use "non-normal modes of cognition."[56] This approach defines divination as "a means of acquiring normally inaccessible information . . . utiliz[ing] a non-normal mode of cognition which is then synthesized by the diviner and client(s) with everyday knowledge in order to allow the client(s) to make plans of action."[57] Peek also highlights the liminal characteristics of diviners who "serve as communicators between worlds, they do not fully belong to either realm."[58] One might better state that they are a lived example of the contextually understood real connection between the seen and unseen. Peek provides us with an understanding that diviners are liminal actors in the community who have access to hidden information through means of divination.

Anthropologist John Beattie (1915–1990), who studied under Evans-Pritchard at Oxford and then completed field research among the Bunyoro of Uganda in the 1950s, organized the means of divination into three categories that reveal answers: "mechanical" divination, divination by augury and extispicy, and divination by spirits.[59] Beattie also distinguished divination from scientific approaches, interpreting it as drama:

> Divination is a rite, and so is essentially dramatic and expressive. This is the central reason why, even though diviners are sometimes wrong, divination is not thereby discredited. A Western theatre-goer does not ask whether a play is "true." He [sic] asks, rather, whether it aptly communicates what it is sought to communicate. And often, divination is a drama no less—perhaps more—than it is a technique.[60]

A number of recent authors follow Beattie with dramaturgical approaches in understanding divination, including René Devisch, Michael Winkelman and Philip Peek.[61]

Godfrey Lienhardt (1921–1993), an Oxford anthropologist who studied the Dinka in Sudan from 1947–1951, writes of the division of divine power and human action both being "permanently present" in the Dinka

---

55. Ibid.
56. Peek, *African Divination Systems*, 193.
57. Ibid., 194.
58. Ibid., 197.
59. In Middleton, *Magic, Witchcraft*, 211–31.
60. Beattie in Middleton, *Magic, Witchcraft*, 231.
61. Winkelman and Peek, *Divination and Healing*.

diviners. Diviners are the connection between spiritual realities and human action.[62] Lienhardt also notes that among the Dinka there are those regarded as higher and lower by the community. Those who are higher are able to divine solutions to problems through the power of a "free-divinity" in their body, while the lower are those consulted in regard to witchcraft.[63]

Lienhardt further describes an example of the lower practitioner as one that can "extract from the patient's body bits of wood, or sand, which have been shot into the body by witches," which sounds similar to Turkana specialists called *akatuwan*, who perform the same duties. In reflecting on his research, Lienhardt states that "the categories [of diviners] shade into each other, but a famous 'person of Divinity' and prophet would be demeaned by being called a *tyet*, a mere diviner."[64]

A more recent study of Samburu *laibon* by anthropologist Elliot Fratkin is helpful for understanding the ways that Turkana *ngimurok* can be imagined as only partially within the category of "diviner." Fratkin perceives Samburu *laibon* as not merely priests who speak to God for people, nor as only prophets who speak from God to humans. Instead,

> they are particular members of an 'outsider' family of Maasai who have mystically powerful gifts of prophecy, divination, and protection from perceived supernatural attacks. Although Samburu laibons occasionally perform public divinations and prophesize future events for the welfare of the community, their predictions are in the main concerned with determining the cause of misfortunes, particularly those believed to be caused by sorcery.[65]

Fratkin's research among the Samburu, alongside the research of Richard D. Waller among the Maasai (1995), is the beginning of a research perspective that places the traditional religious specialists of the Nilotic ethnicities of East Africa in their own category or complex. Are they diviners, prophets or priests? Waller argues "these are different activities and are thought to be manifestations of different powers." He continues, "most prophets in Maasailand are also diviners, though not all diviners have the power of foresight."[66]

With the terms "divination" and "diviner" applied to so many forms of problem solving and religious rituals among peoples around the world,

62. Lienhardt, *Divinity and Experience*, 151.
63. Ibid., 71.
64. Ibid.
65. Fratkin, quoted in Winkelman and Peek, *Divination and Healing*, 221.
66. Waller, "Kidongoi's Kin," 32.

this researcher questions the usefulness of these terms in relation to understanding the epistemology of a specific context. Peek concedes that "such a diversity of organizational schemes would seem to reinforce the stereotype of divination's capriciousness: divination is whatever practitioners call divination" and that "previous typologies are unsatisfactory because the cognitive modes they attempt to distinguish usually overlap."[67] His solution is that "more attention must be paid to emic typologies."[68]

New anthropological studies on divination[69] have continued the understanding that divination is both ubiquitous and infinitely varied. Evan Heimlich contends that what we have been calling "divination" is nothing more than "various conventions for reading different kinds of hidden patterns, in order for their members to locate themselves socially."[70] Heimlich further argues that the study of divination should extend to modern societies' understanding of the terms "random" and "chance" and to describing, "*our own* honouring of oracles."[71] This is a reflexive pursuit in which I hope to join once completing the present research.

In the Turkana context, Mbiti states that "the Turkana believe that the diviner is God's chief representative, functioning as a doctor, purifier of age-sets, predicting raids and soliciting rain."[72] This qualification of "diviner" as an understanding for *emuron* is still only partial. To call Turkana traditional religious practitioners "diviners" is only helpful in acknowledging that these practitioners occasionally use means to solve problems in the community. It does not help us understand the differences and peculiarities of Turkana *ngimurok* from other religious practitioners around the world or within the Nilotic prophet complex.[73] The research presented here, in an attempt to clarify the phenomenon of *emuron*, traditionally referred to as "diviner," is an attempt to provide one such emic typology.

Shamanism

Avvakum Petrovich, a Russian priest deported to Siberia in 1661, first recorded the word "shaman" in a published text in his autobiography in 1672.[74] Throughout the eighteenth and nineteenth centuries, explorers and priests

67. Peek, *African Divination Systems*, 12.
68. Ibid., 13.
69. Curry, *Divination*.
70. Heimlich, "Darwin's Fortune," 177.
71. Heimlich, "Darwin's Fortune," 176; emphasis his.
72. Mbiti, *African Religions and Philosophy*, 68.
73. Waller, "Kidongoi's Kin."
74. Narby and Huxley, *Shamans Through Time*, 18.

described "shamans" from central and northern Asia, mostly as demonic, in league with the Christian devil, or as frauds. Early anthropologists, such as Arnold Van Gennep, attempted to regain control of "shamanism," which had already been used to describe the religions of "Siberian populations, Africans, North, Central, and South American Amerindians."[75] Van Gennep argued that there was no such thing as a shaman based religion, as "shamanism" suggests, and that the word "shaman" or *šaman* is only used locally among the Tungus, Buryats and Yakuts peoples of Asia.[76]

Mircea Eliade, who codified "shamanism" in his 1964 text by the same name, provides general descriptions and definitions of "shaman" based on his extensive fieldwork among Central and Northeast Asian religious specialists:

> Shamans are of the "elect," and as such they have access to a region of the sacred inaccessible to other members of the community. The shaman is the great specialist in the human soul; he alone "sees" it, for he knows its "form" and its destiny.[77]

Shamanic powers are bestowed on shamans in Central and Northeast Asia by: 1. "hereditary transmission", 2. "spontaneous vocation" ("call" or "election"), 3. "of their own free will" or "self-made," but Eliade notes "these 'self-made' shamans are considered less powerful than those who inherited the profession or who obeyed the 'call' of the gods and spirits."[78]

Shamans, even after receiving shamanistic power, are not officially recognized by their community until they have also:

> received two kinds of teaching: (1) ecstatic (dreams, trances, etc.) and (2) traditional (shamanic techniques, names and functions of the spirits, mythology and genealogy of the clan, secret language, etc.). This twofold course of instruction, given by the spirits and the old master shamans, is equivalent to an initiation.[79]

These ecstatic and didactic elements are equally important in the initiation. If only the ecstatic, the shamans would simply be neurotic or psychopaths, as many early researchers suggested.[80] Although they are called out and ecstatic, the mark of the true shaman must also include learned techniques

---

75. Van Gennep, 1903, in Narby and Huxley, *Shamans through Time*, 51.
76. Narby and Huxley, *Shamans through Time*, 52.
77. Eliade, *Shamanism*, 8.
78. Ibid., 13.
79. Ibid.
80. Ibid., 23–27.

that make them useful in the community. This was proof to Eliade that shamans were not irrational:

> The shamanic initiation proper includes not only an ecstatic experience but, as we shall soon see, a course of theoretical and practical instruction too complicated to be within the grasp of the neurotic.[81]

Additionally, shamans are characterized by their abilities to enter into a trance through which their spirit can travel into the world and view people and events from above. This shamanic characteristic was popularized in America by R. Gordon Wasson's descriptions of mushroom induced trances with shamans in southern Mexico. These descriptions were published in the popular magazine, *Life*, and are quite possibly the most popularly read accounts of shamanism ever.[82]

From these accounts we can form a basic definition of "shamanism": *Beliefs centered around a religious specialist, called "shaman" in Central Asia, who reveals knowledge through ecstatic experiences and learned techniques. Shamans are especially known by their ability to travel to and see different locations while their body remains in a trance in one location.* Most scholars agree that the word "shaman" can apply to some Asian and North and South American peoples. There are now also forms of "neo-shamanism," including "cyberian" and "cyburbian" shamanisms.[83]

The Use of "Shamanism" in Africa

Although the category "shamanism" is used regularly to describe religious specialists in Africa as part of what might be called a shamanistic complex,[84] Mircea Eliade resisted the temptation to carry this reified understanding of shamanism into Africa in the manner in which it has been used in other contexts. When describing the core of shamanism or the "archaic techniques of ecstasy" from around the world, Eliade intentionally omits Africa, noting:

> We have omitted Africa; to present the shamanic elements that it might be possible to identify in the various African religions and magico-religious techniques would lead us too far.[85]

81. Ibid., 31.
82. Wasson 1957, in Narby and Huxley, *Shamans through Time*, 141–47.
83. Harvey, *Shamanism*, 447.
84. E.g., Somé, *Healing Wisdom of Africa*; Price, *Archaeology of Shamanism*; Turner cited in Winkelman and Peek, *Divination and Healing*.
85. Eliade, *Shamanism*, 374.

Eliade suggests that if one wants to apply "shamanism" to the African context, one should consult Friedrich, *Afrikaische Priestertümer* (1964), Nadel "A Study of Shamanism in the Nuba Mountains," (1946) and Evans-Pritchard, *Witchcraft and Oracles among the Azande* (1937). However, in my reading, Evans-Pritchard never uses the term *shaman* in application or discussion of the religious system of the Azande.

At the very beginning of his text, Eliade states that,

> If the word "shaman" is taken to mean any magician, sorcerer, medicine man, or ecstatic found throughout the history of religions and religious ethnology, we arrive at a notion at once extremely complex and extremely vague; it seems, furthermore, to serve no purpose, for we already have the terms "magician" or "sorcerer" to express notions as unlike and as ill-defined as "primitive magic" or "primitive mysticism". We consider it advantageous to restrict the use of the words "shaman" and "shamanism," precisely to avoid misunderstandings and to cast a clearer light on the history of "magic" and "sorcery."[86]

For Eliade, the use of the word was intended to be limited to "a religious phenomenon of Siberia and Central Asia, as the word comes to us through the Russian, from the Tungusic *šaman*."[87]

Other recent studies of shamans, including the three volume, *Shamanism* (2004) edited by Andrei Znamenski, and *Shamans, Spirituality, and Cultural Revitalization* (2011) by anthropologist Marjorie Balzer, do not make bold claims that shamanism is a religious category that fits the African context. Even though Balzer considers shamanism to be of ultimate significance for understanding manifestations of religion around the world (12), she does not mention Africa once in her contemporary anthropology of religion study. In Znamenski's anthology of essays, the case is not made for the existence of the shamanic category in Africa. Instead, in the section on Africa, two older essays are included: a chapter from a 1982 text on Kalahari Kung healing, and Edith Turner's 1994 essay, "A Visible Spirit Form in Zambia." Turner notes in her essay that the spirit-guided healers that she observed in Africa were different than the shamans of Asia in that instead of the shaman entering into a trance, it was the client who would enter into a trance.[88]

These popularized and academic descriptions lead me to believe that the term "shaman" is not a helpful category for use in the Turkana context,

---

86. Ibid., 3–4
87. Ibid., 4.
88. Turner in Znamenski, *Shamanism*, 463n6.

nor Africa in general. Eliade shares that common shamanic initiations "involve 'dreams' in which the future shaman sees himself tortured and cut to pieces by demons and ghosts."[89] My research and the research of others has revealed no such occurrences in Turkana *emuron* initiations, although the evil specialists, *ngikapilak*, are known for skinning dead humans and cutting them to use in strong evil curses. But this is a completely different matter. Spirits do not possess Turkana *ngimurok*, nor do they fall into trances in which they travel to different geographical locations. It is my perspective after reviewing the literature of shamanism, that "shamanism" and "shaman" are terms that do not apply to the Turkana context. To reiterate, shamans are specific religious specialists from specific locations in Asia and possibly the Americas. Even in many of those locations we would all be best served if researchers used and described indigenous terminology for religious practitioners.

SUMMARY OF KEY TERMS AND PERSPECTIVES

This chapter has explored the literature and key terms surrounding traditional religious understandings in the world in general, in Africa, and specifically in Turkana. The literature continues to support the thesis that there is no clear agreement on the ways that general terms should be used in religious studies in Africa. From the ethnocentric use of the word "primitive" to the popular understandings and broad application of "shamanism" around the world, the understanding of traditional religious systems have suffered from both over generalizations and the misuse of specific terminology taken far out of context. In the next three chapters I will provide the data from my phenomenological study of religious specialists in Turkana. I will provide descriptions using local terminology and local understandings in ways that clarify who the *ngimurok* and other religious specialists are in Turkana, without over simplifying with broad generalizations. In the concluding chapter I return to the question of Turkana *ngimurok* as prophets, priests, diviners or shamans.

---

89. Eliade, *Shamanism*, 377.

4

A Phenomenological Description of Turkana Religious Specialists

"*The true* ngimurok *are the ones who are chosen by God.*" (i.45, 3.22a)[1]

"*It is a self-fulfilling prophecy that where there are sorcerers and raiders there will also be* laibons. *A modern variant might now add researchers, film-makers and tourists to the list.*"[2]

INTRODUCTION

BASED ON RESEARCH COMPLETED as described in chapter 2, this chapter provides an exhaustive phenomenological description of Turkana religious specialists. Previous descriptions of Turkana religious specialists, specifically *ngimurok*, have relied heavily on two sources: Gulliver's colonial report of his survey in Turkana in 1948–49,[3] and Barrett's 1998 interpretive dissertation on Turkana cosmology. Each of these reports recognizes their limitations and acknowledges that most of their data came from secondary informants and research assistants who were not self-identified as *ngimurok*. Gulliver admits to only having talked with one *emuron*, met one other, and only recorded the

---

1. All quotations and references from interviews are cited by interview number (for example, i.45 is from interview 45, see Appendix B for the full list of interviews and their dates), or by my field notes notebook page number (for example, 3.22a is from notebook 3, page 22, section a).

2. Waller, "Kidongoi's Kin," 57.

3. Gulliver, *Preliminary Survey*.

names of six others.[4] Barrett recounts a strong relationship with only one *emuron* named *Natubwa*, who was not one of the *ngimurok* from an ancestral lineage.[5] In my own attempt to visit with *Natubwa* during research in December 2011, my research participants shared that he has since died. Allegedly, his entire family was shot and killed by cattle raiders in 2007 or 2008 (2.28b).

This is the heart of the problem that this research ameliorates: While research does not doubt the importance of Turkana religious specialist's called *ngimurok*, all recent research in the region that discusses *ngimurok* refers to and builds its arguments upon these two previous narrow, deficient and Linnaean classification focused descriptions. The description of *ngimurok* presented here is supported by lived experience in Turkana communities from 1999–2007 and additionally comes out of an ethnographic-phenomenological methodology employed during an intensive research time October-December 2011. During this research period, more than 50 interviews were carried out in the Turkana language, including significant primary interaction and interviews with 30 self-described *ngimurok* at their homes, with four additional interviews with those who are identified by others as *ngimurok* but deny or clarify their identity as something other than *emuron* in their own self-description.

This chapter provides a phenomenological description based on these experiences and interviews, attempting to describe the phenomena of *emuron* in the words of *ngimurok* themselves. Although all description in social science has been recognized as interpretive in the sense that it cannot help but be affected by the epistemology of the researcher,[6] a phenomenological description attempts a bracketing, or temporary suspension, of interpretive and evaluative description. This phenomenological description should "retain the original texture of things" without explanation and analysis.[7]

In attempting this phenomenological description I first reviewed my field notes (three 60-page notebooks, handwritten), transcripts of selected interviews (104 pages of single-spaced, typed 10-pt font, Turkana language transcripts), more than 70 hours of audio recordings, and 2 hours of video recordings to identify the key terms that my research participants used to describe themselves and other *ngimurok*, the services they provided to their clients, the varieties of rituals performed, the ways in which they receive knowledge, and the objects required for their practices. In accordance with

---

4. Ibid., 240.
5. Barrett, *Sacrifice and Prophecy in Turkana Cosmology*, 16
6. Wolcott, *Ethnography*, 145.
7. Moustakis, *Phenomenological Research Methods*, 58.

the broader goals of my research, I was also careful to record *ngimurok* reactions to and relationships with Christianity and other New Religious Movements in Turkana, these are mostly recorded in chapter 6. I will write here, as much as possible, from the perspectives of the thirty different self-identified *ngimurok* who agreed to participate in my research. While I attempt to use their words, the translation of their words is my own translation, and as the interviewer, I am the one who directed the interviews, asking questions that seemed appropriate to myself and my own line of inquiry.

The Realities of Fieldwork

At the beginning of every interview visit there was a period of multidirectional observation and ambiguity. There was commonly a flurry of excitement upon my arrival to an *emuron* homestead. For some of the *ngimurok*, a vehicle arriving at their homestead was nothing abnormal; yet for others it was extremely uncommon. A few would not allow me to drive a vehicle to their homestead and required us to leave the truck behind at a safe distance and enter the homestead area on foot. Most speculated that I had come to share news of an upcoming meeting or event, either an immunization clinic or a food distribution event that has become so common with the proliferation of development agencies in the region. My normal response, "no, I have come to be your visitor," quickly followed by, "where should we park our truck and prepare our site for sleeping?" piqued the interest of the *emuron/amuron* and his or her family, but left the reason for the visit ambiguous. It also played on what I knew of Turkana hospitality, that when a person arrives at another's home, the host is required to care for the guest, often by providing food and a place to sleep.

The weight of one of the key questions raised during my research proposal, "what if no one is willing to talk to you about their practices and roles as *ngimurok*?" was quickly lifted at the beginning of my research. While I fully expected some opposition to my approach and inquiry, not only from *ngimurok* themselves, but also from the Western Christian missionaries, I was not prepared for the complete transparency on the part of the *ngimurok* we visited the very first week of my research. After spending two nights at the home of the very first *emuron* we decided to visit, James, my research assistant, and I honestly shared our previously unshared doubts about the research before we began: neither of us had expected to be given such complete access by the *emuron*.

At that very first homestead, on the very first day, we were invited to watch the *emuron* as he interacted with his clients in both public and private spaces. On that first day we observed rituals that people had never discussed with me, or even mentioned, when I served in the same region as a missionary for nine years. My assistant felt bold and asked if we could record video of the rituals and we were immediately granted permission. Within the first week of research I had completed three very successful interactions with *ngimurok* who appreciated that I wanted to learn, through their perspective and words, the ways that they work in the community. By the end of that first week I had more data than what I had previously imagined I might be able to piece together in 6 months.

What made the difference from the years I had lived in Turkana as a missionary? Why was I now being told secrets and witnessing rituals I had never heard about as a missionary? Upon reflection I am certain that it had everything to do with my approach as a researcher: First, I made myself vulnerable and relied on the hospitality of the *ngimurok* as a visitor at their home. Second, I had decided that I really did not know who the *ngimurok* were. I had no words of judgment or condemnation. My only understanding was that missionaries and church leaders were not very good at explaining who the *ngimurok* were, and that I had finally decided that it was best that I receive the words directly from the *ngimurok* themselves. Somehow I sounded sincere; I'm hoping it was because I was.

I also believe that one of our keys to initial success was deciding to begin our research in the part of the research area that was the farthest location away from any town. This meant that the initial *ngimurok* we visited did not know that we were coming. Toward the end of our research time we found that some people knew we were coming and were even expecting us to visit with them.

It was never made known ahead of time to research participants that a payment could be received for participating, but I gave a small payment of thanks to each of my research participants based on their willingness to share with us. The amount was small, in monetary value about $7 USD, but they were coveted items from town: a few kilograms of sugar and up to one kilogram of tobacco leaves. In many situations, the monetary value of the food provided to my assistants and me by the *ngimurok* was greater than that of the gifts I gave. I mention these small payments here, which are quite common in research projects, because as the research time progressed, *ngimurok* in different areas began to not only have foreknowledge of why I was visiting, but also knew that there was some sort of payment involved if they would talk to me.

The best research experiences seemed to be early on and after the short breaks we would take in town for me to type my notes and catalog the videos and photos I was recording. I did not realize how fatigued we would become after a number of days of interviews. Some days we would travel to a homestead only to find that the *emuron* was away for an extended period of time. At times we tired of asking the same questions and did not become very interested in the interview unless the participant offered something new that we had not yet heard. We were trying to complete too many interviews in too short a period.

The challenges were numerous. The vehicle we rented was not the most reliable vehicle and we were stuck on more than one occasion in the sand. This, combined with the heat (80-110F), irregular eating schedules (we often did not know when we would arrive or if food would be offered to us), the odd, unexpected isolated rain storm that would prevent us from traveling for a day or two, occasional lack of clean water, days with no opportunity for bathing, and the lack of bathroom facilities, all moved us toward physical and mental exhaustion.

But there were also exciting, refreshing moments: The times when we uncovered new information about *ngimurok* that we had never heard, or times when our interview sessions would turn into a feast. At one point we arrived at a home just as they were about to spear a camel and slaughter it. The amount of meat given and consumed that evening was gluttonous! On another occasion we shared tea and spent the night in a makeshift camp with people who were driven from their homes by bandits and were privileged to document their stories. One evening on the shore of Lake Turkana, we cooked freshly caught fish on a palm frond grill. Most exciting for all of us was discovering a line of hereditary *ngimurok* that previous researchers had never mentioned.

The research participants who accepted us into their homesteads with incredible hospitality, and were excited to share with us what it meant to be an *emuron* in Turkana, overshadowed all of these difficulties and momentary joys. The acceptance I experienced as an alien researcher who asked more questions than was appropriate for the context was beyond what I imagined could be possible. Only on a few occasions did we experience rejection and unwillingness to participate in the research.

Rejection of the Phenomenologist

At times there was reluctance on the part of an *emuron* to fully reveal their practices, especially if they did not know me. Sometimes an *emuron* would initially only talk about the practices that they knew were acceptable to some Turkana Christians, but not the practices that have been rejected by Christians. My advantage in these situations was that after completing many interviews, I was able to talk about the practices I had already discovered from the data of other interviews. Often, simply saying the names of a few hidden practices or of the common medicinal sticks used in rituals, would cause the research participant to laugh and open up to an entirely deeper level of sharing.[8] One such example was on my sixteenth interview when the *emuron* said that he did not use the ritual pigmented clay or ochre (*emunyen*) that Christians often reject. When I responded by saying that I had not yet met an *emuron* from his ancestral lineage of Lokorijem that did not use white and yellow *emunyen* he quickly responded, "oh *emunyen*; that's what I meant when I said water, of course I use *emunyen* . . . " He then proceeded to tell me about the uses for white, yellow and blue *emunyen* in depth. I never called his bluff directly, but no one else in my research referred to *emunyen* as "water." But, as I have said elsewhere, this is the advantage of being able to complete more than 50 interviews in the local language as opposed to talking to one or two *ngimurok* and a few second hand informants through a translator.

Only once did an *emuron* completely refuse to talk to me about his work. This *emuron* is known widely within his area and beyond as both an *emuron* and a church leader, holding the title "bishop," in a local Evangelical mission-initiated church. Upon arriving at his home it was obvious to both my research assistant and myself that this man was about to oversee a ritual, as nearly 50 women were gathered outside his home. He said he knew why I was there (word had travelled quickly and his village was on a main track for vehicles) and did not have time to talk to me. He was too busy with the needs of the community and with preparing for church visitors from America who were coming the next week, he said. This *emuron* had a strained relationship with the NGO I had previously worked with and was apparently concerned that I would share with other non-Turkana who financially support his church and community that he was engaged in traditional ritual activities.

For him, these activities are not mutually exclusive from Christian faith or even leadership in the church, a view that most people in his community also seem comfortable with. Yet, in spite of his liberality to oversee traditional rituals as an *emuron* in the community, he has chosen to hide these practices from Westerners associated with the community and his church, and denies his role as *emuron* when directly asked. I covet the opportunity for him to someday share with me openly how he reconciles both traditional Turkana ritual and Christian theology, but during my research time he refused every possible opportunity to visit with me. I know that he has been judged harshly by Western Christians in the past and that his level

---

8. Examples of hidden practices not commonly revealed to outsiders, and especially Western missionaries, include: the use of special sticks, offerings made to ancestors and the use of ritual ochre.

of trust in sharing with outsiders is very low. Yet, in spite of being harshly judged by Western Christians, he still actively seeks their financial support. This further points to his ability to hold both Christianity and traditional religious practices together, even if in tension.

I entreated one of this man's sons, after thoroughly explaining my research, that I had a genuine desire to understand how his father reconciles Christianity and traditional Turkana ritual, and the guarantee of his anonymity in my research reports, in an effort to encourage his father to talk to me. He responded, "I understand what you are trying to do and I agree with it; I also trust you, but my father is a very strong and difficult man. I cannot tell him anything."

On one other instance an *emuron* was not helpful because he was highly intoxicated, which was reportedly his normal condition. When I found him, he assured me he would still be able to help me and led me to his home, first in our vehicle, then on foot since he did not want the tracks of a vehicle leading directly to his homestead. Once inside one of his large houses, with his family surrounding us, he would begin to answer questions but then refuse, demanding payment before he would share information with me. While he did demonstrate the ritual offering of both sugar and tobacco to his fathers, eventually he became belligerent with loud requests for large sums of money and large animals.[9] His wives and older sons were observably embarrassed and the oldest son even apologized as we were walking away toward our vehicle.

A third *emuron* did not refuse to talk and was openly sharing with me until his older son, a church leader who identified me as a missionary, arrived at his father's home during the interview. The son began to answer questions for his father in ways that he thought a Christian missionary would want to hear. When I asked the son to not answer for his father, but to let his father answer the questions, his father also began to change his approach, stating that now that he was a follower of Jesus, he no longer did the things he had just described to me, in detail.

In spite of these rejections, I was able to have very open dialogue with many *ngimurok* who willingly shared from their own perspective who they are and what they do as *ngimurok* in their communities. In fact, on more than one occasion it was very surprising how open the participants were. I did not expect such honesty and hospitality. My sense is that Turkana *ngimurok* are weary of being identified as 'evil' by outsiders and those who follow the traditions of outsiders. They are also very aware that rapid change is occurring that threatens their positions of authority and respect

---

9. This exchange was video recorded, 038.MOV (10/26/11).

in communities. Multiple *ngimurok* were happy to hear that the things they were telling me would be written down so that their children and grandchildren would be able to someday read their words. When I would begin by saying there are many words about *ngimurok* all around, but that I wanted to hear words from the *ngimurok* themselves, there was a desire on the part of the *ngimurok* to assist me in that endeavor.

Who Do You Say You Are?

One of the main aims of my formal and informal interviews was to explore the complexities of the term *emuron*. For those who are self described as *emuron* and for those described by others as *emuron*, what does the title mean? The English translation of *emuron* has almost exclusively been "diviner," following Gulliver.[10] As seen in the previous chapter, "diviner" has such a broad range of meanings in both religious studies and anthropological literature that it is unhelpful in understanding the local Turkana phenomenon of *emuron*. In contrast to these general understandings of "diviner," what are the ways that traditional religious specialists in Turkana define, describe and categorize *ngimurok* themselves?

During my field research, no research participant, either self-described or described by others as an *emuron*, was willing to say that all *ngimurok* were essentially the same. Important differences were distinguished along the lines of ancestry, revelation, clans, techniques, and even morality.[11] Although I found variation in the ways *ngimurok* were viewed, potential general categories of *ngimurok* revealed themselves through the course of the research. These general categories were self-described by research participants and were mainly based on revelatory patterns, that is, the way in which *ngimurok* received knowledge.

And so, an initial question for the research participants was often: If not all *ngimurok* are the same, what are the different *ngimurok* you know about? Quickly followed by the question, even if I was certain that I already knew the answer, "which *emuron* are you?" or "Where are you among all these *ngimurok* that you have described?" These category questions opened the way for descriptions based on Turkana traditional religious and cultural categories, as described by the religious specialists themselves.

---

10. Gulliver, *Preliminary Survey*.

11. "Morality" here refers to the virtue of the *emuron* as evaluated by the community. In general, *ngimurok* were evaluated as "good" (*luajokak*) unless they were driven by jealousy and greed (*etereku*) or participated in practices that were taboo, i.e., the skinning, cutting, or use of dead human bodies, which are the known practices of the *ekapilan*, that is, *ngimurok* who have been filled with greed (*etereku*).

One common response was based on verbal descriptors of *ngimurok*. These included: "The ones who dream," "the ones who exegete/read[12] certain objects," "the ones who remove objects." Often these types of attributive verbs would be unhelpful, as when a participant would simply state that an *emuron* does *amuronut*. This would be somewhat akin to describing what a lawyer does by saying "a lawyer practices law." In this context, the best translation for "an *emuron* does *amuronut*" might be, "a ritual specialist does rituals," or, following Gulliver's use of "diviner," "a diviner divines." Thus, these general categories help to provide some structure, but are limited without further description.

Many *ngimurok*, when asked to list all the different kinds of *ngimurok* that they knew of, would also begin to list specialists who helped with specific medical problems, had a specific practice or ritual that helped with one specific problem, and then would clarify that that one wasn't exactly an *emuron*. Also, when an *akatuwan* (the one who ritually removes things from the body) was interviewed, even though every research participant, including other types of *ngimurok*, state that an *akatuwan* is an *emuron*, the *akatuwan* preferred the term *akatuwan* for herself. It is thus recognized in this research that any proposed general or specific categories will likely continue to be contested both internally and externally.

DIFFERENT TYPES OF *NGIMUROK* PRESENTED BY THE RESEARCH PARTICIPANTS

Through the research process I began to discern categories of *ngimurok* based on their practices, the way they receive knowledge and validation, their lineages, and the variety of problems that were brought to some more than others; in other words, their specializations. I have intentionally attempted to avoid using Western categorizations, thus any categorization found in this description has come out of the *ngimurok* descriptions of different types and terminologies used for Turkana religious specialists.

Because of my fairly wide range of interviews, I did come across *ngimurok* who do not fit the categories that other *ngimurok* describe. I do not consider these to be anomalies, and as such, invalid research participants. Instead, I offer their perspectives as valid in their own right, in a way that I believe presents a current context for *ngimurok* that cannot be

---

12. The Turkana verb for prophetic reading is *akisemere*, whether the object being read is a bag of tobacco leaves, a one hundred shilling note, the intestines of a goat, or some other object. I have argued for (and use) this Turkana word as a dynamic equivalent for "exegesis" when studying the Bible. See Lines, "Exegetical and Extispicic Readings."

neatly packaged into a singular, well-defined category. In many ways, although the data shared here provides a much richer description of *ngimurok* than previous available, it also adds to the complexity of the meaning of *emuron*, often frustrating my own attempts at clear-cut classification and exacting definitions.

Four categories of *ngimurok* were self-described and are listed here. These four categories are the *emuron* of the head, the *emuron* of the sandals and intestines, the *emuron* who reads (tobacco and money), and the *emuron akatuwan* who exorcises foreign objects from the body. Although the *emuron akatuwan* interviewed preferred to use the term *akatuwan* in her own description of herself, she did also describe herself as an *emuron*, and every other ritual specialist in this research described the *akatuwan* using the word *emuron* or the feminine form, *amuron*.

In addition to these four self-described categories, five other *ngimurok* categories were described by the research participants, two of which are viewed as evil actors in the community. In addition to these nine, five more categories were described, including those who are similar to *ngimurok* in their roles, but are not *ngimurok* by their own or others' descriptions, although they are described in the context of *ngimurok* discourses. See Table 1 below.

Table 1. Categories of *Ngimurok* Revealed from the Research

Self-identified categories of *ngimurok*	Other described categories of *ngimurok* (contested)	Categories of "similar to *ngimurok*" (contested)
Emuron a akou, lo erujait **Emuron of the head, who dreams (22 interviewed)** From one of three ancestral lineages. Specialist in community wide problems: rain, gardens, cattle raiding (prevention and protection), sicknesses, protection of wealth (domestic animals and daughters). Fathers visit and speak in dreams to identify and protect against problems before they occur.	***Ekasuban*** **The Doer/Curser** The evil one who does curses by manipulating stolen objects. Curses with the eye when people are eating. Works against the rituals of *ngimurok*. Motivated by jealousy, personal gain, or payment for services. Many are siblings of successful *ngimurok*.	***Emalaikat / Legio Maria*** **Angels/Legio Maria Church** Some leaders in this imported new religious movement are now seen as specialists in problems with spirits and ancestors. Some of the *Legio* specialists travel around visiting homes to hold prayer services for those with spirit related problems. They are at times possessed by particular saints or angels who speak through them to clients.
***Emuron a ngamook ka ngamaliteny, Emuron of sandals and intestines* (8 interviewed)** Specialists in identifying the cause and solution of problems in individuals and families by throwing sandals and reading goat intestines. Help in identifying a thief, *ekasuban* or *ekapilan*. No ancestral lineage although one clan is known for this (*Esigerit*).	***Ekapilan*** **Hidden evil curser** Causes death, circles around at night when people are dying, digs up fresh graves, skins and cuts up dead human bodies and uses body parts for cursing. Traditionally killed if found skinning/cutting a body.	***Ngikarikok a ngikanisae*** **Church leaders in various protestant and Catholic churches** Numerous *ngimurok* noted that church leaders are *ngimurok* who teach from and follow different traditions, but attempt to do the things of the *ngimurok*, especially when praying for rain, healing, and protection against evil.
Emuron lo esemere etaba/ ngaropiae **Emuron who reads tobacco/ money (2 interviewed)** Specialist in reading words from *Akuj* (God) that are revealed when looking at tobacco or paper money. Some are also specialists in particular problems, such as barrenness.	***Emuron a akomwa*** **Emuron of the termite mound** Ritually perambulates four times around a large termite mound for the purpose of cursing those who have stolen animals. The termite mound will fall to the ground during the ritual and is connected to the effectiveness of the curse.	***Akariton*** **The one who rubs/pulls** The *ekariton* specializes in helping in the delivery of a child, often by massaging the abdomen to help the baby be in the correct position for childbirth. Traditionally female, some have recently heard of male practitioners.
Akatuwan/ Amuron a etio/auono **The one who removes evil things from the body (1 interviewed)** Uses rituals to remove actual physical objects that are causing pain or pressure inside the body. These objects, often sticks, meat or hair, have been placed in the person by a curse or the eye of an *ekasuban*.	***Ekadwaran*** **The one with a bitter mouth/saliva** Note that "bitter" and "prophesy" are the same root word in Turkana. This specialist uses his/her bitter prophesying saliva to spit on boils and abscesses on the skin, causing them to open and heal.	***Ngikarikok/Ngikasikou a ngadakarin*** **(also *Eketamen*)** **Leaders/Elders of the community** Men who lead in the traditional prayers and blessings (*agata*) at group events, especially meat roasts, weddings and initiation ceremonies (*akinyonyo, asapan*). These are respected men in the community, but not *ngimurok*.
	Dakitari **Swahili for "Doctor"** The one who knows ritual/medicinal sticks and herbs (*ngikito*), specializes in their gathering and uses, but is not a "dreamer" or "reader." Same term is also used for practitioners of Western medicine.	***Lu Nyeyenete*** **"Those who don't know"** This category covers a range of practitioners who have either made up their own practices or imported practices from elsewhere and are seen as deceivers (*ngimokorae*). Often found in the markets of Lodwar town.

EMURON OF THE HEAD WHO DREAMS, THE EMURON OF GOD

> *Emuron a akou (a ngakeis), lu erujae* (2.1a) *a naju* (2.3b), *ngimurok a Akuj* (3.9b)

> "*God has given me this work to lead the people, to take care of the animals, to take care of sickness*" (1.11b).

Twenty-two of the religious specialists interviewed identified themselves as an *emuron* of the head (*akou*, s., *ngakeis*, pl.), an *emuron* who dreams (*erujae*) when sleeping (*a naju*), or as an *emuron* of God (*Akuj*). These terms are used interchangeably for self-identification. All the *ngimurok* in this category receive revelation from their fathers while dreaming and can recite their *emuron* lineage back to one of three great *emuron* ancestors: three of the research participants identify themselves as descendants of Lokedongan, four as descendants of Lokerio, and 16 as descendants of Lokorijem. At the most, each of the *ngimurok* interviewed were no more than five generations removed from their named great *emuron* ancestor; the closest was an *emuron* who is the grandson of Lokorijem. Of the descendants of Lokerio, the closest interviewed was the great-grandson of Lokerio; the two interviewed descendants of Lokedongan were great-grandchildren (one male and one female); all could name at least one more ancestor one generation beyond this great ancestor *emuron*. The descendants of Lokorijem most often shared the name Siangale when referring to the father of Lokorijem; the father of Lokerio was named Tepis; the few remaining descendants of Lokedongan name Atol as the father of both Lokedongan and Lokorijem. While this ancestral connection was made between the lines of Lokedongan and Lokorijem, no connections were made between the lineages of Lokorijem and Lokerio.

Extreme positive statements were made concerning these *ngimurok* ancestors:

> My fathers [Lokorijem and his descendants] were the *ngimurok* of God [*Akuj*]. They were the good ones who brought rain, healed sickness and protected people with ochre. They are the *ngimurok* who were appointed by God long ago. (3.9b)

Of these 22 research participants, five were women: one from the family of Lokedongan and four from Lokorijem. The women identified themselves in the same ways as the men ("the one who dreams," "of the head" and "of God"), but used *amuron*, the feminine form of the noun. I will discuss issues specific to these five female *ngimurok* later in this chapter.

Patrilineal validation of the emuron of the head

The identity of the *emuron* of the head is validated by the direct connection through dreams to his or her father, who was also an *emuron*, for both guidance and revelation. Often, *ngimurok* in this group would respond to questions concerning their practices by simply stating, "I am an *emuron* like my father" (2.26a), or, "the *ngimurok* of the head, they are the ones who follow the traditions/laws of their father" (2.27a, i50). For this type of *emuron*, it is very important that the father was also an *emuron* and that the father visits in dreams.

Both the father and grandfather are reported to visit in dreams to talk to and instruct their *emuron* descendant. Most explained that the visits in their dreams were very realistic, but that these visits always occurred in their sleep:

> I am an *emuron* of the head (*lo akou*); I dream when I am resting, in my sleep." [Who speaks to you when you are dreaming?] "My father and his father of my father. He comes to speak to me." [Your grandfather is Lokorijem and your father is Lodip?] "Yes, they are always coming to speak to me, Lodip and even Lokorijem. They are certainly all my fathers." [Did you meet the face of Lokorijem long ago when you were young?] "No, I had never met him. I meet him these days." [If you never met him long ago, how do you know it is him who is coming to speak to you?] "He just comes and sits with me, just like you are sitting here. He certainly comes and sits like this. (i22:2; 2:17b)

The continued relationship with the fathers provides credibility and identity to the *emuron* of the head. These visits do not take place during an induced trance and the *emuron* does not perform any special ritual in order to induce the fathers to visit. They visit only during normal sleep. It is possible for the fathers to be upset and not visit a particular *emuron* for an extended period of time, even weeks or months. In this case the *emuron* discerns what must be done to appease the father. The instructions are most often presented to the son by the father in a special dream-visit.

As an exception, the ancestral connection to great *ngimurok* is not patrilineal in all cases. That is, some male *ngimurok* validate their ability to be an *emuron* through the ancestry of their mother, who in each of these cases was found to be the daughter of a male *emuron* and was known as a practicing *amuron (f.)* who received dreams (3.2a, i26). Although this situation seems rare, and is met with skepticism by other Turkana and some other *ngimurok,* two male *ngimurok* from different families validated their identity as an *emuron* through their mother during the research. These men did not claim that their mothers speak to them in dreams, but that their maternal grandfathers are the ones who visit them in dreams and provide guidance.

Priority of Ancestral Lineages: Lokorijem, Lokedongan, Lokerio

> "The ngimurok who know sandals and intestines, God helps them some days, but the dreamer is in front of them all." (2.1b)

Those who identified themselves as *ngimurok a akou*, "of the head," or *ngimurok lu erujae*, "the ones who dream," were more likely to denigrate the abilities and powers of others called *emuron* who did not come from an ancestral lineage of *ngimurok* or, even further, who did not come from their own specific lineage of *ngimurok*. For all other *ngimurok* (those not from ancestral lineages), while their own practice was seen as integral to the lives of their clients, there was certainly deference toward those *ngimurok* from ancestral lineages in regard to the community-wide problems of drought, community wide sicknesses and cattle raiding.

Other *ngimurok* were likely to refer to the *ngimurok* who dream as the ones who performed the greatest works to help the community. One non-ancestral *emuron* of sandals and intestines exemplified this deference by stating:

> I don't really know anything about the family of Lokerio. The family of Lokorijem are the *ngimurok* who are living. They are the ones whose fathers could call down rain. I've not met those of Lokerio. (2.17a)

As will be described below, the ability to "call down rain" is seen as the ultimate role of the *emuron* of the head. This statement also provides an example of the view that the descendants of Lokorijem are the dominant active *ngimurok* in Turkana today.

The descendants of Lokerio did not try very hard to dispel this view of the priority of Lokorijem and his descendants. Instead, they often took the position that they were equal, but different lines of tradition. One *emuron* descendant of Lokerio admitted that the family of Lokorijem are now the leading *ngimurok*. One of the greatest *ngimurok* in the Lokerio family, Lokinei, according to those from all three traditions, had recently died. His brothers and sons among the descendants of Lokerio had yet to identify any one *emuron* who could compare to Lokinei's leadership and rain-making abilities. This death and lack of leadership among the family of Lokerio is certainly a contributing factor to their recent decline in influence and their deference to the descendants of Lokorijem.

Other responses from the *ngimurok* descendants of Lokorijem and Lokedongan concerning those of Lokerio range from views of equality, indirect criticisms, to outright insults. Sometimes the statements reveal that irrespective of how one personally evaluates the other ancestral *ngimurok*, it is not beneficial to say anything directly negative about them:

> Those ones of Lokerio, I don't know their work. I can't say anything about them. (3.11b)

> Both the descendants of Lokorijem and Lokerio are the same. There are two fathers but no one is greater than the other. (2.26b)

One *amuron* great-granddaughter of Lokorijem revealed that she was not certain about the relationship of the Lokorijem and Lokerio families, but that she does know the most famous story of Lokerio. This is the story that is told of Lokerio dividing Lake Turkana so that the warriors could cross and return with the camels they had stolen,[13] which also explains the origin of camels in Turkana:

> I don't know about Lokerio. They have their own people. I don't know if we, the people of Lokorijem are related to Lokerio or not, but I have heard the story of Lokerio dividing the lake. I only know the *ngimurok* of my own ancestors. (2.22b)

Another *emuron* descendant of Lokorijem positively emphasized the priority and past greatness of Lokerio, but spoke harshly of the work of his recent descendants in comparison, going so far as to say they have become evil, working out of envy and greed:

> The people of Lokerio were the first *ngimurok*. These *ngimurok* can bring rain, yet some are ruining their reputation with *asubes* (cursing for the purpose of jealousy or greed). They have become *ngikasubak*. Some are *ngimurok* like those before, like Lokine. His *amurote* could throw down rain. But certainly long ago in this place, my father became first among them. In the past the *amurote* of those of Lokerio has sometimes been ahead of those of Lokorijem. (i22:5)

I would commonly ask: which of the lineages are the true *ngimurok*? Rarely would there be a direct answer from the Lokorijem line, sometimes a descendant from the Lokerio line would say the Lokorijem are now more powerful. While such responses were rare, the following two statements of Lokorijem *ngimurok* are more evaluative, displaying a categorization of those who are legitimate or true (*luaiteni*) from those who are not:

---

13. This famous story of Lokerio is also recorded by Barrett, *Sacrifice and Prophecy*, 144–45; and Lamphear, "Aspects of 'Becoming Turkana,'" 96.

> The children of Lokerio? Yes, they are also *ngimurok*, somewhat (*cha*). [Somewhat? Does that mean they are not real, legitimate *ngimurok*?] Now if you say they are not legitimate, they will tell you by their own words that they are legitimate. Only they themselves know about their own legitimacy. But, we [of Lokorijem] disregard those of Lokerio; they are not legitimate. Those of Lokorijem are legitimate. (i15:7)

> The people of Lokerio follow us [*ngimurok a Lokorijem*]. They have dreams, but we are before them. The true (*luaiteni*) ngimurok are those who dream, from the family of Lokorijem, they are from the *ebilait* clan (*emachar*). (3.2a)

One *emuron* from Lokorijem's line refused to disparage the descendants of Lokerio directly, but instead pointed out the results of their work:

> I don't know [which family is better], but in [Lokerio's descendants'] place, rain is missing when people go to them, but there is rain on this side in this place [where Lokorijem's descendants live]. (1.8b)

One of the most interesting statements, which I had previously never heard (and is missing from the *ngimurok* literature), yet was confirmed multiple times during my research, relates to the differences in the ancestral origins of both Lokerio and Lokorijem:

> The family of Lokerio are descendants of the baboon (*echom*). The fathers of Lokerio were baboons who became people (*ngitunga*). The ancestors of Lokorijem were all people who came from Karamoja [the Western mountain region just across the border of Uganda where the Karamojong people live]. (3.3a)

As I sought to interpret the statement that the ancestors of Lokerio were baboons, I was reminded of one of the patterns that allows for the carrying out of ethnic violence, dehumanizing the other. This is the primary precondition for ethnic violence or even genocide; the other must be seen as less than human, as either an animal or an insect.[14] But that is not what is happening here in this situation. First, no one called the descendants of Lokerio, "baboons;" the baboons were only the ancestors of Lokerio. Second, it was viewed as an origin myth that was accepted by many people, both *ngimurok* and non-*ngimurok*. It must be noted that the descendants of Lokerio do not accept this origin myth as their own, pointing to the conclusion that there must be something disparaging about the idea. It could

---

14. Chalk and Jonassohn, *History and Sociology*, 27–28.

even be, as more than one person pointed out during my research, that people are commenting on the physical characteristics of the descendants of Lokerio, especially their commonly darker skin color, which is generally looked down upon in Turkana.

Only a few distinct differences in traditions were noted between Lokorijem and Lokerio descendants. First, Lokorijem's descendants are all from the clan, or *emachar* "brand," *Ngibilae (pl.)* or *Ebilait (sing.)*. The tradition of the *Ebilait* clan is that women can only use the skins of wild animals for carrying their children. They are often seen carrying children in the skin of the gazelle instead of the normal domestic animal skins. Food taboos for the *Ngibilae* include never touching the brain or lips of a cooked animal and never eating the head of a sheep or camel. The common understanding is, "if you eat the brain you won't be able to dream and if you eat the lips you can no longer speak truth . . . it cools the mouth" (2.16a). The descendants of Lokerio are from the clan, or "brand" *Emeturanait*. They have no taboos about eating any part of the animal and women carry their children in the skins of domestic animals like all other Turkana (2.15b).

Is Lokedongan a third ancestral line of ngimurok a akou?

All written descriptions of Turkana *ngimurok* mention only two lines of ancestral *ngimurok* of the head: Lokorijem, who seem to currently have a primary status as revealed in my research, and Lokerio. But my research discovered a possible third *emuron* ancestor, Lokedongan, who was frequently mentioned by the descendants of Lokorijem. Confusion, in the form of inconsistencies, was displayed among the descendants of Lokorijem regarding this ancestor named Lokedongan. Some believed he was either the grandfather of Lokorijem or the brother of Lokorijem:

> Our house of *ngimurok* [Lokorijem] started with a Karamojong named Siangale. I think the father of Siangale was Lokedongan. I also know of the sons of Lokerio. Lokinei [a great grandson of Lokerio] was an *emuron* of rain. (2.24a, i24:1)

A large group of *ngimurok* and other Turkana, estimated to be about 75 people, had recently visited the grave of Lokedongan, who had called some of the *ngimurok* of Lokorijem's family to offer sacrifices at his grave to bring rain (see photo in Appendix E). This was intriguing, as a number of the descendants of Lokedongan were not present at this offering and do not believe that the descendants of Lokorijem are the descendants of Lokedongan. Most of the descendants of Lokorijem who purported to know the history of Lokorijem claimed Karamojong ethnicity for the ancestors of Lokorijem.

Ngimurok descendants interviewed for this research who identified themselves as the descendants of Lokedongan recount a lineage that separates the family of Lokedongan from Lokorijem. The narrative from Lokedongan's descendants includes stories from a generation beyond Lokedongan and Lokorijem. Two brothers, Kaalinyang and Atol, were captured from Samburu and taken into the Turkana *Ngitira* (*Esigerit*) clan. Atol became the father of the brothers Siangale, Lokorijem, and Lokedongan. Not much is known about Siangale and it is even possible that Siangale was captured from the Karamojong or even that Siangale was not a brother, but was the wife of Lokorijem. Thus, the descendants of Lokorijem claim Karamojong ancestors and the descendants of Lokedongan claim Samburu ancestors.

The story continues that Lokedongan married a beautiful wife named Abakoedung and they had two children: a son, Liman, and a daughter, Lokorijem, a namesake of her uncle, before Lokedongan died and was buried near Lorengalup. When Lokedongan died, his brother Lokorijem wanted to take Abakoedung as his wife, which was customary. Uncustomarily, she refused and left with her daughter Lokorijem south to the lands of the Pokot, where they became Pokot prophetesses and began a line of women prophets that reportedly still exists today.[15] Liman, the son of Lokedongan, remained and had at least eight children through which an *emuron* of the head tradition was passed down.[16] I was able to meet and interview a grandson, granddaughter and great granddaughter of Liman who are practicing *ngimurok* in the ancestral line of Lokedongan and to whom both Liman and Lokedongan visit in dreams. As far as they are aware, they are the only surviving practicing *ngimurok* in this tradition. My research assistant and I were led to this family by a church pastor in Lodwar who is the great-great grandson of Liman, and who says he does not have dreams in which his ancestors visit him.

This discovery of a third line of ancestral *ngimurok* of the head, previously unmentioned in the literature, combined with hearing the stories of

15. Although I do not have any first-hand Pokot verification of this class of female religious specialists, I have found mention of Pokot female specialists called *chepsokoyon*, described by one researcher as "a female diviner concerned with the problem of witchcraft," O'Dempsey, "Traditional Belief and Practice;" and by two other researchers as female "milk diviners," Jónsson, "Pokot Masculinity," 130; and Bianco, "Songs of Mobility," 29.

16. This history was recounted by multiple descendants in interviews 49 and 50, Dec 8 and 9, 2011.

ancestors from Karimojong and Samburu, reveals the futility in attempts to identify a static Turkana *emuron* tradition. While *ngimurok* of the head are clearly validated by their ancestral lineages and the success of their rituals today, it is evident that boundaries of such clear-cut validation were different in the past. This is consistent with historian John Lamphear's view that assimilation of many different peoples and traditions has always been part of what it meant to be "Turkana," especially in the nineteenth and early twentieth centuries when large areas of pastoral migration and inter-ethnic conflict gave the Turkana an advantage over other ethnicities.[17]

During this period, people were not only forced to assimilate through conflict, but willingly joined Turkana villages for protection.[18] Indeed, the situation may not have been that the Samburu ancestors of Lokorijem and Lokedongan were captured and brought to Turkana, but instead, that the Turkana moved into the current area of Turkana district where the Samburu were already living.[19]

While the idea that Turkana identity was formed fairly recently through migration and assimilation is certainly speculation, it is an idea that is consistent with the self-ascribed descriptions of important ancestral lines of *ngimurok* only four to six generations removed. For the Turkana *ngimurok* who are "of God," "the true ones," "who know the traditions of the fathers," to say that their great ancestor was from another ethnicity, or even a primate, belies our often-Western-romantic desires to study groups like the Turkana as timeless "primitives" with traditions "as old as time." We instead find that they are a complex people, with a history of mixing and assimilating, who only at this time in history have ever been the way they are now.

This is an important digression that helps us answer the question, "are the descendants of Lokedongan a third, separate line of Turkana ancestral *ngimurok*?" Yes, according to those who are the descendants, they are, and that is sufficient validation for a phenomenological study. Furthermore, such a "discovery" reveals that there likely have been and will be other ancestral lines of *ngimurok* in Turkana as well.

Revelatory Relationship with the Father (Apa)

> "*Unless my father tells me what to do, I can do nothing. My father taught me the* etal *(tradition)*" (1.8a).

---

17. Lamphear, "Aspects of 'Becoming Turkana.'"
18. Ibid., 95.
19. Ibid., 93.

When asking the *ngimurok* of the head how they know what to do for the problems brought to them, or how they know what problems may happen in the future, the answer is almost always, "God tells me," or "My father tells me" in dreams. This dreaming experience occurs while sleeping, normally at night. Sometimes dreams in which the father or grandfather visits do take place while sleeping during the day, but it is not an induced sleep or hallucinogenic aided state; just normal sleep, mostly occurring at night. The sleep of an *emuron* of the head is so important that they are never awakened if found to be asleep.

Descriptions of visits with the fathers in dreams were very similar with only minor variations for all *ngimurok* of the head. The father or the grandfather, or both, come in the same form that they had when they were alive. They provide specific directions for specific problems by speaking and by providing visions:

> [When you are dreaming during your sleep, who speaks to you?] It is my father who comes. My father comes to speak with me. [Your father?] My father. He always comes; he comes just as he was (*itemem*) long ago, exactly as he was (*ikwaan*) long ago. He comes to give me a word, saying 'do this word about such and such a thing like this.' He says 'do these things for these problems like this.' Sickness is coming, rain is coming to this or that place like this; an enemy is coming. Take the *ariwo* (ritual sacrifice) and kill it. He shows me which *ariwo* by the color of the skin of the animal. He shows you the very skin so that you see it. In fact, you even see that animal, whether it is a goat or a sheep or whatever, you see it standing there. You even see the pen it is standing in. You see the very animal in its pen wherever it is. If the place is Katir, then you see the home where it is in Katir. If it is in Turkwel, then you see the home where the goat is there. Then I tell a person to go and find that goat. (i15:6)

Sometimes the *emuron* father or grandfather is only heard and not seen:

> My grandfather, Lodip [the eldest son of Lokorijem], comes to me in dreams when I am sleeping and talks with me. Sometimes it is only a voice that is heard. Sometimes I see him. I know it is him because his face is the same, but somehow his head is different. I don't see his body. (i23:2)

While the fathers will provide specific solutions to specific problems that clients have already brought to the *emuron*, many times the fathers foretell the *emuron* that a certain problem is about to happen. A solution is provided that will prevent the problem from happening. Often, these future problems, including enemy raiders and human and domestic animal sicknesses, have the possibility of affecting entire communities. The solution protects the community:

> He [my father] shows me saying, 'there is a sickness coming.' Before the sickness even comes he tells me, 'Take this certain ochre (*emunyen*) and spread it on the people.' I tell the people in the area to have that ochre put on them, it is like an *ariwo* (protection ritual). (i22:3)

Ochre, or specific pigmented clay or mud is often one of the solutions provided by the fathers.[20] The specific color is important for an effective treatment of a problem:

> When I am sleeping my father and grandfather show me which ochre should be used for a problem. (2.24b)

Some *ngimurok* described more extensive interaction during the dreams. The fathers are not only speaking to them, but they are also speaking to the fathers in conversation. The dream experience is understood as such a vividly genuine event that food can even be consumed in the dream:

> When I am talking to my fathers in a dream sometimes they even feed me food. Then when I am awake I don't feel hunger. (3.18b)

These dreams are extremely realistic events for the *ngimurok* of the head. The visits of their fathers were described as the way a visitor comes to your home to sit next to you and talk. Often it was explained that the dream experience was identical to the way I was sitting and visiting with the *emuron* at his or her home, engaged in conversation. These visits from the fathers are of the utmost importance. Without words from the fathers, the *emuron* of the head will not proceed with providing ritual instructions to the people seeking answers for problems.

I repeatedly tested the extent of this total reliance in every situation on words received from the fathers. Was there not a pool of specific knowledge and practices from which the *emuron* could draw on their own, I queried? There seemed to only be a limited number of possibilities: a limited number of types of animals, colors of animals, colors of ochre. One might consider it reasonable that an *emuron*, having successfully dealt with the same situations any number of times, could rely on previous formulas. To test this, I constantly asked the question: "If someone comes to you and you have not received a dream from your father telling you what needs to be done, do

---

20. See "*Ewosakin Emunyen*," chap. 5, for more on Turkana ritual ochre.

you ever just think on your own what worked for that type of problem in the past and do it?" This was always quickly and emphatically answered in a way similar to one of my early interview responses, "No, you never think on your own in your head, you only do the words of your father" (1.9a). Even as an *emuron* was explaining a ritual to me, I interrupted and asked, "Before you do this, do you know what to do on your own or does something tell you what needs to be done?" To which the immediate response was: "Who else could bring me this but my father" (i22:5)?

This reliance on the fathers was further confirmed with statements that asserted the dishonesty of an *emuron* speaking when the father does not speak:

> There are days when my father does not come in dreams. In those days I can't tell people what to do. We [the *ngimurok*] are not supposed to lie. We do not lie to the people; we only tell them what our father says. (2.2a)

As will be shown throughout the rest of this description, this is a major difference between the *ngimurok* of the head and all other types of Turkana *ngimurok*. While other *ngimurok* have set rituals and divination techniques that reveal information and solve problems, the *ngimurok* of the head are completely reliant on their fathers for revelation concerning problems and the specifics of rituals to be performed.

Passing on the Traditions to the Next Generation

Because of reliance on revelatory dreams from the fathers, one does not become an *emuron* of the head until the father has died and begins to visit in dreams. While children of the *ngimurok* of the head observe and even participate in rituals overseen by the father or mother from an early age, they are not described as *ngimurok*. Even older *ngimurok* were reluctant to say that they had chosen any of their children for specific training or as successors.

When asking, "Now that you are very old, will one of your children replace you?" a common response was, "Right now they are all helping me, but there is not one of them that I have given this work to possess. But now they can do the work when I spit on them (*amak*) to do my work" (2.25b). Spitting (*akimak*)[21] on a person in Turkana, in general, is seen as a blessing. This spitting of an *emuron* is a commonly understood method of officially assigning a task to another person. When a person, normally a child or wife, stands before the *emuron* and the *emuron* spits upon the head or hands of that

---

21. Or the dialect variant *akimuak*, see Vermi, *Turkana Dictionary*, 126.

person, it is understood that any task immediately carried out by that person is done with the instruction, authority, and blessing of the *emuron*.

I often noticed that the daughters of an *emuron* were the ones who did much of the work of the ritual slaughtering of the animals; for example, holding the animal down while it was being killed, especially for the methods of suffocation, cutting the throat, or *tongeere*; that is, the cutting open of an animal while still alive. The authority needed to participate in these rituals was given by the *emuron* ritually spitting on his children and wives who would be assisting. Other rituals that family members were appointed to carry out included the application of ochre on the bodies of clients and the throwing of water onto the clients. These same daughters and wives were also the ones who cooked the meat from the sacrifices.

While the children of the *emuron* of the head learn the mechanics of the rituals normally carried out as they are empowered to assist in the rituals of the *emuron*, the role of the *emuron* of the head cannot be handed over to a child until the death of the *emuron*. It is not until after the death of the *emuron*, when the *emuron* father begins to visit in the dreams of the child, that one can be considered the *emuron* of the head. It is not until after death that the *emuron* father selects his successors. It is quite possible that the dead *emuron* will not visit all of his children in their dreams. At times, the fathers only visit one of the children in their dreams.

Ambiguity and Interchangeability of the Terms God (Akuj) and Father (Apa)

An ambiguity was sometimes noted in the ways the *ngimurok* of the head referred to revelation coming either from God (*Akuj*) or a father (*apa* "father," or *aapa* "paternal grandfather"). The God and father terms often seemed interchangeable in the casual discussions with *ngimurok*. When I would directly attempt to gain clarification, the explanations often revealed a complex, seemingly contradictory, unified understanding of the relationship between God and *ngimurok* paternal ancestors. One of the most interesting responses, "the God who is my father," came out of the following exchange:

> My *apa* (father) comes and tells me words/things to do. *Akuj* (God) comes and tells me things when I am asleep and dreaming. [Which God? (*Akuj ani?*)] God who is my father (*Akuj ngesi apakang*). (2.1a)

And again, the first person possessive pronoun was at times used in parallel with both father and God:

> My God (*Akuj kang*), my father (*apa kang*) tells me to come to his grave when he needs something. (2.27a, i50, descendent of Lokedongan)

Yet, at other times, God and father were held as distinctly separate sources for revelation, as if the possibility was that God could speak to the *emuron* separately from the fathers:

> God (*Akuj*) comes to talk to me in my dreams to tell me what to do; sometimes my father (*Apa*) comes. (2.3b)

> God (*Akuj*) speaks words to me in my sleep. Yes, God even sends my father in my dreams. Both my father and God are always coming. When it is God I just hear a voice. When it is my father I can see him I know him by seeing his body, we sit together and talk back and forth in the way you and I are talking now. (2.11b)

> God comes to me when I am dreaming and tells me what to do, and my father is always coming also. When my father comes, he comes together with God, he comes to tell me: save this person here (2.15a, 34:00).

One *emuron* from the line of Lokorijem even described his ancestor as *Akuj Lokorijem*, suggesting that Lokorijem was the same as God or that there was very little distance between the concepts of father and God. Both my research assistant and I were astonished to hear this and checked the recording from the interview to verify that he was not saying "the god *of* Lokorijem." Then, in the very next sentence, the *emuron* continues by using "Lord" (*ekapolon*), a term normally reserved for "God" (*Akuj*), with *apakang* (my father):

> For rain, a camel is killed, or a goat is killed. I tell them that we are not killing the animal for nothing. It is certainly killed because God Lokorijem (*Akuj Lokorijem*) began it, saying to me, 'go, the camel for rain is this color, tell those people saying go and kill it, rain will come.' Sometimes the camel is brought here to my homestead and killed, other times I am told by the Lord my father (*ekapolon apakang*), 'kill it at some other place.' So once the animal arrives it is speared or sometimes it is held and then *tongeere* (ritual disemboweling while alive). Then I throw water on the people, saying, 'God (*Akuj*) help us, provide these people with rain, and now go well.' I call to God. (2.18a; i22:3)

Another *emuron* explained the connection by simply stating that "the fathers have become one with God, so they are the same as God. They came long before the churches came" (3.9b). This explanation, that the fathers have become one with God, was not offered by any of the other *ngimurok*. Yet, it provides a perspective that does explain the ambiguous usage of the terms. If the fathers, over time, are farther away, then they must be closer to God.[22]

Visiting the Father's Grave

Occasionally, when the fathers and other paternal ancestors of the *ngimurok* of the head visit their *ngimurok* descendants in dreams, they make requests related to their physical needs and the condition of their graves. The *emuron* is expected to visit the grave and fulfill the requests of the father or other ancestor. The most common complaints from the ancestors that need attention are hunger and scarcity of shade covering the grave. These occurrences were described multiple times in the research and can be summarized with a few representative statements. The first two statements display the priority of the father in deciding when there is a need for the *emuron* to visit the grave and a few of the normal activities at the grave to appease the father:

> Sometimes my father comes to me in a dream and tells me he is hungry or that the sun is burning him and that I need to come and feed him or re-cover his grave with tree branches. So I go to my father's grave and do what he has asked. I will sleep there and feed him meat and tobacco. I cover the grave with sticks. Then I go home. Sometimes I feed my father at my home. (2.4a)

> Yes, my father calls me to his grave. Sometimes he says the sun is burning him and the grave should be covered with sticks. Sometimes I give him water. Other times I feed (sacrifice) a sheep to him. (3.11a)

Another *emuron* describes regularly attending to the needs of the father, even when not instructed by the father:

> I go to my father's grave about two times each year, both on my own and when my father tells me to come. I bring him a sheep, tobacco and sugar; sometimes I even bring him a bull or a camel. (2.12b)

---

22. My initial reaction to this ambiguity in the usage of the terms God (*Akuj*) and father (*apa*) was to wonder what Turkana Christians are hearing and understanding when Jesus talks of the Father in reference to God, especially in passages like John 8:8–14, or even in instructing his followers to pray, "Our Father, who is in heaven." Are they understanding the "Father" as God, the father of Jesus, or as God our ancestral father? This is a topic that needs further investigation.

A third example describes a significant time requirement for the visit:

> When my father tells me I go to his grave for about 4 or 5 days to feed him. (2.19b)

The following example is unusual in that the *emuron* describes the father as coming like a spirit who intends to cause problems (*ekipe*); perhaps the request to visit the grave is seen as burdensome because of the distance:

> Sometimes my father says 'kill me a goat' and I go to his grave and kill it. Sometimes he comes like a spirit (*ekipe*) to my house to tell me what he wants. His grave is not near here; this is not my place; we came to this place because of famine (*akamu*). (2.26b)

One *emuron* revealed that for especially difficult community-wide problems he would go to his father's grave, offer an animal and await revelation concerning the problem to come in a dream. While he can take care of individual problems at his home, when large groups come, especially those groups seeking rain, he is compelled to go to his father's grave and wait for a dream to show which action should be taken. Normally he sleeps at his father's grave for four days; during these days a certain animal is revealed while he is sleeping that needs to be killed as an *ariwo* sacrifice (1.11b).

Most ancestral *ngimurok* reported visiting their father's grave at least once or twice each year, typically sleeping by the grave for four nights. These visits are almost always prompted by the father or ancestor visiting the descendent *emuron* in a dream, at home, in which the ancestor requests the visit. At other times, especially when an area is in need of rain, multiple *ngimurok* descendants of the same ancestor will visit the grave together, along with other friends and relatives to sacrifice multiple animals. An *emuron* recounted one such very large recent gathering of *ngimurok*:

> A large group recently went to Lokedongan's grave, which is why we have had rain. Our fathers were angry with the people. That was the cause of the recent drought (*akamu*). There were maybe 70, maybe 100 of us who went to his grave and did what we were told. We killed six goats and two camels and brought tobacco. We slept there in August for four days. On the fifth day it rained. (3.18a)

Gatherings such as this one are considered rare, but are seen as especially effective in times of great community need.

From these responses we find that for the ancestral *ngimurok*, the grave of the father is an important location for both placating an *emuron* ancestor and receiving revelatory dreams from the ancestor when large community-wide problems, such as drought, are occurring. Common means for appeasing the requests of the ancestor include the ritual feeding of the ancestor and the covering of the burial mound with freshly cut thorny branches from an acacia tree. The feeding of the ancestor is accomplished by sacrificing a domestic animal, or multiple animals, at the grave. Those present will eat the roasted meat, except for portions of the meat designated for the ancestor, which are placed in the branches covering the grave. Other forms of ritual feeding include throwing small amounts of chewing tobacco, sugar or water on the grave.

Gender and Ngimurok of the Head

Even though Turkana family units are highly patriarchal, there are some women who are known and self-describe themselves as *ngimurok* of the head. Five of the research participants in this study were daughters of ancestral *ngimurok* of the head,[23] currently married to men from non-*ngimurok* clans.[24] All five openly shared about their work as an *amuron* (the feminine form of *emuron*). One was only practicing in hiding, at night, at her home, waiting until her husband died before openly working as a full *amuron* (i.23). The other four were practicing openly.

One of the openly practicing *ngamurok* had one of the wives of her *emuron* brother living with her to assist with her practices (i.15). This *amuron* was disabled and had limited mobility, making the assistance of her sister-in-law (*nakamaran*) invaluable. The sister-in-law explained her help to the *amuron* in this way: "When she tells me I fetch water, I bring the sticks, I butcher and cook the goat that has been ritually killed. I cook; am I not a wife? I am her wife (*aberu*)." (i.15:3). There were no sexual connotations in this statement, but it served to underscore the uncommon occurrence of a woman practicing openly as an *amuron*. A husband who is not from an *emuron* of the head family would not be able to help with the rituals of his *amuron* wife. In this situation, the wife of an *emuron* brother is able to help in the ways that the wife of an *emuron* would be able to assist her husband in carrying out the laborious aspects of particular rituals.

An *amuron* of the head, as self-described, is not limited in her ability to perform rituals or receive revelations from her father and other ancestors

---

23. I spoke to these five women in interviews 15, 23, 40, 41, and 49.

24. That these five women are all married to husbands from non-*ngimurok* clans is not surprising, as men and women in Turkana are expected to find a spouse exogamously. What is surprising is that they have retained the traditions of their fathers from within their husband's clan.

A Phenomenological Description of Turkana Religious Specialists 93

in dreams. At one point in an interview I asked an *amuron*, "Are you an *amuron* (feminine form of the noun) or *emuron* (masculine form of the noun)?" I received an extended reply that suggests an *amuron* of the head is not limited by her gender:

> [I am an] *amuron*; an *amuron* that is a married woman. I am not a man like Ekomolo [a recent ancestor *emuron* in the line of Lokorijem]. I am a woman that does rituals (*emuroe*) and that dreams (*irujae*). I dream just like Ekomolo dreams. Bad things happen and God tells me words about someone or another; the camel of this person, the camel of this person is the one that will throw down rain (*echakuni akiru*), the camel is at this certain home, of this certain hair color. I go straight away and ask for (*kilipun*) it myself, I bring it and kill it. [Do all people come to you with problems or only women?] Everyone comes; even men come with their struggles for me, even women dance. Women and men come. And even more when the camel is killed for me in the middle of my home, when it is finished, I certainly give back (*ealak bocha*) the meat to the people. And if it is rain that they wanted, the rain falls. It [the rain] brings things back to life and the grass comes up. Water becomes common (*topetun*). (i15:4)

This response reflects her full participation in the community as an *amuron*. She is leading the rituals connected to the most important role of the *ngimurok*: prayers and sacrifices, guided by her fathers, to bring much needed rain.

While this participant is able to practice openly as an *amuron*, one research participant described the difficulty of being seen as dishonoring her husband by practicing openly as an *amuron*. The adult daughter of a great *emuron* of the head in the *Ebilait* clan, she is now married to a wealthy husband in the *Esigerit* clan. She explained the dilemma of being known as a successful *amuron* while trying to honor her husband:

> Yes, I am an *amuron*. My father was a great *emuron* (*emuron lo apolon*). I do the things that my father did and the things he tells me in my dreams. I do them, but I only partially do them. When I married, I left many of those things to his sons. I must respect my husband. For if you do this work when your husband is here, God will see this evil and say, 'Why is this married female person (*itwaan niberu*) doing this work while staying with her husband?'... The tradition (*etal*) that I was long ago born into is very different from this tradition of my husband. I must respect my husband; I certainly can't kill (*nyedonyori*) my husband. The wife must take and hold the tradition of her husband. I only do

> this work if there are people of my household here who have a sickness like congestion (*arukum*), since in this place the hospital is far away. I might take some water and throw it on them. I might take a little mud and use it as ritual ochre. I get soil from the river here and spread mud (*echoto*). God then saves the person. It is acceptable for me to do these things, but I cannot do them in the open so that I respect my husband. (i23:1–2)

Later, she explained how she hides her work at night and that when her husband dies she will work openly as an *amuron*:

> Yes, they are always coming. But they come in small groups at night so that people don't see. I am afraid other people will see them and I will be called a thief who is stealing from my husband. They don't bring many problems. They come saying they have hunger, bless us so we can go and find what we are looking for at someone's home, in order to find food. They don't bring problems here like, 'I want to go kill a person.' I throw water on those who are looking for food. [What about those groups of men who are going to look for animals (i.e., going on cattle raids)?] The groups that are going other places to the east, I certainly throw some water on them so that they can go and return without being killed there. (i23:4–5) [Does God show you the *ariwo* sacrifices in your dreams?] Yes, I see the *ariwo*, but many times I don't tell anyone. I need to show respect to my husband. [When your husband dies, will you do this work openly?] Yes, I will no longer have to hide my work from my husband. My sister was the same. Her work was unseen while she was married, but now she is a great *amuron*. (2.22a)

These descriptions clearly identify the *amuron*'s work as equivalent to that of an *emuron*, but also display a tension among some to outwardly defer to the traditional patriarchal tendencies. This creates tension for the *amuron* who must balance what is considered a moral trespass against her husband by dishonoring him with a moral trespass against God or the *emuron* ancestor who reveals rituals to her in her dreams. Yet, in spite of these known tensions, people continue to visit the *ngamurok* of the head who are known as successful in solving problems.

Common Problems Brought to the Ngimurok of the Head

> "The problems that people bring are rain and sickness. They want me to throw water on them and use the *emunyen* (*ochre*)" (2.26b).

Most ancestral *ngimurok* who participated in this research project explained that the major problems[25] they help with in the community include lack of rain, sickness among people and animals, and bandits or cattle raiders. Ancestral *ngimurok* were also found to be active in directing and blessing the community during specific activities such as planting gardens or traveling with animals. Community-wide problems are normally reserved for the eldest *emuron* in a family, or those who are known for their success in providing favorable results. Illnesses in individuals are taken to more local *ngimurok* or to an *emuron* known by the community to be successful in solutions for a specific problem. In this section I provide a description of each of the common problems brought to the *ngimurok* of the head. Many of these problems are not exclusively dealt with by the *ngimurok* of the head, but are also the domain of other categories of *ngimurok*. Of all the problems brought to the different *ngimurok* and other religious specialists in Turkana, lack of rain is the one problem that is the exclusive domain of the *ngimurok* of the head.

Rain (*akiru*)

> "The problems my father dealt with were rain (akiru), sickness (edeke) and enemies (ngimoe)" (2.24a).

The ability to receive the community at one's home and prescribe the correct rituals that will produce rain during extended dry periods is one of the most important roles of the *emuron* of the head as noted by my research participants. The stories of great *ngimurok* of the head often include those who could make rain fall immediately after leading a community ritual. All three *ngimurok* of the head ancestors relevant to this research, Lokedongan, Lokerio and Lokorijem, are known as those who could make rain "hit" (*taram akiru*) immediately following sacrifices with the called community. At times when there is extended drought and individual *ngimurok* have been unsuccessful at triggering rain, multiple *ngimurok* will gather together at the grave of an *emuron* ancestor to receive dreams and offer the prescribed sacrifices, as described earlier in this chapter. One of the greatest

---

25. The Turkana words that I am translating as "problems," most often used in the context of issues brought before the *ngimurok,* are ngakiro and ngichen. Ngakiro is the plural form of *akiroit,* or "word," and is a more generic term that can be understood as "news," "words," "things," "incident," "story," or "issues." Ngichen (alternative spelling, ngican, in Barrett, *Turkana-English Dictionary,* 55), is understood as "disaster," "trouble," "affliction," "crisis," or even as "tragedy." I have decided that, in the context of bringing ngichen and ngakiro to the *ngimurok,* the best translation is "problem." "Problem" reflects that there is not only a "trouble" but that there is also the expectation of a possible solution that can solve the problem.

ngimurok with rain-producing success in current memory is Lokinei, from the ancestral line of Lokerio. Since his recent death, none of his brothers or sons have been able to replicate or match his abilities.

Normally, the eldest *emuron* of the head in each family is the one who receives the community at his homestead for rain rituals. One *emuron* described the priority of the elder *ngimurok* in his family concerning rain:

> People come with their problems both in groups and as individuals to my home. They come to have me intercede for sicknesses. They come when they are preparing to drive animals far away so that an enemy will not take them. I do the intercession (*agatakin*) and the ritual sacrifice, and then they are good to travel. But, I don't pray for rain; there is an *ekapolon* ("great one, elder") who does that. I have older uncles, so that is their work; I can't do it when there are elders. (2.15b)

Thus, priority is given to the eldest *emuron* in each ancestral line when the community concern is rain. While there is not truly a system of hierarchy or status among the *ngimurok* of the head, as each *emuron* serves the problems of their local area, it does seem that the ability to cause rain to hit through ritual means is what distinguishes the great and legendary *ngimurok* of the head from all the others. The presence of rain, even in small amounts, makes a huge difference in the semi-arid climate of Turkana.[26]

Normally the *emuron* of the head will have a dream revealing from the fathers the specific rituals to be done in order for rain to come to an area. After receiving a revelation, people in the area are called to come to the home of the *emuron* with appropriate gifts for the rituals and for the *emuron*. The event might take only one day or could be as long as four days, and also includes shared feasting of the meat by all those present. Because the fathers in the dreams dictate the specific rituals, there is not one formula of ritual acts that are always carried out to bring rain.

Sickness (*edeke*)

> "*I pray for rain and people bring problems of sickness to me*" (2.11b).

Categories of illnesses (*edeke*, sing., *ngidekesinei*, plural) reported as treatable by *ngimurok* of the head during my research include: general illness or

---

26. The average annual rainfall in Turkana County is 120mm (4.72 inches). A recent report listed 2004 as a very good rain year in Turkana, with a total of 243.1mm or 9.57 inches. See Arid Lands Resource Management Project II, "Drought Monitoring Bulletin, April 2011: Turkana County," Government of Kenya, April 2011.

weakness of the body, barrenness in women, specific illnesses such as infections, swelling, fever, malaria, sexually transmitted diseases, difficulties in childbirth, and spirit (*ekipe, ngipean*) and ancestor (*ngikaram*) possession. While any *emuron* of the head can find possible solutions to these problems, some were considered specialists who have success or special revelation concerning one specific problem.

One research participant was known for, and identified himself as a specialist in barrenness, and is known to have a high rate of success in helping women become pregnant through prescribed rituals for the woman and the extended family. Barrenness is not viewed as a problem with the body of the woman, but as a problem in the entire family that can be solved through ritual activity.[27]

Another research participant is a self-described specialist in sexually transmitted diseases who claims success in curing a number of illnesses by concocting a drink of specific roots and the urine of domestic animals that was revealed to him by his father in a dream. HIV infection is among the diseases he claims to be able to cure. While the local government discourages these types of claims, he is well known in his area for his abilities.

While most *ngimurok* work with clients dealing with illness from within their local areas, a known successful specialist will have clients that come from other areas and great distances, and has clients who are referred from other *ngimurok*. Clients at one specialist's home had travelled approximately 300 kilometers (about 180 miles) for a consultation. At another specialist's home, a husband and wife had journeyed on foot nearly 100 kilometers, accompanied by their local *amuron*. This *amuron* was an *akatuwan* (see below), who, while accompanying the couple to the home of the *emuron* for their consultation regarding barrenness, also provided her own specialized services to the *emuron* himself for pain he was feeling in his own body. This is where it was first explained to me that all *ngimurok*, even the *ngimurok* of the head, are very limited in their ability to heal themselves and must rely on the services and revelations of other *ngimurok* for the healing of their own illnesses.

There are multiple traditional ways to deal with illnesses without visiting an *emuron*. There are women known for cutting the body to relieve pain and pressure and also women and men who specialize in the delivery of children. Although some in the western missionary and medical community have associated the practices of cutting the body during illness with *ngimurok*, these practices of cutting and of being present at the delivery of

---

27. For a specific ritual prescribed to one woman and her family, refer to the transcript from the video recording (VN 2–3).

a child are not part of the role of the *emuron*, but part of folk healing traditions often carried out by elders in the family.

Clients who go to the *emuron* for treatment of an illness are normally seeking answers and solutions to the factors that may have caused the illness. The present physical symptoms and discomfort are not necessarily the primary concern but have prompted an interest in discovering the unknown or hidden causes of the illness, whether it is a curse, the anger of a disgruntled ancestor, or some other cause. These causes are the greatest concern of the client and the *emuron*. Many times the visit to the *emuron* is preventative in nature, as the client seeks a ritual (for example, *ewosakin emunyen*, the spreading of ochre on the body) or a medicinal stick (*ekitoe*, for example, the *ebata*) to wear on a necklace or bracelet. For treatment of the symptoms themselves, many Turkana now rely on western medicines and treatment at both Kenyan government and privately sponsored medical clinics. The *ngimurok* of the head are not opposed to these clinics or Western medicines and will often tell clients to go to these clinics to receive medicine.

One *amuron* of the head did describe her suspicion of the abilities of the clinics to heal people in the ways the *ngimurok* were capable of healing, yet confirmed that clinics and hospitals were good for people who were sick:

> Long ago there were no hospitals or clinics, the only thing a person could do was pray to God. It is the same now for the people of Turkana who have problems, while some may be close to a hospital, others who live far from town can only go to the *emuron*. Even when people go to the doctors [in town], they take their medicine and don't get better, and then they return to the *ngimurok*. When they come here [to the *emuron*] they are healed. Even the people in my family go to the clinic for some illnesses. None of these things are bad, even the hospital is good; they are all the help from God. (2.13a)

While Western medicine and facilities are seen as "help from God," they are also viewed as lacking in their ability to discern the relational and unseen causes of Turkana illnesses that are revealed to the *ngimurok*.

Enemies and Bandits (*ngimoe* and *ngingoroko*)

Other common problems brought to the *ngimurok* of the head are those relating to *ngimoe* (enemies) and *ngingoroko* (bandits). The term *ngimoe* most commonly refers to people of other ethnicities who come from outside areas to steal animals in a home area or who seek to steal animals that are grazing in other areas. *Ngimoe* also includes those seeking to defend themselves and their animals when Turkana men are raiding their animals.

The main difference with the term *ngingoroko* is that while *ngimoe* are from other ethnicities, *ngingoroko* are normally Turkana seeking to take animals from other Turkana. Groups of Turkana *ngingoroko* will form from local communities and often travel from village to village near their home areas in order to recruit other young men, receive blessings and meat from the elders, and to visit *ngimurok* for advice, rituals of protection, and information regarding the timing of planned cattle raids either into other areas of Turkana or into the areas of other ethnicities.

Cattle raiding is illegal according to the Government of Kenya, is reliant on illegal firearms, often results in the killing of those involved in raids, and can lead to cycles of retaliatory violence. Because of this, most *ngimurok* in my research, even when assured anonymity, did not speak openly about their personal involvement in supporting or offering protection to those embarking on cattle raids. One *amuron* did describe in surprising detail a ritual undertaken to keep the raiders alive while on a raid (see the section on *ariwo* rituals in chapter 5). This *amuron* openly described herself as a specialist in the protection of cattle raiders: "The two main things I help with are protecting those who want to steal animals and those who are struggling with work" (3.19a). It was unusual to hear such an open discussion of the *emuron* role in cattle raiding, and the few of the other *ngimurok* who mentioned it did not speak so directly.[28]

Another older *emuron* insisted that stealing animals was merely "asking" or "begging" for animals, choosing his wording carefully. He then explained a rationale for why *ngimurok* bless raiders and raiders share their spoils with the *ngimurok*:

> [Are you able to provide protection for those going to the place of the enemy to capture animals (cattle raiding)?] You say they are going to capture animals, isn't it that they are traveling around to ask for animals? They are only going to ask (*eloose akilipa*). Anyone who wants 'to ask' says let's go here where there is water (blessing) before going 'to ask' for something." [You mean even those young men who are going to meet in fights with young men from across the lake?] "Yes, even those ones on the other side [of the lake]. That thing is like 'asking.' And when they return here, they certainly give you something for throwing water on them before they went; they will pass by you here. This is what every person does, certainly before they go 'to ask' they

---

28. While only a couple *ngimurok* verbally affirmed their role in aiding cattle raiders, an interview with a former cattle raider (interview 42) and the above very open statement did help to reaffirm my desire to further research the connections between religious specialists and the persistence of cattle raiding in the region.

go to their good friend (*lopaekeng*) to be blessed with water. If I bless him with water, will he not think of his good friend who helped him once he receives what he asked for in that place? He will come and say, 'I have come to bring this to you from when I was away, take this, friend (*ekone*).' If he doesn't bring something in this way, he owes a debt to God (*Akuj*) who says, 'you have forgotten your good friend who helped you in the past. Will you forget him forever, not giving him even something small, as you finish all the food yourself? If you find that you have finished all the food yourself, will you also be able to hold all the problems yourself? (i22:4, 54:26–57:13).

While this *emuron* was one of the most candid concerning the process of blessing those going on raids, most participant *ngimurok* only shared their role in protecting the local community from outside *ngimoe* and *ngimurok*. The killing or maiming of *ariwo* sacrifices most often offers protection from enemies and bandits. The father or grandfather of the *emuron* of the head reveals the specific animals for these *ariwo* sacrifices.[29]

The extended quote above also reveals a direct benefit to the *ngimurok* after a successful raiding party returns to the local area. "If I bless him with water, will he not think of his good friend who helped him once he receives what he asked for in that place?" Although the *ngimurok* themselves refused to talk about it, many Turkana shared that there are some *ngimurok* who have become very wealthy by protecting and blessing successful animal raids. The *emuron* who did share about this role must know that his success in this regard is quite obvious: As we were leaving his homestead, I noticed a large number of sheep of a different breed with markings that I had never before seen in Turkana. My assistant informed me that they are a breed of sheep that are commonly found in Samburu. There were too many to count.

The quote above also displays that there are negative effects to not providing the *emuron* who blessed you with a portion of your animals after a successful raid. It is suggested that even God is involved. The raider who does not compensate the *emuron* appropriately is at risk of owing a debt to God, and this will surely bring problems into one's life. This leads to the rhetorical question presented by the *emuron*: "If you find that you have finished all the food yourself, will you also be able to hold all the problems yourself?" The meaning is explicit: if you don't give what you should, what is owed or

---

29. Specific *ariwo* rituals and examples are provided in the *ariwo* ritual section in chapter 5. A brief definition of the *ariwo* includes: any of a number of animal sacrifices that either serves as protection from evil forces (both people or ancestors) or is directly aimed at scaring and preventing those who intend to commit acts of evil or violence from harming others.

what is adequate, to the *emuron*, God will send problems, and because you have kept everything for yourself, you will also be on your own when the problems come. The *emuron* will not be helping with those problems.

During the research period in 2011, raiders from the south and east across the Kerio River had recently attacked two villages on the west side of the Kerio River in the Kangirisae-Nakor area, less than one week before my visit to these villages. Three people had been killed and nearly 400 people were displaced, building temporary homes in safer areas to the west. Groups of young men with rifles from the villages were organized into patrols in an attempt to protect the area and keep track of the movements of the bandits. In a situation that was very tense, the people were angry that the police had not yet arrived to protect the area.

During this time I happened to be interviewing one of the main area *ngimurok* of the head at his home when the government appointed official for the area, the "chief," arrived on his motorcycle. Their interaction that followed, which I recorded with their permission on video, revealed that the chief wanted to call all the people together immediately for the *emuron* to do an *ariwo* protection sacrifice. The *emuron* responded in a way that made it clear who was to take the lead in dealing with protecting the people:

> If you [the chief] speak to the people now, how will I [the *emuron*] be able to initiate the *ariwo*? When the moon returns I [the *emuron*] will lead the people of Kangirisae back to their homes and do the *ariwo*, but the people who live on the other side of the river will need to decide if they are going to return. After that I'll lead the people of Nakor back to their homes and do the *ariwo*. (10/25/11 020.MOV)

After this exchange the chief implores the *emuron* to do the *ariwo* first in the Nakor village as that is his home village, but the *emuron* refuses. This exchange revealed that even in situations where raiding seems immanent, it is the protective practices of the *emuron* that take priority over the actions of the local government administrators.

Another *emuron* during that same visit disclosed that there was an *emuron* across the river that was doing the protection rituals (*ariwo*) and blessings for the bandits who were raiding on this side of the river. At the same time, the *ngimurok* on this side of the river were doing the *ariwo* to protect the people and their animals from the bandits. This can help us understand the local connection of the *ngimurok*. While the *emuron* is capable of sending out bandits with protection and blessing, he or she is also capable of performing rituals that will protect the people of their local area from bandits.

Opening the Gardens (ATANGAA NGAMANAT)

Traditional Turkana community gardens are planted either in rain catchment areas of certain plains or in the flood plains along the seasonal flowing rivers. These gardens are almost exclusively comprised of sorghum, *ngingomwa* (*Sorghum bicolor*), which is the fifth most popular grain in the world and is highly adapted to arid and semi-arid environments like Turkana (Ngugi and Maswili 2010:166).

The most water is needed for these gardens just after the planting during the germination and initial growth period. Thus, the timing of the planting to coincide with the rains or the flooding of the river is of critical importance. Some *ngimurok* of the head are specialists in knowing when just the right time is to plant the sorghum gardens. The planting of the gardens does not begin until the *emuron* calls the people to his or her home and ritual offerings of previous sorghum harvests are made along with other particular rituals; even the hands of the ones who will be planting are blessed with water and ritual ochre. Only then can the community begin to plant the sorghum.

Multiple *ngimurok* described this "opening the gardens," *atangaa ngamanat* role alongside their other roles:

> The main problems that people bring to me include opening the gardens when it is time to plant sorghum, sicknesses, problems with the animals, when women are barren, and to pray for rain. (2.17b)

Once the gardens have been planted there are other specialized rituals that certain *ngimurok* perform to protect the crops from both insects and birds.

Wealth and Employment (EBARI KA ETICH)

Many young people who are in school or have completed school are looking for employment in Turkana. The Kenyan unemployment rate is estimated at 40 percent and is one of the highest unemployment rates in the world.[30] Even those who have employment are nervous about their ability to keep their position. This is another area of life in which the *emuron* can find solutions. One *amuron* described these problems as "struggling" or "wrestling."

> Many people bring problems of struggling (*kipio*) with work. They are struggling with money. They are looking for work. The

---

30. Central Intelligence Agency, World Fact Book: https://www.cia.gov/library/publications/the-world-factbook/rankorder/2129rank.html, last accessed 3/28/2013.

two main things I help with are protecting those who want to steal animals and those who are struggling with work. (3.19a)

The *emuron* is able to provide encouragement and success through rituals. "I know how to pray for a person, to take water and to pray for them, 'God, help this person'" (2.15a). One *amuron* provided me a list of government officials, a veritable "Who's Who" in Turkana, who regularly drive out to her remote homestead in order for her to provide blessings and ritual protection for their work.

Problems with The Ancestors: *Ngikaram* and *Ngipean*

There is fluidity in the ways that different *ngimurok* understand the problems of *ngikaram* and *ngipean*, in that the terms seemed to be used interchangeably; for, just as I thought I had finally come to a definition of each, someone would completely switch the terms based on the definitions I had previously received. I finally came to a consensus over the course of my research, although it should be known that these terms continue to be fluid and contested within the context.

The *ngikaram* are typically characterized as ancestors who are unknown, the spirit of an ancestor that had died long ago. It is never considered a good thing for a person to be visited by *ngikaram*; in fact, it is commonly thought that the *ngikaram* are the cause of strange problems in a person's head, causing people to become crazy or insane (*kerepit*).

In contrast with the *ngikaram*, the *ngipean* are the ancestors recently deceased that the living family members know and recognize by voice (2.4a). This is still problematic and not desired, but the ancestor that is known will often speak through the family member being possessed, giving a reason for the possession. "When there is a problem with *ngipean*, the solution is to listen to the *ngipean* at the home and do what it says to do" (2.3a). With the *ngipean* there is often a solution to correct the situation and end the ancestor's intrusion, but with the *ngikaram*, it is more difficult to find a solution. Some *ngimurok* of the head stated that they can only occasionally solve the problem of *ngikaram*, or that they cannot do anything for that problem at all.

While it seems odd that an *emuron* of the head would admit that they are unable to help in certain situations, this was the way it was explained in the case of *ngikaram*. One response to the question, "Can you help a person who is sick with the *ngipean* or *ngikaram*?" displayed astonishing transparency in regard to the limits of their ability:

> I am able to help some, but I am not able to help others. For when *ngikaram* come, *ngikaram* are very bad, the person that they seize they just take away. It is very difficult, they just want to kill, but some you can just beat with *ariwo* rituals and they collide with the *ngikaram* and that person is quickly healed. But some defeat you forever, some you fight with *ariwo* rituals. (i15:7)

The problem of *ngikaram* in some situations is so difficult that nothing can be done, even though multiple suggestions are made for possible solutions:

> But some are so bad that no one can help them. You can even take them to the government [hospital] and they are defeated and the person dies. Sometimes the *akatuwan* can help by beating them with the gourd, but for some there is nothing you can do, they hold on no matter what you do. They beat the gourd to remove it, but they fail; they call the Christians and they fail; they bring the person to the *emuron* and they fail. They transport the person to Lodwar [hospital] and there is nothing that helps. They are defeated and the person dies. (i15:7)

Even after visiting different types of *ngimurok*, even after the prayer of Christians, even after being taken to the hospital, in some cases there is nothing that can be done for the person afflicted by *ngikaram*.

A response from an *emuron* who reads intestines suggests that in some situations they might serve a client with *ngikaram* better than the *emuron* of the head would:

> If a person has *ngikaram*, the house of Lokorijem can help them. But, if they have seizures it is not possible for them to heal them. There are only two ways to heal the seizures: the medicine of the government/white people[31] and with reading the intestines. (3.9a)

Another *amuron* admitted that her father could help people with these problems, but that,

> It is not possible for me to help with *ngipean* or *ngikaram*. It is difficult. My fathers were able to remove the *ngikaram* by putting ochre and spit on the heads of those with the problem. They would say, 'shinde, shinde ekipe' (be defeated, spirit) and they were healed (*tojoker*)" (2.22b)

---

31. Literally, "yellow ones who arrived," *nangolenyang*, a colloquialism for "the government administrators," now understood generally as "government," even though there are now no "yellow ones" in the government administration in Turkana.

Finally, the oldest *emuron* of the head I interviewed shared with me a rather colorful description of the ways he used to deal with the *ngikaram* and *ngipean*:

> I helped people who had these problems [*ngipean* and *ngikaram*] in days past, but I am old these days. A long time ago I healed many people who had *ngipean*. I would throw water on them the same way and also grind *ebata*. I would put the ground *ebata* into the head through the nostrils. I grind and soak the *ebata* and put it into the head until mucous comes out, different mucous, then it opens. I grind the *ebata*, I soak it in water, it turns yellow then I separate the water from its solute. The wet solute remains, I put it in the nostrils and they start fighting. That is the person of *ngipean*, the one that *akuj* possesses. I would do this and they would be healed. It always worked. (i24:5)

In spite of this isolated incidence of confidence, the *ngimurok* of the head seem to be confounded by the difficulties of the *ngikaram*, even though this and the repeated possession by *ngipean* are regular problems brought to the *emuron*.

Summary of the Emuron of the Head

The Turkana traditional religious category "*Emuron* of the head" was self-described by a majority of my research participants. 22 one and two-day interviews were conducted with those who identify themselves in this way. The *ngimurok* of the head were the easiest *ngimurok* to find, normally practicing openly in the community, not only in ritual leadership, but also as political and judicial leaders, except in the cases of a few women *ngimurok* of the head who did not practice openly in deference to their husbands.

Three key characteristics described in this study separate the category, "*Emuron* of the head," from all other categories of religious specialists studied. First, the *emuron* of the head is an ancestral position in which the specialist is recognized as an *emuron* because of his or her relationship to a father *emuron* in a specific ancestral line of *ngimurok*. This research confirmed the continued presence of two ancestral *emuron* lines: the descendants of **Lokerio**, currently a minor line of *ngimurok* and the descendants of **Lokorijem**, currently the major line of *ngimurok* in Eastern and Southern Turkana. Additionally, this research uncovered a third active hereditary line of *ngimurok* through the ancestor named **Lokedongan** stretching into Western Turkana.

The second key characteristic is the direct reception of knowledge from the ancestor and/or God (*Akuj*) in the dreams of the *emuron*. It is only through these direct communications that the *emuron* can know which ritual, carried out in a specific way, will protect the community or solve the problem of individuals. Ritual devotion to the ancestor, often at the grave of the father or another *emuron* ancestor, is important for placating so that the revelatory dream relationships will continue with the father/God. The ambiguity of this father/God relationship was explored.

The third characteristic of the *emuron* of the Head is that the problems most commonly dealt with are those affecting the entire community: rain, planting gardens, traveling with animals, banditry, and community-wide sicknesses. This research found that the other categories of *emuron* are often specialists in specific individual or family problems. While the *emuron* of the head is able to provide solutions to individual problems, if the father/God reveals the solution, the *emuron* of the head is best described as a specialist in those problems that affect the entire community.

We will now turn to the research findings concerning the other three categories of self-defined *ngimurok*: the *emuron* of intestines and sandals, the *emuron* who reads (tobacco and money), and the *emuron* called *akatuwan* who removes evil items from the body.

EMURON OF INTESTINES AND SANDALS

> *Emuron lo esemeere ngamaliteny ka elamlam ngamuk* (The *emuron* who reads intestines and throws sandals)

During the research, eight *ngimurok* were interviewed who consistently identified themselves as part of this second category of self-described *emuron*. These *ngimurok* are specialists in identifying the cause and solution of problems in individuals and families by means of a cycle of both throwing sandals and reading animal intestines.[32] Even more specifically, they are seen as useful in identifying thieves or one of the evil ritual practitioners, the *ekasuban* or *ekapilan*. Although one clan, the *Esigerit*, is traditionally known for producing more *ngimurok* of this type, no ancestral *emuron* ancestry is required for the *emuron* of the intestines and sandals.

The idea that this is a clan specific practice is contested by many *ngimurok* of other clans:

> Long ago our family was the only one who knew how to read the intestines, now everyone does it and says that they know how to do it. Some clans are now even considered specialists in

---

32. The details of how the sandals provide answers when thrown and the general ways the intestines are read are described in the next chapter, especially Figures 3 and 4.

sandal and intestine reading [specifically the *Esigerit* clan], but the ritual (*emuronot*) was originally ours. (2.16a)

While the *ngimurok* of the head consider the abilities of the *emuron* of the intestines to be less than their own, they are seen as helpful in the community. As one *emuron* of the head affirmed: "The reading of intestines is a thing that helps (*akingarakin*) the community" (2.26a).

For these *ngimurok*, there is an observed revelatory relationship between the throwing of sandals and the reading of the intestines. When a problem is initially brought to the *emuron* the sandals are consulted. This first throwing of the sandals will confirm the problem and provide an answer to the question of which goat should be sacrificed for the reading of the intestines. Both skills are held by this *emuron*. This process was described by both *ngimurok* of the head and the *ngimurok* of intestines and sandals.

> Yes, the *emuron* who knows how to read sandals and the *emuron* who knows how to read intestines are the same person. The one who knows sandals takes the sandals and throws them first and it tells him there is this goat, kill the goat that has this or that color hair (*taara akine ajulot be ati*). So, they go and find and kill that specific goat and then unfold (*tanganya*) the intestines. Yes, they look and certainly rectify the sickness (*Ee, kingolik kipak robo edeke*). (i15:4)

The two part process is further explained as one in which the sandals provide the specific information concerning the goat to be killed. Then, the intestines of the goat are examined as if they were a map of the local area that can be 'read.' This reading is done in the context of the community of men who will consume the meat of the goat once roasted. While reading (*akisemeere*), the men look for any anomalies, aberrations, or spots that should not normally be present in the intestines. More often than not, a spot is found. After discussion, the *emuron* will decisively share who the spot represents in the community. The meaning of the spot might be connected to a person in the community who is known to be sick or the meaning of the spot could also be a prediction that someone in the community is about to become ill, and that the illness is preventable if the correct actions are taken.

The process is here described in the words of an *emuron* of the intestines:

> When we throw the sandals we find out what color the hide of the goat should be that we will kill. Then the person brings the goat and when we kill it we read the intestines. When reading the intestines it is like a map, there is the river, there are the

homes, there are the mountains. I look for something that is out of place, something that should not be there, like a small spot. That spot will tell us what person the problem is going to effect. I can tell what person it is by the color of the skin, it matches the color of the spot. The other old men around me during the reading of the intestines also help to point out things, but I am the only one who speaks out what the problem is or what the spot represents. They do not disagree with me because I am the one who knows the intestines very well. (2.16b)

In dealing with a specific illness in humans that is already known, the family of the sick person may visit the *emuron* of the intestines and sandals. After the sandals reveal the coloring of the animal to be killed, the *emuron* will go to their homestead to kill the animal. One *emuron* explained:

The sandals will show us which animal should be killed as the *ariwo*, then the person will be protected from the illness. First, the person who is sick comes to me and I throw the sandals. When they bring the *ariwo* that was revealed, I go to their home to kill the *ariwo* there to protect them. (i19, 22:00–23:30)

In regard to the *ariwo* ritual, which was mainly observed among the *ngimurok* of the head, the killing of the animal is clearly understood here as providing life and defending against the sickness already present in the homestead.

The Absence of Revelatory Dreams

In conjunction with this particular revelatory cycle of sandals and sacrifice for the reading of the intestines, a key differentiating characteristic of the *ngimurok* of the sandals and intestines from the *ngimurok* of the head is the absence of dreams. Direct revelations are not received from the fathers or *Akuj*; instead, *Akuj* speaks through the learned divination practices.

One significant discourse revealed that the absence of revelatory dreams served as a limitation in some situations. While the reading of sandals and intestines could help in many situations, there are limits, and referrals would be made to the *ngimurok* of the head. The *emuron* of the sandals and intestines responded to my questions:

[Do you dream in your sleep?] No, I throw sandals and read intestines. That is what I am known for. [So why does someone come for you, what is the difference between the *emuron akou* and you, that someone would want to come see you instead of the other *emuron*?] The problems that are brought to me are simple, short illnesses that are common, the more difficult problems go to the great ones (*ngikapolok*) [the *ngimurok* who dream] who don't throw sandals. If there is a problem with *ngipean* or *ngikaram*, they are taken to the *emuron* who dreams. Sometimes a person comes here and the sandals reveal that the problem is with *ngikaram*, when that happens, I send them to the *emuron* who dreams. (i19, 27:00–28:30)

Revelatory use of Ngipean

It was further discovered in the research that the *emuron* of sandals and intestines, in the absence of direct revelation from fathers/God, is not relying soley upon their own skill in regard to their readings, but also state that there are spirits that provide direction to the sandals when they are thrown. Again, there was ambiguity in the language used to describe these supernatural directive forces. I had observed numerous times that the *emuron* often removed some of the tobacco brought as a payment from the client and sprinkled it over the sandals before beginning to throw them. A description was provided when I asked one *emuron* of the sandals and intestines about payment from their services:

> [What do people pay you when they come?] some people pay with animals, some pay with money and tobacco. Tobacco is important because I sprinkle it over the sandals before throwing them. [Why sprinkle tobacco over the sandals?] The tobacco is for the *ibore* (thing) of the sandal, the *ibore* that is inside the sandal. It is like *ngipean* (spirits/ancestors) and it is what reveals things to us. It eats the tobacco. If I give it tobacco it will accept to reveal things to us. If there is not tobacco the sandals will only sit there, they won't say anything. (i19, 31:20–33:00)

The ambiguity is evident in the language used. The *ibore* in the sandals is what is consuming the tobacco and directing the way the sandals land when thrown. The word *ibore* is a very general, non-descriptive, gender-neutral term used to denote a "thing." While an *ibore* often refers to something that is unknown by the speaker, it can also refer to something that the speaker is referring to but does not want to name directly.

What is more revealing is the use of the term *ngipean* in this situation. While we have seen that possession of people by their recent ancestors, or *ngipean*, is a negative problem to be solved, here we find the *ngipean* as active forces animating the sandals to reveal information unknown to people, but known to the *ngipean*. Here the *ngipean* are viewed in a positive light, revealing the type of sacrifice, or even the specific animal that should be prepared for the shared roast and its intestines read. This more positive view of the *ngipean* is difficult to reconcile with the common Christian interpretation that strictly defines the *ngipean* as "demons" or spiritual powers working against *Akuj*/God and seeks to harm people. This is a discussion beyond the scope of this research. What is clear is that although the *ngimurok* of the sandals and intestines do not receive revelatory dreams with direct messages from the fathers/God, they do not claim to receive revelation only through their specialized skill at throwing sandals. Instead, there are *ngipean* to whom an offering is given at the time of the sandal throwing who direct the placement of the sandals.

To further confuse an attempt at a logical explanation, solutions to problems received through this process are not attributed to the *ngipean* or the *emuron*, but are instead attributed to *Akuj* (God). When asked if revelation came from the *emuron* skill in throwing sandals, one *emuron* responded, "I didn't do that with my own hand; God (*Akuj*) made the sandals show that" (2.15). Thus, while the special skill of the *emuron* is found in the reading of the sandals and finding and interpreting the anomalies found in the intestines of the sacrificed animal, it is *Akuj*/God who is credited with directing this revelatory process, even if indirectly through the *ngipean* and *emuron*.

Even with these revelatory differences, there are similar practices. Similarities of practices between these *ngimurok* and the *ngimurok* of the head include the throwing of water as a blessing and the spreading of different color ochres (*emunyen*) on those who are afflicted with various problems. While the color of the ochre to be used is directed by the father/God for the *ngimurok* of the head, sandals can reveal not only the color of the animal whose intestines are to be examined, but also the color of ochre to be applied to those afflicted in specific situations.

One *emuron* of sandals and intestines disclosed both the ever present practice of blessing with water and the importance of specific sandals:

> Yes, I throw water and spread ochre, but I do not use sticks (*ngikito*). I make my own sandals for throwing out of camel hide. It must be my sandals that are used. The sandals tell me which color ochre to use and which color *ariwo* needs to be killed. But throwing water always happens, it happens before the other things, before throwing the sandals. (2.17a)

Like this *emuron* of the sandals and intestines, most were in possession of a special pair of sandals that were reserved for throwing. Traditional camel hide sandals were preferred to the newer sandals cut out of the tires of vehicles, a very popular convention in Turkana.

Problems Brought to the Emuron of Sandals and Intestines

When an animal or a group of animals go missing, the *ngimurok* of sandals and intestines can reveal important information. One *emuron* explained that the animal in question must still be alive to find answers:

> The sandals can tell if the missing animal is still alive or if it has been eaten. If it has been eaten, they can't show where the animal is or who stole it, but if it is still alive, the sandals can show where it can be found without fail. (i19, 46:00–47:00)

Many illnesses are attributed to practitioners of evil rituals in the community. At times the sandal/intestine cycle could reveal the location or identity of an *ekapilan*, but more often provides the specifics for practices of protection:

> People come who have fever/illness (*elekes*), especially malaria. These illnesses come from an *ekapilan* who wants to kill a person. I use the sandals and the intestines to discover the problem. The sandals will show us which animal should be used as the *ariwo* to protect against the sickness. (2.16b, i19, 21:00–23:26)

It was made clear that there are limitations to the illnesses that sandal/intestine reading can help:

> There are four sicknesses that I cannot help with the intestines [and sandals] for which I tell the people to go to the hospital: 1. *Elepot* (gonorrhea), 2. *Lokwakel* (HIV), 3. Boils that require surgery, and 4. Complications with pregnancy. The traditions (*etal*) can take care of the other problems. Even if a woman has been unable to have a child, the intestines will show why. (3.8b)

An example of a specific illness *ngimurok* of the sandals and intestines could heal that the *ngimurok* of the head are unable to solve was also provided:

> If a person has *ngikaram*, the house of Lokorijem [the *ngimurok* of the head] can help them. But, if they have seizures it is not possible for them to heal them. There are only two ways to heal the seizures: the medicine of the government/white people and with reading the intestines. (3.9a)

While the *ngimurok* of the head are consistently sought to engage the problems of the larger community, the *ngimurok* of sandals and intestines, as with the other *ngimurok* in this study, are known as specialists providing solutions to a narrower set of problems. The common problems brought to the *ngimurok* of sandals and intestines include: assistance in locating lost or stolen animals; identifying the geographical location of problems in general or more specifically the geographical origin of problems in the community; solutions for specific illnesses in individuals, especially fever/malaria; identifying the reason for barrenness in women; and most specifically, the healing of seizures that the *emuron* of the head is unable to heal.

Summary of the Emuron of Sandals and Intestines

The *ngimurok* of the sandal and intestine reading cycle are specialists in their abilities to divine answers from the throwing of sandals and subsequent extispicy. While they credit *Akuj* with revealing answers to them through the sandals and intestines, they do not receive direct revelations from their fathers or God through dreams. There is also ambiguity between the stated attribution of revelation to *Akuj* and the role of the *ngipean*, specifically in directing the position of the sandals in the sandal-throwing portion of the sandal/intestine cycle.

Although they are traditionally known as being from one clan, today these *ngimurok* are not from any one specific clan or lineage. Many Turkana will claim the ability to answer questions by throwing sandals and will throw sandals for entertainment. Likewise, many male elders will gather around the intestines of an animal at every roast to inspect them for signs, but only certain members of the community are considered specialists in these practices. These specialists are within the broader Turkana category *emuron* as described by themselves, by other *emuron* practitioners, and by others in the community.

It is made clear through this research that while the *ngimurok* of the sandals and intestines are within the category *emuron*, they are substantially different from the *ngimurok* of the head. These differences were self-described in their specific practices, their source of revelation, and the problems for which they are most commonly consulted.

EMURON WHO READS (TOBACCO, MONEY)

Emuron lo esemere etaba, ngaropiae

Reading Dried Tobacco Leaves

During the research, one *emuron* who specializes in the reading of tobacco leaves was interviewed and observed at his home over a period of two days. This *emuron* is characterized as one who has a special ability to discern the answers to problems by reading the tobacco leaves brought by a client.[33]

---

33. Payment made to the *emuron* who reads tobacco requires at least one small bag

The *emuron* who reads tobacco does not come from an ancestral line of *ngimurok*, but has received this special ability from God directly. God can speak directly to this *emuron* as he reads the tobacco.

Like other self-described *ngimurok*, the one who reads tobacco uses multiple rituals and sacrifices to aid in providing solutions, but the specific solutions are unknown until the reading occurs. Common problems brought to the *emuron* who reads tobacco include illnesses, appeasement of ancestors (*ngipean*) who are troubling the family through possession or illness, and most commonly, the problem of infertility.

While the fathers of the *emuron* of the head reveal which specific animal should be used in an *ariwo* sacrifice in a dream, and the spirits in the throwing sandals provide revelatory knowledge to the *emuron* of the sandals and intestines concerning the *ariwo*, the *emuron* who reads tobacco is given a direct message from *Akuj* in the tobacco leaves. This direct message likewise most often applies to the *ariwo*:

> People who are sick come to me to consider (*akitamun*) the thing that has caused the problems. I use the tobacco to tell me what the skin of the goat for the *ariwo* should be. (3.2b)

Given full access to two readings inside the main house of the *emuron* at the center of his homestead, I was able to observe tobacco readings for two women who have had difficulty having children.[34] The first woman was in a common situation: her husband had sent her back to her father's house because she had not yet become pregnant. He was not going to pay the bride price unless he knew that she could become pregnant. The second women had experienced three miscarriages and had not been able to carry a child to full term.

During each individual session the women sat on a woven mat on the floor of the mud house while the *emuron* sat on a platform built with sticks about 3 feet off the ground, directly across from her. Holding a clear plastic bag filled with tobacco leaves, he would gently adjust them with his fingers and then move his fingers back and forth over the leaves as if reading from a book. When asked, the *emuron* explained, "I read the tobacco here just the way you would read a letter. I see words right here and I read what they say."

---

of tobacco for the reading in addition to some money. The amount of tobacco or money is not predetermined, but depends on each individual situation. If a client is seeking or requires an animal sacrifice, then two animals are brought to the *emuron*, one for the sacrifice and one for the *emuron* to add to his/her herd.

34. These tobacco readings were video recorded on 10/22/11, followed by a video recorded interview, 092.mov.

Sometimes he and the client would sit in silence as he read the leaves, but both of the women would wait for him to ask a question before speaking.

For the first woman, he began by asking her why she had come; had she come wanting the ritual ochre (*emunyen*)? Her words were striking, "I want to find out some things that you can tell me from the tobacco that I can tell my father about me." In her situation, she was now unwanted; unwanted by her husband and at risk of being unwanted by her father if he could not find someone to pay for her as a wife. Since being sent away from her husband, she had completed a cleansing ritual (*amook*) for herself, but the husband had refused to do any rituals.

After reading the leaves again, the *emuron* provided two words of advice: first, that there is nothing to be done about the man who refused to do the prescribed rituals. The *emuron* said that he cannot control other people, "my role is to perform the rituals (*amuronut*); the one who would benefit is that man, not me." Second, the *emuron* said that she would be given the blessing of water (*ewatakin ngakipi*), and that no problems will follow her because she is blameless and has not committed adultery.

The first woman stood up and silently walked out of the room. The next woman, who had been waiting in the small entry room of the hut, entered silently and sat down in the same spot as the first. There was silence as the *emuron* read the same tobacco. "Do you remember the things you were told to do? Have you done them?" The woman who had now lost three children responded that they had not done the things and she needed more clarification on what was to be done. The *emuron* listed the specific rituals that were to be carried out by the men in her family, including her father and her husband together. These rituals included the hitting of the goats in her father's goat pen with a certain leafy branch, to create a dust in the air. This will cause the spirit (*ekipe*) that is causing the problems to come out, then the oldest of the men should throw water on the goats in the pen. For four days[35] they should be left alone, with no shedding of any animal's blood. After these four days, the animals should be let out and the problems will be gone. Then they should return to the *emuron* for a blessing.

The *emuron* who reads tobacco leaves, who was interviewed during this research, is well known for his ability to solve fertility and barrenness problems with great success. As we travelled throughout the region, he was repeatedly identified by other *ngimurok*, even the *ngimurok* of the head, as the primary *emuron* specialist who knew how to solve fertility problems. People, from wealthy government officials to day laborers, regularly paid for transport

---

35. "Four days" for the *ngimurok* means two days and two nights, or what we would call two days by a Western calendar.

from the administrative district capital, Lodwar, more than 100 kilometers away, to consult with this particular *emuron* when the couple is unable to get pregnant. This particular *emuron* is so well respected that when we arrived at his home during a time of nearby cattle raiding, we found that the regional government official had stationed two armed administrative guards at the *emuron's* homestead to protect both the *emuron* and his clients.

From each of the research interactions with the *emuron* who reads, it is clear that the *emuron* is receiving revelation from *Akuj* through the tobacco reading not merely to deal with a medical or physical problem related to fertility or pregnancy. The words received and given reveal a concern for the relationships of those in the lives of the women, allowing each woman to be received back into her family. While the spoken problem may initially be barrenness, the ultimate problems revealed are relational.

Reading Paper Money

A similar type of reading was also described as done by an *emuron* who reads money. In the same way as the *emuron* who reads tobacco, the clients bring money to the *emuron* to pay for a reading relating to a specific problem that requires a solution. Instead of reading tobacco, the *emuron* has the ability to read one of the paper money bills provided by the client. Again, messages are read by the *emuron* that reveal very specific ritual solutions for the problem. There are no great, widely known *ngimurok* who read money. One *akatuwan* is known as a reliable reader of money, but this is not seen as her main work as an *emuron*.

Summary of the Emuron *Who Reads*

The *ngimurok* who read attribute both their ability to read tobacco or money and the messages that come through the readings to God, *Akuj*. They do not receive messages from their fathers in dreams and do not receive their abilities in a hereditary manner. They do not throw sandals for clients or read intestines. They do not host communities at their homesteads to pray for rain; instead, they focus on specific problems and become well-known for a record of successfully solving problems through reading messages from God on tobacco leaves and money. Yet, even with these distinct differences, they are self-described as being within the category *emuron*, and all others in this research also referred to these readers as *ngimurok*. This is clearly a separate category of *emuron* with an important specialized role in the community, helping not only with specific physical problems, but what are often seen as the relational causes of those problems.

AKATUWAN

> *lo etio (ka elepit) lu etuate: tolema akong a itwaan kori ngikito a itwaan* (2.5b).
>
> The one of the gourd and wooden milking container who removes the eye or the stick of the evil doer.

The *akatuwan* is another type of specialized *emuron* with the ability to locate and remove internal (presumably interstitial subcutaneous) foreign bodies from their clients. Evil and secret *ngimurok* have the ability to place items in the bodies of others that will cause discomfort and pain with the intention of eventually killing their victim (see *ekasuban* and *ekapilan*, below). When one suspects that this has occurred, and it is confirmed by other *ngimurok*, then the *akatuwan* is sought to physically remove the foreign body from the client. This is accomplished ritually, without excision, and produces the actual object that was in the body. This object can be seen by the client, but not touched, and is then disposed of by the *akatuwan*.

One of the best descriptions and validations I received of the work of an *akatuwan* first came during an interview with an *emuron* of the head:

> When the *ekapilan* has seen you eating and puts something in you, you must go find your *ngimurok*. You go to one *emuron* who says you have been cursed by the *ekapilan* then another *emuron* throws sandals and confirms it is true what the *emuron akou* has said. That one takes water and throws it on you. Is there not also another *emuron* called an *ekatuwan*? He exorcises (*etuwae*) people with the *elepit* (wooden milking container); this one is also an *emuron*. It is very difficult for another *emuron*, even those who dream, to remove this. The *akatuwan* is the better one, who can remove this thing out of you forever. The other *emuron* can only relieve the pain in your heart, but can't remove it. (i22:5)

This description provides an understanding of the *ngimurok* as interrelated in their ritual services to the community, with different roles for different problems: the *emuron* of the head identifies that you have been cursed, the *emuron* of the sandals and intestines can provide more specific information and confirmation of the curse, but the *emuron akatuwan* can actually remove the physical object of the curse from your body. While different types of *ngimurok* can offer similar ritual services to clients, this ritual ability to remove (*katuwa*) objects seems to be a service that is exclusive to the *emuron akatuwan*.

During the research, I stayed two days at the home of an *akatuwan* in hopes of observing a ritual that produced a foreign body removed from a client. I had originally met this *akatuwan* at the home of another *emuron* where she had accompanied her clients who were having difficulties with fertility. While at the home of the other *emuron*, she had performed the removal ritual on the *emuron* early one morning. My research assistant and I had heard the shaking of the gourd in the main building of the *emuron* but did not know what we were hearing until interviewing the *emuron* later that morning, in which he revealed that he had asked the *akatuwan* to remove an object that was causing pressure in his body. When we interviewed the *akatuwan* that day, she invited us to visit her at her home (about 150 kms from where we currently were), sharing that she could not perform a ritual for us to observe unless there was a client with an actual problem.[36]

It would be 26 days before we arrived at the home of the *akatuwan* who invited us to her homestead. The first day we were invited into the shelter where she performs the ritual of the gourd and milking container to remove foreign bodies. During that interview, (i.38) she showed us the objects used, explained the process and also explained how she received the ability and authority to performs these rituals from her mother, who was also an *akatuwan*. She used her older son to physically demonstrate the way the ritual objects were handed directly from her mother to her when she became an *akatuwan*.

Receiving of the Ritual Objects of an Akatuwan

The ritual objects were passed on to the *akatuwan* from her mother in this way:[37] She sat across from her mother with her hands together, palms facing up. A goat had been ritually killed and the chyme (*ngikujit*) was rubbed on the outside of the *elepit* (milking container). In the same way, the *etio* (hollow gourd) was covered with the *ngikujit* by her mother's hands. Then her mother placed the *etio* in her outstretched hands and covered it again with more *ngikujit*. With the *etio* still resting in her open palms, her mother, with hands facing palm down, would link fingertips with her and they would pull against each other and her mother would release her fingertips. They would link fingertips and repeat until her mother had released the *etio* to her four

---

36. This was the response of all the *ngimurok* when we requested to observe rituals. Each ritual is specific for the client and could not be performed without the presence of a client with a problem. On two occasions, each with an *emuron* of sandals and intestines, we convinced the *emuron* to show us a ritual without a client. In each of those situations, I became the client and words were revealed about my personal situation and this research project.

37. As recorded 11-29-2011, 002.mov.

times. Then her mother finally also placed the *elepit* in her hands and it was finished. She had received the objects and was now an *akatuwan*.

Problems Brought to the Akatuwan

People visit the *akatuwan* when they suspect that something evil has been placed in them that is causing pain or sickness in their body. This suspicion is confirmed by other *ngimurok* and often identified as being caused by the evil eye of the *ekapilan* or from a curse received while you are eating causing the food to enter a wrong part of the body, becoming wedged interstitially where it can cause pressure, pain, and eventually cause death. The client is expected to pay the *akatuwan* 3,000 KSH[38] or 3 goats for each session. Most of the time, 2–4 sessions are required to completely remove everything from the body that is causing problems.

Akatuwan *Ritual Observed*

Once received at the home of the *akatuwan* and paying the fee, the client waits at the homestead until summoned for the ritual. There are factors that can interfere with the removal ritual. The first day we visited with the *akatuwan*, she was unable to perform the ritual because of the presence of clouds in the sky. The next day there were still a few clouds and she left us in doubt about the effectiveness of the ritual that she was about to perform on an old woman. We video recorded the ritual anyway, and to our amazement the ritual produced a foreign object that had been lodged either in or behind the left eye of the client. What follows is a description from that video recorded session (11-29-2011, 007.mov).

The client, an older woman, lay down on a woven mat in the ritual shade of the *akatuwan*. The instruments of the removal ritual were brought to the *akatuwan* by her older children: the wooden milking container (*elepit*) and a gourd (*etio*) partially filled with dried sorghum. The empty *elepit* was partially filled with water by the *akatuwan* from a plastic water container kept in the ritual area. Like the water used for blessing at the homes of other *ngimurok*, this water is not used for drinking, but only for the ritual. The partially filled *elepit* was placed directly on the part of the client's body suspected to have the foreign body. In this case, the *elepit* was placed on the side of the head directly behind the eye on the temporal bone, or temple.

The gourd was then shaken and used to beat all over the body, but especially in the area where the offending object was suspected to be. The *akatuwan* then tapped the outside of the wooden *elepit* four times, reached

---

38. Approximately $45, or about one month of wages for a day laborer in Lodwar.

in, and pulled out an object that was, at that moment, removed from the body. The object can be a stick, the eye, meat, hair, or even the blood that had remained in the body after a miscarriage. In this case, it is a small stick (3.16a, video:11-29-11, 007.mov).

This ritual removal session lasted only three minutes in total. With the *elepit* next to the eye and covering the eye, the *etio* was shaken first for 42 seconds before the *akatuwan* placed her right hand into the water of the *elepit* to remove an object. One object was removed. The *elepit* was repositioned slightly and the *etio* shaken again for 37 seconds. This time her hand came out of the *elepit* empty. The *elepit* was placed directly over the eye and the *etio* shaken a third time for 10 seconds. A second objet was produced and removed from the *elepit*. The *elepit* was repositioned a fourth time with 17 seconds of shaking the *etio* with no result. The client was then asked to sit up and the *elepit* was positioned directly on top of her head. The *etio* was shaken for 20 seconds, the *elepit* was searched and nothing was produced. The *akatuwan* quickly emptied the water from the *elepit* onto the ground and sat both the *elepit* and *etio* on the ground near the two produced objects. The client stated that she was already feeling some relief from the pressure that had been around her eyes.

Again, with all of this happening so quickly, within 3 minutes, I asked the *akatuwan*, "Is that all? Is it finished?" She replied that because of the clouds that were in the sky only a few things could be taken out. She explained that the best times for the removal rituals is when there are no clouds in the sky and it is still the first three hours of the day.

We asked about the dark, wet objects that had been taken out from the woman's head or eye, as they were now lying on the ground next to the *elepit* and *etio*. The *akatuwan* replied, "They are small sticks. Look, this one is like a person, dark like the one who put it in there." She took a small palm leaf and stood the removed object up on end without touching it with her fingers, "See? It looks like a person." It is not uncommon that the object would in some way resemble the person, the *ekasuban* or the *ekapilan*, who had placed it in another person.

I further asked about the two objects, specifically how they are disposed. The *akatuwan* said that they are just thrown out on the ground outside of her homestead; they are of no consequence and have no power in themselves. Once they have been removed, they are just trash and cannot harm anyone. This is something I would want to further explore in the future, as the *akatuwan* was clearly not willing to touch the objects with her hands.

Akatuwan Imitators

Because of my Western scientific skepticism and disbelief in the ability of an *akatuwan* to remove foreign objects from the body of a client without cutting the skin, I asked other research participants about the possibility that an *akatuwan* was performing 'slight of hand' in some way or another. The response I received was that this is not 'slight of hand,' but that the ritual of the *akatuwan* is known to work. I was told that there have been those who tried to imitate the removal ritual of the *akatuwan* through 'slight of hand,' but that they are always caught. If someone is caught acting as an *akatuwan*, but does not produce results or is seen producing the exorcised objects by slight of hand, they are beaten and chased out of the village.

During my research there was one mention of a type of *akatuwan* who removes objects from the body by the use of sisal or rope. It was said that they take the stalk of the sisal plant and beat it until it is like an *athante* (a fibrous brush). They soak the *athante* in water and then place it on the part of the body where there is a problem. The *athante* pulls the problem out of the body. This was described by an *emuron* of the head with the clear distinction that "this one is not an *emuron*" (3.9b). The *akatuwan* confirmed that this was not a true *akatuwan*, but instead was someone making up their own rituals.

During my interviews with the *akatuwan*, she also lamented that others are beginning to copy her work in untraditional ways, especially those from the new religious movement Legio Maria:

> Many Legio Maria are becoming *ngikatuwak*, but they are not using the traditional ways; they are using oil and rosary beads to pull the evil things out of the body. Some people even take those with *ngipean* to the Legio; they say they are better than the *ngimurok*, but I don't believe them. (3.17b)

This was further evidence that the work of the traditional *ngimurok* is being challenged not only by Western Christianity, but by outside NRMs that were adapting to the Turkana context.

Summary of the *Emuron Akatuwan*

The *emuron akatuwan* is recognized as an *emuron* with the ability to perform a very particular ritual that can remove objects placed in the client's body by those with evil intentions. The *akatuwan* does not provide or receive revelations from dreams or readings, and does not even provide any spoken unknown information. Instead, the *akatuwan* produces an actual physical object through the removal ritual. The removal of this object provides relief from pain for the client and also terminates the power of a curse placed on the client by an *ekasuban* or an *ekapilan*. The knowledge, authority, and ritual objects of the removal ritual are handed to the *akatuwan* by another *akatuwan*. The role does not need to be hereditary, but in most cases is passed from parent to child. Most *akatuwan* are identified as women; no male *ekatuwan* was identified by my research participants, although the possibility exists.

The *akatuwan* interviewed normally receives clients at her home, but can also travel to the home of the afflicted to perform the ritual. This particular *akatuwan* is very well known throughout all the research areas and is even known on the eastern side of Lake Turkana, where she travels by boat at least once a year to serve the needs of clients. It was noted, by those in her village, that the last time she returned from the other side of the lake, she returned with at least 50 goats that she had received in payment for her services.

SUMMARY OF THE FOUR SELF-IDENTIFIED TYPES OF NGIMUROK

This research revealed four types of Turkana traditional ritual specialists that were unanimously referred to by the term *emuron* throughout the research: the *emuron* of the head, the *emuron* of the sandals and intestines, the *emuron* who reads (tobacco and money), and the *emuron akatuwan* who exorcises foreign objects from the body. All the *ngimurok* interviewed and all research participants referred to and described these four types of *ngimurok*. The research participants in each of these four categories of religious specialists were also self-identified as *ngimurok*. Yet, the descriptions provided by the participants have revealed that there is clear variation within the category *emuron* in regard to the ways of becoming an *emuron*, ways of receiving knowledge, the problems brought to them by clients, and the ritual objects required to perform various rituals. A brief summary of these four types of *ngimurok* are provided here through these categories.

Becoming an Emuron

The *emuron* of the head becomes an *emuron* through hereditary means. In almost all circumstances, the *emuron* of the head must be the child or grandchild of an *emuron* of the head, and is not truly an *emuron* until the deceased father or grandfather *emuron* begins to visit in revelatory dreams. The *emuron* of sandals and intestines becomes an *emuron* through learning their specific sandal and intestine reading skills from others. For many, this is learned from their fathers and uncles, but the learned reading skills are not required to be passed in a hereditary manner. While many Turkana men know a little about throwing sandals and reading intestines and may engage in both for entertainment or homestead purposes, those who are called *emuron* of sandals and intestines have proven themselves successful in their readings.

The *emuron* who reads tobacco or money has received a special gift from God (*Akuj*) in their ability to read. Their ability is not learned from their fathers or any others. Some tell of a near-death initiation story in which God revealed the ability to them. The *emuron akatuwan* becomes an *emuron* through the success of her learned removal rituals and objects that have been passed on to her from another *akatuwan*. In the self-description of the *emuron akatuwan* in this research, the rituals and objects were passed from mother to daughter, but the role of the *akatuwan* is not known to be limited to any one clan and is not strictly hereditary.

Receiving Knowledge

The *emuron* of the head is the only one of the *ngimurok* who regularly receives knowledge through dreams. While many in Turkana will receive dreams and dream interpretation is a regular part of Turkana discourse, an *emuron* of the head exclusively relies on dreams to receive foreknowledge of upcoming situations in the community and specific solutions to specific problems in the community. During these vivid dreams the *emuron* will host the father or grandfather *emuron*, or both, and will verbally communicate with them. The audible voice of God may also be heard in these dreams, and there is a close relationship between the ancestor *ngimurok* and God *Akuj*.

The *emuron* of sandals and intestines receives knowledge through the cycle of throwing sandals and reading the intestines of specific goats. The sandals answer questions by means of *ngipean* who are within the sandals and who are appeased with tobacco at the beginning of the sandal throwing session. Knowledge is revealed through the reading of intestines through the interpretation of anomalies found during the inspection of the intestines. This knowledge is available to anyone skilled at reading intestines and is often discerned through group reflection over the intestines. It is logically assumed that an animal that grazes and roams a certain area will have signs readily available in the intestines that describe the occurrences in that area.

The *emuron* who reads tobacco and/or money states that knowledge is received from God *Akuj* through their readings. The object being read is like a letter, in which a message has been written for a purpose and a specific reader. While the *emuron akatuwan* may receive some knowledge about the one who cursed or placed a foreign object inside their client after its removal and examination, the removal ritual is not intended to reveal knowledge. Instead, the *emuron akatuwan* is focused on primarily removing evil objects from their clients through ritual.

Client Problems

The *emuron* of the head is known for primarily receiving problems related to the larger community, including lack of rain, timing for the planting of gardens, protection for and from cattle-raiding, community-wide illnesses, and the protection of wealth in the community (animals, daughters and jobs). Clients often include groups representing an entire community, instead of simply individuals. While individuals with smaller specific problems such as illness, curses, or ancestor/spirit possession may seek the assistance of the *emuron* of the head, these problems are often directed to the other three types of *ngimurok* who specialize in those individual problems.

The *emuron* of sandals and intestines is specifically known for their ability to geographically locate the sources or solutions to problems. Thus the major problems brought include lost or stolen animals, particular illnesses that require particular solutions, and seeking to identify the location of an evil hidden practitioner, the *ekapilan*. The *emuron* of sandals and intestines also specializes in identifying the particular sacrifice needed for the *ariwo* protection rituals and the *amook* cleansing rituals.

The *emuron* who reads tobacco was described as most commonly dealing with the problems surrounding fertility and childbirth, individual illnesses, protection from curses, and problems with spirit/ancestor possessions. The *emuron akatuwan* is most commonly sought when it is suspected that an evil practitioner has placed an object inside the body with harmful intent. The *akatuwan* is sought to remove the foreign object from the body, without excision, through the removal ritual.

Ritual Objects and Structures Required

All of the following ritual objects used by the *ngimurok* are described in more detail in chapter 5, but are listed here to help summarize the similarities and differences of the four types of self-defined *ngimurok*.

Because the *emuron* of the head relies exclusively on dreams from the fathers for revelations, it is important for the *emuron* to have a separate sleeping place, set apart from the rest of the family. This separate space is called the *eteem* and most often is an almost completed circle of upright *edome* sticks, about 20 feet in diameter. The *eteem* does not have a covering or roof, and the opening/doorway always faces the West. Often, this opening faced the main *anook*, or nighttime circular animal pen, and between the *eteem* and the *anook* would be a place set apart for ritual sacrifices and the cooking of sacrificial meat. At either side of the *eteem* opening there was often a stalk of sorghum stuck between the sticks rising above the walls. These were seen as watchmen guarding over the *eteem* to prevent those with evil intentions from entering inside. The homestead of the *emuron* of the head is arranged in such a way as to accommodate very large groups. In all observed homesteads, groups of people numbering in the hundreds would be able to be present between the *eteem* on the east and the *anook* on the west, surrounding the central sacrificial and meat roasting area. The houses of the wives of the *emuron* would be placed to the north or south of the *eteem*.

Almost all of the ritual objects required by the *emuron* of the head are kept in the main *eteem*. These include traditional wooden bowls for mixing and holding different colors of *emunyen*, or ochre, large wooden *elepit* containers for holding water to be used in water blessings, and pieces of special sticks (*ebata, ekeriau, engeso*, etc.; see chapter 5) used in rituals. In the *eteem* would also be camel skins for sleeping on the ground and the long traditional spear (*akwaara*) to be used for ritual sacrifices.

The *emuron* of sandals and intestines has some similar, even identical ritual objects, including bowls for *emunyen*, *elepit* containers for water, and a traditional spear for sacrifices. An open *eteem* is not found at the homestead of the *emuron* of sandals and intestines; instead, a special *akai*, or palm leaf covered stick hut is found containing the ritual objects of the *emuron*. In this *akai* are kept the special sandals for sandal throwing, normally made in the traditional style with either camel or rhinoceros skin. These sandals are not worn by the *emuron*, but are reserved only for sandal throwing. Clients are brought into the special *akai* for the sandal throwing, but sacrifices are made just outside of the main homestead, and it is at the place of the sacrifice and eating of the roasted meat that the intestines are read.

The *emuron* who reads tobacco also has the same wooden objects for water blessing and *emunyen*. A central *akai* is built for meeting with clients individually and reading the tobacco. This is also where the *emuron* will sleep and is the place where the main wife will divide cooked sacrificial meat into appropriate portions for those present at the homestead. It is important that everyone present at the homestead, whether family, client or visitor, eat some of the meat offered for the sacrifices each day. There are no special ritual objects required for reading the tobacco. Clear plastic bags purchased in town are used to hold the tobacco leaves during the readings, and are the same common bags used by all people for holding tobacco, food, cooking fat or other items purchased in town or at small shops in villages.

The *emuron akatuwan* again has similar wooden objects for holding *emunyen* and water, but also has the two specialized objects for the removal ritual, an *elepit* for holding water, through which objects are removed, and the small gourd (*etio*), filled with sorghum seeds, for shaking around the *elepit* and the client. An area set aside for the removal ritual is found within the main homestead, but is not built as an enclosed *akai* or and open *eteem*. Instead, it is built more as a shade, open on one end with a palm leaf cover.

Through these descriptions of the four types of self-identified *ngimurok*, I have begun to piece together their similarities and differences. While they each have similar integral roles in their communities, it can also be seen that there are distinct differences. It is also important that these four types of *ngimurok* seem to work in concert with each other in nearby communities instead of in competition. Competition is observed more between *ngimurok* of the same type in closer geographic proximity than among the different types of *ngimurok* in the same area. Clients are referred to other types of *ngimurok* to confirm a diagnosis or to meet with a specialist for a problem that has been revealed by another. While some *ngimurok* of the head may claim priority over those of another ancestral heritage, these *ngimurok* are spread out to serve different geographical areas, with clients first seeking help from the *emuron* of the head in their own area.

I now turn to the descriptions of other ritual specialists for which there is no unanimity in the research for using the term *emuron*. First I will provide descriptions of those ritual specialists described as acting malevolently in the community, the *ekasuban* and the *ekapilan*. Then I will describe the six other categories of ritual specialists described during the research as being similar to *ngimurok*.

MALEVOLENT TRADITIONAL RITUAL SPECIALISTS

There are two types of malevolent ritual specialists that were consistently mentioned during the research, but not always consistently described. The most consistent descriptions came from those who identified themselves as *ngimurok* in the interviews. These two types of malevolent specialists are the *ekasuban* and the *ekapilan*. All people generally fear both. The major distinction is that the *ekasuban* is often known in the community and secretly hired by clients seeking to harm other individuals, whereas the *ekapilan* is not known and brings evil into the community through ritual activity with parts of the dead bodies of animals, especially the bodies of humans.

Ekasuban

Research participants consistently described the *ekasuban* as an *emuron* who deviates from the ways of his father and from God because of jealousy. Yet, even though they may have their origin within the lineage of ancestral *ngimurok*, for those self-identified as *ngimurok*, the consensus was clear, "*ngikasubak* are not *ngimurok*" (2.3b). The *ekasuban* is further described as one who knows secret rituals that are accomplished with objects either from or representing the person being cursed or obstructed.[39] These actions are seen as connected to jealousy; jealousy of successful *ngimurok* of the head, maybe even their own siblings who receive dreams from the father while he or she does not have dreams; jealousy of the wealth of other *ngimurok* or Turkana elders; jealousy of the acclaim of the great *ngimurok* that brings many clients.

One *emuron* of the head described how the transformation from *emuron* to *ekasuban* takes place as deviation from the ways of God:

> I heard there was an *ekasuban* in this area who wanted to ritually harm (*katosub*) and even kill me so that he could inherit this area after I was dead. He dreams his own *ariwo*, his goat, and does it for the purpose of killing me just near by here. [Are these *ngikasubak* truly *ngimurok*?] They are somehow called *ngimurok*, but they have deviated. [Does that mean that even the son of an *emuron* can become an *ekasuban*?] He certainly becomes an *ekasuban*. That's right, there is no other person it could be. Once he deviates, God no longer speaks to him clearly. He has left behind the path that in the past he was supposed to follow. His other path is to *asub* (to curse, manipulate, obstruct with objects), the path of *asub* is a very evil path. (i22:4)

This perspective might also reveal that the term *ekasuban* is used as a disparaging term for *ngimurok* who are in conflict or competition with *ngimurok* from the same geographic area. Only an *emuron* could inherit an area from another *emuron*, yet the one who actively seeks to do so is called an *ekasuban*.

Another *emuron* from the lineage of Lokorijem described how those who become *ngikasubak* will not profit through their work. Instead, they are "digging their own grave:"

> An *ekasuban* is one who is taken by jealousy to do *asub*. The emuron that steals things from people and does secret things

---

39. Incorporating both contagious and homeopathic forms of sympathetic magic as traditionally defined by Evans-Pritchard.

with them is an *ekasuban*. They are very bad. My father, a great *emuron*, said to his children, 'if you do the things of the *ekasuban* you are digging your own grave.' I only know of one in Akelerio's family, some others occasionally stray away and seek to kill with their hearts, and in their anger they curse, but only this one who has become an *ekasuban* is digging his own grave. He is even known and people pay him to harm other people. There are also other *ngikasubak* from outside of the ancestry of the *ngimurok*. They are mostly men." (2.23a)

This description also explains that the *ekasuban* is not always from a hereditary line of *ngimurok*. Yet, it must be common for an *ekasuban* to come out of the home of an *emuron* if a great *emuron* would warn his children about the possibility. One *emuron*, in acknowledging the possibility of an *ekasuban* coming out of an *emuron* family, explained the possibility without blame to his male *emuron* lineage: "If there are any *ngikasubak* in our family it comes from his mother's side" (2.24b).

The jealousy of the *ekasuban* explains the desire to want to ruin the rituals of the *emuron* that bring benefit to the community:

> Some of the *ngikasubak* are those who are the children of *ngimurok* that become jealous of the success of other *ngimurok*, so they begin to take small items from the rituals of the other *ngimurok*, specifically the chyme from a sacrificed animal for rain. They do this to use the chyme in secret rituals to prevent rain, to make the rituals of the others ineffective. This will keep the other *emuron* from being successful. The *ngikasubak* always work against rain; they don't want rain. (2.14a)

That the *ekasuban* is driven by jealousy is a given, but some even insisted that the *ekasuban* has lost his or her sanity: "*Ngikasubak* are like the *ebu*, the hyena that has gone mad. He might act like a person who is drunk, but he is not intoxicated" (2.12a).

Because the person and the specific practices of the *ekasuban* are normally hidden, there was much more variation in the descriptions of their practices. This is consistent with the explanation that many of their ritual practices are created by themselves and are not used by the *ngimurok*, and that they do not receive knowledge from dreams or the intestines of goats as the *ngimurok* they are jealous of are able to do: "Ngikasubak don't dream, they don't read intestines. They take small things and do their own things because of their jealousy (*etereku*)" (3.2b). Some of their various practices include, "tak[ing] human feces, urine, saliva, cooking it in small containers, tying the container shut and then burying it in the ground" (1.9a); "cursing people by taking their footprint [the soil/sand from the impression of a footprint], then they take spit, urine and feces and cook them until it boils" (2.5b); even incorporating the killing of an evil creature: "the *ekasuban* kills the *anakanak* [monitor lizard, *Varanus albigularis*] and uses fresh pieces from it in his sorcery" (2.1b).

The *ekasuban* is also seen as an evil coward, as a thief who hides his activities, sneaking around collecting the objects that can be used in an attempt to ruin the effectiveness of the *ngimurok*:

> *Ngikasubak* are not *ngimurok*, they are like deceptive thieves (*ngimokorae*). He takes the footprint of a person and curses them. And he is hidden; he does not want people to know that he is an *ekasuban* because people will refuse the things that he does. (2.15)

Finally, the morality of the *ekasuban* is not ambiguous within the Turkana community:

> The *ekasuban* is evil. We all refuse (*engerit*) the *ekasuban*. The one who makes people run afraid is evil." (2.16b)

During the research I was only able to briefly interview one person identified by others as an *ekasuban*. This interaction took place in front of a crowd of nearly fifteen others, including a few Turkana church leaders who were nervous about my association with a known *ekasuban*. The supposed *ekasuban* was acting as if he was intoxicated and suggested I should buy him some local alcohol. I learned very little from this interaction other than to confirm the description that *ngikasubak* were like wild hyenas who acted intoxicated. My sense was that he was completely in control of his faculties, that he was fully aware and even calculated in his words and actions, yet I was unable to have a coherent conversation with him.

At no point did he ever identify himself as either an *ekasuban* or an *emuron*, but if he considered himself an *ekasuban*, it would have been inconsistent for him to announce such a fact in front of others. Those who identify themselves as an *ekasuban* risk the ire of a community that might attempt to reverse their transformation from an *emuron* to an *ekasuban*:

> The *ekasuban* is like an *ekapilan*. A true *emuron* is one who helps people, but the *ngimurok* who fall away end up becoming *ngikasubak*. No one teaches them, they just do it on their own (*kisiak bon*). And their practices, they just make them up (*akirok*). Sometimes if you beat them they will become good again. (i24:5)

From the descriptions provided by the *ngimurok* research participants, the *ekapilan*, though possibly a former *emuron*, is a separate category of ritual specialist from the *emuron*. They are known for being driven by greed, their engagement in individual sympathetic magic practices, and seeking to obstruct the beneficial activities of the *ngimurok* in their communities, or even their own family.

Ekapilan

Similar to the *ekasuban*, the *ekapilan* is considered by many to be in the same category as the *emuron*. But for my *emuron* research participants, a clear distinction is made between the work of the *emuron* and the *ekapilan*. One similarity to the *ekasuban* is that the *ekapilan* "learns their rituals initially from their father" (2.12a). But, the differences are striking once one hears of some of the obscure evil practices of the *ekapilan*:

> These are different than the *ngikasubak*. These are the ones who come at night and skin the dead person's body. They dig up the graves of people who are recently buried, cut up their bodies and then make their soup. [Does he really eat it?] He eats the liver. He burns the feces of the donkey as his charcoal and when the liver is cooked, he eats it. He runs crazy, going wild at times. (2.15)

No other ritual specialist in Turkana is described as using the parts of deceased humans in their rituals, which is far removed from acceptable behavior in Turkana. Sometimes the *ekapilan* is referred to as the *ekayangan*, "the one who skins," in reference to their practice of digging up the bodies of those recently deceased and then preparing the body for their secret rituals by first skinning it.

Not only is the *ekapilan* known for using the bodies of those who are dead, but also for circling those who are near death at night. People know that,

> the *ngikapilak* go round and round (*akirimrim*) the place where a person is sick or dying. People fear him the way they fear death. When someone is getting weak they must sit up and act as though he or she is not weak because of fear that the ekapilan will see him or her. (2.23b)

It is also said that the *ekapilan* has special abilities to cause problems or curse someone by means of an evil eye, the *akongo*, especially when the person being cursed is eating food. Any sort of choking or other gastrointestinal problems encountered while eating is often attributed to an *ekapilan* who was observing his or her victim unaware. As one *emuron* explained, "Don't they curse your food? And then when you eat it, what happens? You are cursed. These are the things of the *ekapilan*, to curse the food and also to skin people." The *emuron* continued,

> he also has the eye (*akongo*) that can curse anything, even the animals and anything, so that they will be killed. That's what is different about the *ekapilan* [from an *ekasuban*]. He has the eye, he is the one who curses, other *ngikapilak* are those who skin and cut up dead people. (i24:6)

Because of these very strange practices and very negative roles understood in the community, *ngikapilak* remain in hiding and do not openly practice in the community. If found in the community, especially when caught in the act of handling or skinning a deceased body (and the *emuron* of the sandals and intestines employs rituals that help identify the *ekapilan*), "there are two responses for what the community should do with an *ekapilan*." The first is startlingly described: "Those ones are evil, the ones who cut up and skin people, if we find those we quickly run the stick through them. It's true, for evil things an evil thing enters" (i24:6; i25:5). To "run the stick through" a person is a death sentence that is reserved only for the *ekapilan*. In response to the reversed order of acceptable societal behavior, a branch of a tree is removed and sharpened on one end and used to impale the *ekapilan* from the terminal end of the intestinal tract into the torso. Such an extreme death sentence is reserved for the *ekapilan* who is caught in the act of skinning or dismembering a corpse. A second option for punishment is a similar prescription as one offered for the *ekasuban*: restoration to the original state through an *emuron's* blessing. "The *ekapilan* can have peace with God when an *emuron* throws water on them and the person is healed (*ejoker itwaan*)" (3.12a). A beating by the elders of the community is normally carried out before seeking the blessing of the *emuron* in these situations.

In summary, the *ekapilan* is an extremely feared ritual specialist who remains hidden and keeps their work secret. Even the name, *ekapilan*, is difficult for the Turkana to say when others are around. The *ekapilan* engages in extremely abhorrent practices, the use of the bodies of recently dead people, and killing someone with the glance of an eye when a person is eating. Because of their extreme practices, an extreme form of punishment is carried out on those proven to be an *ekapilan*. They are either beaten or killed with a sharpened stick. Again, clearly the *ekapilan* is different from any other *emuron* and should be clearly distinguished from the four types of self-described *ngimurok*.

WORDS USED TO DISTINGUISH THE ACTIONS OF THE *EMURON, EKASUBAN,* AND *EKAPILAN*

The actions of religious specialists were described in various ways during the research, with specific verbs and nouns commonly used with specific religious specialists. This is another way for us to classify the types of specialists and their understood roles in the community. As described earlier, while it initially seems unhelpful to learn that an *emuron* is one who does *amuronut,* or, that the ritual specialist does rituals, contrasting the understanding of *amuronut* with descriptions that the *ekasuban* does *asubanut* and the *ekapilan* is known for *akapelanut,* might further help in understanding the local classification of these religious specialists.

Amuronut

Amuronut is described and understood as a more general term for rituals, but specifically positive, helpful rituals that are performed to remove obstacles, restore health from illness, appease the ancestors, provide protection in raiding, and purify people or homes after a defiling event. The bad things (*ngakiro naaronok*) are removed from the person or situation. It is clear that *amuronut,* among the *ngimurok* interviewed, includes rituals that bring about positive ends in situations. It will be explained through the results of the Turkana Christian survey (chapter 6) that many non-*ngimurok* would include the negative results of *asubanut* and *akapelanut* in the same category as *amuronut*. But from those who practice *amuronut,* there is a clear distinction that helps to define important differences between the *emuron, ekasuban,* and *ekapilan*.

Asubanut

Asubanut is known as the hidden rituals of the *ekasuban*. The *asubanut* is used to curse people, to manipulate situations, or to obstruct the *amuronut* of the *ngimurok*. The verb *asub* is related to the verb *akisub,* "to do." Thus, the *asubanut* is the action of the *ekasuban* that only he or she knows how to do. Both the verb *asub* and the resulting *asubanut* are exclusively described by *ngimurok* and non-*ngimurok* alike as a negative activity motivated by *etereku,* "jealousy."

Akapelanut *(Akapel and* Akirikar*)*

Two verbs, *akapel* and *akirikar,* are used to describe the activities of the *ekapilan*. These are "evil rituals," *akapelanut,* not merely with negative intentions, but with the ultimate evil intention to bring both pain and death to the intended person. A translation of *akapel* is understood as "to ritually curse to death." This type of cursing with the intent to kill is differentiated from the more common verb for cursing, *akilam*, in that *akilam* is a cursing of another with words from the mouth without a physical ritual, an activity in which anyone, whether a ritual specialist or not, can participate. To curse someone in this manner of *akilam* may cause problems for the one cursed, but it is a curse that can easily be remedied through the blessing of an *emuron*. The ability to curse someone through ritual is *akapel* that is only known by the *ekapilan*. This type of curse will certainly lead to death unless more extreme measures are taken, including the *ariwo* rituals.

The term *akapel* is understood as so harsh and extreme, even to the point of instilling fear at the sound of the word; most of my research participants would prefer to use the verb *akirikar* when describing the actions of the *ekapilan*, even though *akapel* is the root word of the name for this evil ritual specialist. *Akirikar* has the weaker meaning, "to violently and completely destroy," and is also used in other contexts, such as cattle raiding and battles with enemies from other ethnicities.

OTHER TRADITIONAL RITUAL SPECIALISTS

In addition to the four self-described categories of *Emuron* of the head, *Emuron* of sandals and intestines, the *Emuron* who reads, and the *Emuron Akatuwan*, the research participants described five additional contested *ngimurok* categories. The first two of which are viewed as evil actors in the community, and were described above in the previous subsection: *Ekasuban* and *Ekapilan*. These five categories of *ngimurok* are described as contested because even though they have a close relationship with the practices of the first four types of *ngimurok*, and they are often grouped together in the larger category of *emuron* by outsiders, the self-described *ngimurok* participants in my research were not unanimous in their usage of the term *emuron* in describing these five. In fact, some were adamantly opposed to the usage of the term *emuron* in regard to these five.

In addition to these nine (the four self-described and the five contested), I am including descriptions of five more categories of religious specialists encountered in my research. These five additions include those who are described as **similar** to *ngimurok* in their roles, but are not *ngimurok* by their own or others' descriptions, although they are described in the context of *ngimurok* discourses.

THREE ADDITIONAL RELIGIOUS SPECIALISTS (CONTESTED)

Emuron a Akomwa

EMURON OF THE TERMITE MOUND

The *emuron a akomwa* is known as the ritual specialist who ritually walks four times around a large termite mound for the purpose of cursing those who have stolen animals from their clients. The termite mound will fall to the ground during the ritual and is connected to the effectiveness of the curse, symbolically representing the destruction or cursing of the one who has stolen the animals. The ritual is not meant to kill the animal thief, but to bring about a positive end to the situation as related by one of the *ngimurok* of the head:

> When someone steals their animals, the *emuron a akomwa* goes around the *akomwa* four times, then the *akomwa* collapses and the person guilty of stealing animals will become sick. They become sick and over time they become very sick and realize it is because they have stolen the animals, so they admit the truth of what they have done and they pay for the animals. Then they will get better. (i15:3)

During the research, all of the research participants could similarly describe the *emuron a akomwa*, but none could think of where I might be able to find one to interview.

I am unable to ascertain how they are self-identified. Whether or not they are part of the category *emuron* is clearly contested as demonstrated by the following descriptions from the research participants. First, they are described as "an *emuron* in their own way (*emuron a lowae kech*). They learn from their parents, but they are from different ancestors [not Lokorijem, Lokerio or Lokedongan]; but, they are not *ngikasubak*" (2.14a). Second, some view them negatively: "The *ngimurok a ngakomwae* are among the bad *ngimurok* because they can cause people to die" (i15:5). Finally, one respondent laughed when asked about the *emuron a akomwa*, simply stating, "these are crazy people, they are not *ngimurok*" (3.9b).

Ekadwaran

THE ONE WITH A BITTER MOUTH/SALIVA

This emuron is not a prophet who tells the future as the root *-dwar-*, or "prophesy," might imply, but is related to the other meaning as the root word for "bitter," *edwar*. A person seeking relief or treatment for something like a boil or abscess on their body will visit the *ekadwaran*. The *ekadwaran*, whose mouth or saliva is bitter (*edwar akituk keng*), will spit on the boil. This causes the boil to break open and pus to be expelled, initiating the healing of the boils or abscesses. While some refer to the *ekadwaran* as an *emuron*, it was made clear that "the *ekadwaran* doesn't dream" (2.11b, interview 14).

Dakitaria

Swahili loanword for "Medical Doctor"

Some ritual specialists have particular knowledge of the use of ritual or medicinal sticks and herbs (*ngikito*), specializing in their gathering and uses for physical healing. These specialists are not "dreamers" or "readers," but are identified as similar to the Western medical specialists present in the region at hospitals and clinics: doctors, nurses, and clinic dressers. This is the same term (*daktari*) that is also used for these practitioners of Western medicine. This category also includes those who can help with fertility, pregnancy, or even those adept at pulling teeth. Because of their limited revelatory knowledge, the *dakitaria* are not considered *ngimurok* by almost all of the research participants. In addition, as with the *emuron akomwa* and the *ekadwaran*, I was not directed to these specialists for interviews during my research. Unable to interview these specialists, I cannot provide self-descriptions.

FIVE OTHER DESCRIBED RELIGIOUS SPECIALISTS (SIMILAR TO *NGIMUROK*)

Emalaikat *(Legio Maria)*

Angels/Legio Maria Church

An independent church movement that split from the Catholic Church in South Nyanza district in Kenya in 1963, the Legio Maria Church, or Legion of Mary Church, was initially exclusively comprised of those from the Luo ethnic group. Today, estimates of the number of Legio Maria adherents range from 400,000 to 1.2 million.[40] In this regard, the Legio Maria Church is one of the most resilient and successful of the African Initiated Churches (AICs) in East Africa. While the Legio Maria Church began exclusively as a movement among the Luo people, it is now found scattered across Kenya and even has significant numbers of communities among the Turkana in northwest Kenya.

---

40. Schwartz, "Dreaming in Colors," 159.

Some leaders in this imported new religious movement are now seen as specialists in Turkana communities in regards to problems with spirits (*ngikaram*) and ancestors (*ngipean*). They are called *Emalaikat*; the Swahili loanword that is used in the Turkana Bible for "angel" or "messenger." This name is descriptive of the Legio practice of each believer having a spirit, catholic saint, or Biblical figure (sometimes an angel) who acts as an intermediary between the believer and God during times of meditation and prayer. When asked how the Legio Maria are able to communicate with the Turkana spirits and ancestors, the response is that because they already have spirits they regularly talk to it is assumed they are able to also communicate with other spirits. One *emuron* even explained the phenomenon of the Legio ability to speak with spirits by using a story from the Turkana Bible:

> When Legio pray for the people they get better. Remember the story about Jesus and the *ekipe* named 'legion?' The Legio are able to talk to the *ngipean* like that; when they tell the *ngipean* to leave, they leave (*akitourakin*). They can even do this with the *ngikaram*. (i12:2)

Some of the *Legio* specialists are now known for traveling around visiting homes to hold prayer services for those with spirit related problems. At times, Legio *emalaikat* are possessed by particular saints or angels who speak through them to clients who have problems. Possession by spirits for the purpose of solving problems is a practice that is not found among Turkana *ngimurok*, and is clearly a practice from outside of Turkana religious tradition.[41] Yet, it seems the Legio are introducing this practice as a powerful way to solve problems that is consistent with both their own teaching about spirit saint guides and Turkana understanding that the *mgimurok* receive direct messages from the fathers to solve problems.

In some larger villages I visited, where Legio communities are well established (Legio live separately on the edge of main Turkana communities in Legio "villages."), it was apparent that more clients were beginning to prefer the Legio for spirit related individual concerns rather than visiting the *ngimurok*. I asked the son of an *emuron* of the head, "Where do people now go when there are problems?" His response surprised me the first time I heard it: "They go to the medical clinic first and then to the Legio. People only go to the *ngimurok* for the big things: rain, *ariwo* (the protection sacrifice), *edeke* (illnesses), *ngibaren* (problems with animals), or when the *emuron* specifically calls a person to his house [because of

---

41. While possession by the spirit of an ancestor does occur regularly in Turkana, it is viewed very negatively as a problem requiring a solution; certainly not something desired to solve other problems as the Legio Maria are seeking.

a dream the *emuron* has received]" (i12:3). Another *emuron* of the head complained, "those other *ngimurok*, the Legio Maria, are bothering us by taking people who are sick. Now once it has rained, no one comes to us [the ones who dream]" (2.25b).

The Legio Maria in Turkana are clearly contesting the understanding of traditional religion and the category *emuron*. Whereas some may not include the Legio in the category *emuron*, enough self-ascribed *ngimurok* in my research did describe them as such that I have included them briefly here in the category of contested *ngimurok*. The new rituals of the Legio in Turkana communities and the ways they have been able to appropriate some of traditional *ngimurok* roles is intriguing and should be further explored.

Ngikarikok a Ngikanisae
Church leaders in various Protestant and Catholic churches

Analogous to the recognition of the new roles and competition of the Legio Maria in Turkana communities, numerous *ngimurok* noted that many church leaders are also acting like *ngimurok* who teach from and follow different traditions, but attempt to do the things of the *ngimurok*, especially when praying for rain, healing, and protection against evil.

Some point positively to church leader roles as *ngimurok*:

> The leaders of the churches, they are also another type of *ngimurok*. Those ones are teaching the path of life. Those ones who are doing work are not evil, those who are teaching children to read are not evil, those who are building houses and building school houses for our children are not evil" (2.24a, i24:1).

In addition to participating in the positive development of the community, one *emuron* of the head explained that, like the Legio, the new church leaders and pastors were also "removing the *ngipean* and *ngikaram* . . . when there is worship at the church, the person goes in front of the church and pastor, then believers and the pastors pray for that person" (i12:3).

Just as with the new roles of Legio Maria in Turkana communities, more research is needed on the roles of Christian ministers and missionaries in Turkana communities. While many Turkana Christian pastors might be appalled to hear that they are identified as *ngimurok* by some of the very *ngimurok* with whom they see themselves in opposition, the casting out of spirits and ancestors, and prayers for blessing and healing are clearly in the realm of *emuron* activity in the community. *Ngimurok* perspectives of

Turkana church leaders stemming from the tension between these competing roles are further presented in the beginning of chapter 6.

Akariton (f.), Ekariton (m.), Ngikaritok (pl.)
THE ONE WHO RUBS/PULLS

The *ekariton* specializes in helping with the delivery of a child, often by massaging the abdomen to help the child be in the correct position for childbirth. Traditionally female, some have recently heard of male practitioners (2.11b, 3.1b). The *ekariton* was described during the research as similar to an *emuron* because of their specialized knowledge and ability to provide positive assistance in the community. The *ekariton* does not come from any specific lineage and receives specialized knowledge that aids in childbirth from other *Ngikaritok*.

Ngikarikok/Ngikasikou a Ngadakarin, (Eketamen, Ekapolon)
LEADERS/ELDERS OF THE COMMUNITY

During community events, especially meat roasts (*akipeyos*), weddings (*akuuta*) and initiation ceremonies (*akinyonyo, asapan*), certain elders in the local community are regularly called upon to lead in the traditional prayers and blessings (*agata*). These are respected men in the community, but normally are not the *ngimurok*. The men who lead these events are often the most influential elders in the community, and are seen as the leaders of both the elders and the *ngimurok* in the community (2.11b).

Some self-ascribed *ngimurok* describe these men as different (*egela*) from the *emuron*, but still with an important role in the community. Contestation is present as other *ngimurok* negatively described these community event leaders as *lu pasiek*, "they are of no consequence; they are nothing." Other terminology used to describe the elders' roles in the community included, *eketamen* (the one who teaches) and *ekapolon* (the one who leads). This category of ritual leader was surprising as my assumption at the beginning of the research was that a recognized *emuron*, of one type or another, was always expected to lead in community rituals. This is clearly not the case, as the *emuron* seems to have a more limited role in the leadership or rituals in most communities, even while the *emuron* may even exhibit control over the actions of the political leader in the community. See the section "Other Roles in the Community," below.

Ngitunga Lu Nyeyenete

"Those who don't know"

This category covers a range of practitioners who have either made up their own practices or imported practices from elsewhere and are seen as deceivers (*ngimokorae*) by those self-identified as *ngimurok*. Often found in the markets of Lodwar, "these are the ones who make up things but are not *ngimurok*" (2.26a).

I was able to interact with one of these practitioners in Lodwar. He would use multiple devices, such as the balancing of a feather tied to a stick on the tip of the client's finger, to measure which medicine would help the client. Jars full of medicine were on display, and the practitioner would prescribe and sell the appropriate medicine for any problem conveyed by the client. While most of the clients of such practitioners are not ethnically Turkana, there are increasing numbers of Turkana who seem to be attracted to the medicinal answers provided.

OTHER DESCRIPTIVE THEMES

As I analyzed the data from my interviews in Turkana, I have identified a few recurring themes in the discussions that are not connected to any one specific type of *emuron* and have not appeared in the previous descriptions of *ngimurok*. These include the validation narratives of *ngimurok* who are not validated as *ngimurok* through their ancestral lineage or clan, the limitations of the *ngimurok* to perform rituals during the days of the new moon, recurring significance of the number four, responses to questions regarding payment for *emuron* services, discussions regarding the morality of the *emuron*, and finally, other roles, both political and non-political, in the community.

Non-lineage validation and initiation stories

While almost all the *ngimurok* participants in the research claimed validity of their self-ascription as *emuron* either through a patrilineal *emuron* lineage, a clan who held specific knowledge, or the passing of the title and ritual objects directly from a parent, a few claimed validity through other means. These exceptions include a matrilineal validation narrative and a non-lineage initiation narrative event.

EMURON VALIDATION THROUGH THE MOTHER

At one of our *emuron* interviews, my research assistant became confused when the *emuron* recounted who his fathers were. None of them seemed to be part of a known *emuron* lineage, as we would expect from an *emuron*. He was not even from a clan that is known to produce *ngimurok*. When questioned, the *emuron* responded,

> Yes, it is true that none of my fathers were *ngimurok*. I learned to read the intestines from the fathers of my mother, from my uncles who were from the *ngisiger* clan, even though I am *emosorokoit*, I learned these things from the *ngisiger* clan. (i19, 21:00)

This was the only example of an *emuron* in our research who claimed validity as an *emuron* through the fathers of his mother. This seems to be a rare exception. One might question if he truly was an *emuron*, but we did not find resistance from other *ngimurok* participants regarding the validity of his claim. It was also clear that in spite of a rare connection to an *emuron* clan through his mother, he had many clients and was successful in providing solutions.

NON-LINEAGE INITIATION NARRATIVES

While illness and unseen spiritual callings are common in many ritual specialist initiation stories around the world, I have made the claim, based on my research, that this is not characteristic of Turkana *emuron* initiation stories.[42] Yet, in the research we came across one very popular *emuron* that only claimed validation as an *emuron* through a miraculous initiation narrative. This is one of the *ngimurok* who has the ability to "read," through which God provides visions and words that answer the specific needs of his clients. Again, this is a rare exception, and, even though it further complexifies my attempts at a clear understanding of the phenomenon *emuron*, I provide it here as an example of religious specialist initiation that still does not fit the form for "shamanism" as presented by Eliade et al. What follows is my translation of the narrative:

> When I was still young, before I was married, I had become very sick. I had a very bad eye infection and was sick. I was sleeping with the herd of animals that night and something came to me at night. I could not move, I could not wake up, but I knew that something was there. It was God (*Akuj*). I was told by God to go

---

42. See "Shamanism" in chapter 3, 61–65.

to the lake with five women and five men. The next day I visited an *emuron* that we knew, but he was no help. Later I was just sitting and I saw a vision. I was to go to the lake with 5 women and 5 men and I saw in the vision a ram I was supposed to take with us to sacrifice and eat at the lake. At that point God was directing me and I could hear him talking to me as I led the others to the lake. We walked over the mountain to the lake on the other side. God led me into the water and the others stayed on the shore with the ram. They could not see or hear the one who was leading me. God said I should walk with him into the water to an island where we would find another ram. This ram would be for him and I to eat. The ram we brought would be for the others. I followed deep into the water, deeper, until the plants growing in the lake started grabbing my hair. He told me to return to the shore where my friends were waiting. I arrived there and I was wet, naked and very cold. I just sat there and the men killed the ram. This was the ram we had brought with us. It was not tied with palm leaves as we went to the lake and even while we were there; it just stood there quietly until the time it was killed. I saw a vision describing the way they were supposed to butcher and cook the animal. The contents of the stomach were rubbed on me and I fell asleep for a long time. When I woke up I could just see well and my sickness was gone. Then God instructed me to kill one other animal and gave me a vision of the animal. We went and found the animal. God told me how to cook this animal also. It was cooked in two pots as a soup the traditional way with the intestines and viscera in one pot and the other part in the second pot. I was told to pour the soup on the ground from the first pot and it would rain. It was about the fifth hour (11am), there were no clouds in the sky; there was no thunder, but as soon as I poured the soup out to the ground it started to rain. It rained for a long time. It was then that the people who were there started to believe that God had given me these visions and really was talking to me; and I believed myself. (1.5a,b; i1:1)

While this initiation narrative certainly fits Eliade's second type of shaman initiation, "spontaneous vocation," it is the story of an event that took place while conscious, before a group of witnesses, which is very different from standard shamanic initiation narratives.[43] What is important in this *emuron* initiation narrative is God's initiation of the calling. Belief comes to the witnesses and the *emuron* himself after following God's visions and seeing

---

43. Eliade, *Shamanism*, 13

results: healing of sickness, knowledge of ritual sacrifice with a compliant animal, and the instant miraculous occurrence of rain. All three of these are activities that continue to validate an *emuron* before their clients.

For most, especially the clients who receive effective benefits from the rituals of the *emuron*, this validation narrative of this *emuron* is true. As one *emuron* was able to explain such an initiation narrative: "the true *ngimurok* are the ones who are chosen by God (*Akuj*)" (3.22a). If God has chosen the *emuron*, and the actions of the *emuron* are effective, who can question the *emuron*? Still, for some of the *ngimurok*, particularly those of the *ngimurok* of the head, it is difficult to accept even this rare exception. One such *emuron* recounted that those possessed by spirits or made crazy or sick, and then healed to become an emuron; "these are different (*egela*) than those who were chosen by God long ago" (3.9b). Again, this specific example follows a pattern that is not commonly seen among Turkana *ngimurok* but is more commonly seen in other parts of Africa.

Limitations During the New Moon

One phenomenon that was repeatedly encountered during the research was the inability of the *emuron* to perform rituals that have any effect during the four days of the new moon, known as the days "when the moon is dead" (2.2b).[44] On these days, clients do not visit the *emuron* and rituals are not performed. All the *ngimurok* of the head said that they did not, or even could not, do their *amuronut* when there was no moon. During the phase when the moon is new, one *emuron* said that, "When the moon is dead, you close [the work]. Not until the fourth day of the new moon do you start again" (2.2b).

Arriving at an *emuron* home on one of these days often meant finding that the *emuron* was not at home, having gone to visit at the homes of others or gone to visit the animals where they graze. During these days the ritual objects are left to sit and the bowls containing the ritual ochre are found dry with the residue of the clay after all the water has evaporated. On any other days of the month, one would find containers of wet ochre, ready to be applied on a client at any moment.

This was found to have broad implications during my research. At one point when a community I was visiting was responding to bandits from across the river, I witnessed the conversation between a government appointed administrative chief and the local *emuron*. They both believed that

---

44. "Four days" in Turkana count as two calendar days. Twelve hours of light and twelve hours of darkness counts as two days in Turkana time keeping, especially in regard to ritual activities.

the continuing threat of attack from across the river was over, and the chief was ready to speak to those who had evacuated their homes near the river to tell them to return to their homes. But, it was during the four days of the new moon. The *emuron* responded to the chief, "If you speak to the people now, how will I open the protection/obstruction sacrifice (*ariwo*) when the moon is dead?" (VN4). At this point, the chief decided it was best to wait until the moon had again appeared.

No one could explain the relationship between the phase of the moon and the ability of the *emuron* to perform rituals. This is something to be further explored at a later date. It should be noted that many community events are centered around the days of the full moon. Most rituals are seen as more effective when they are done on a day close to the full moon.

Importance of the Number Four

While there are four inactive days for performing the rituals of the *emuron* each month, the research also revealed that there was some type of relationship with the number four (*ngoomwon*) and Turkana ritual practices. Four is a common symbolic number in many religions and among traditional people. In Turkana it is connected to the phases of the moon (28 days, 4 phases (new, half waxing, full, half waning), four opposite directions, four legs of an animal, symmetry of 4 fingers, and maybe related to the four sections of ruminate stomachs. One *emuron* instructed his clients before an *ariwo* sacrifice that they were to rub the head of the goat from the forehead to the chest four times. (2.4a). Whatever the symbolism might be or was at one time, no *emuron* was able to tell me why four was important, only that it was a ritually significant number if things were to be done the correct way. "Four is sacred (*italiunitoe*)" (3.10b).

Payment for the Emuron

All *ngimurok* participants in the research require payment from their clients in one form or another. Most commonly, payment is received in the form of an animal, especially if the *emuron* has prescribed an animal sacrifice. Descriptions of payment often included a discussion on whether or not those with little means, those without a herd of animals, were also expected to make equal payments as other clients. As seen in the excerpts included here, these discussions normally ended with the statement that in all circumstances, something must be paid. Those who are unable to pay may not be able to participate in all the rituals required by the *emuron*.

When animal sacrifices are required, clients are expected to bring two animals to the *emuron*: one for the ritual sacrifice (most often the *ariwo* sacrifice), and one as payment to the *emuron*. This was the most common arrangement described in the research: "Normally people bring two goats to me when they are sick, one for the *ariwo* and one for my goat pen" (2.2b). Variations to this expectation included a few *ngimurok* who read intestines who are willing to accept the sacrificed animal itself as payment, because they are sharing in the consuming of the meat. One *emuron* of the intestines explained,

> I follow the tradition of my father in reading the intestines. No one pays me. When I read the intestines for someone I eat the meat from that animal with him and his family. The meat that I eat is payment. (3.9a)

As described earlier, the reading of the intestines is often likely to reveal a second animal that must be found and sacrificed. Yet, even among the *ngimurok* of the intestines, a second animal as payment, to add to the *emuron* goat pen, is expected. The most expensive payments encountered during the research were those required of the *emuron akatuwan*. Treatments of the *akatuwan* often require 3–4 sessions, each requiring payment of at least 3 goats; for a person working as a day laborer in the Turkana administrative capital, Lodwar, these sessions could end up costing the equivalent of 3–6 months of wages.

Some *ngimurok* describe payment from the client being based on what the client is truly seeking or how serious the client is concerning the matter at hand that caused them to seek the *emuron*. Two such *ngimurok*, in response to whether there is a specific amount people are supposed to pay when they visit the *emuron*, described payment as related to what people are seeking:

> For every person there is their due reward. Only the person who comes to the *emuron* knows what they should bring. If they come without anything, the *emuron* will pray for them, but the person will certainly bring something to the *emuron* in the future. But if my father says there is a certain animal that must be used for a ritual, they must bring that one. They might bring something else, but no one tells them what they must bring. (2.15b)

> You take your money and you go to the *emuron*. You visit the *emuron* to open things up, to find things. God sees these things; that you went to the home of the *emuron*. Then you will meet

with school, you will meet with employment. You will meet with
your lover, you will find your life and find great wealth. (i15:2)

Both of these explanations take the perspective that whatever the payment, it is worth the cost because you will find what you seek. While the first of these two explanations prioritizes any explicit instructions from the *emuron* concerning payment or a sacrificial animal, both these descriptions explain that in the end, payment is left up to the client. It should be obvious that the client would want to pay an amount commensurate with the things they are desiring, and often, those things are very important: getting into a good school, finding a job, finding a lover, wealth, and even life itself.

How do *ngimurok* respond to those who have little to no domestic animal wealth? Responses like the following, to the question "if a poor person comes who is sick, what do you do?" were consistently telling: "I throw water on them" (2.2b). That is, people who come to the *emuron* and cannot pay, do not receive full ritual treatments. They may only receive the blessing of having water thrown on them, which, for a normal paying client is only the beginning or ending of a larger ritual. It seems the final word is that everyone seeking knowledge or treatment from an *emuron* must pay something, no matter how poor:

> Even a poor person must bring something for payment, even if
> it is small. The tradition (*etal*) is that you have to pay something.
> (2.13b)

In summary, payments to the *ngimurok* are expensive, but the results are viewed as effective and worth the cost. Clients are expected to bring whatever the *emuron* requires, but in some situations can pay whatever they sense is commensurate with the result or blessing they seek. There are variations: the *ngimurok* who read intestines do not always require a second animal as payment, and the *emuron akatuwan* often requires much larger payments. The tradition is that everyone must pay something and those who find themselves in the position of being unable to pay will not be able to participate in the animal sacrifice rituals.

Good (Luajokak) and Bad (Luaronok) Ngimurok

One of the more fruitful questions asked in the research, that helps to provide a clearer insider understanding of who the *ngimurok* say that they are, was a simple question that has to do with morality. Because I had received so many negative responses from Turkana Christians evaluating the *ngimurok* as morally bad or evil (see chapter 6), I asked each of the *ngimurok* this question: "I have heard that some *ngimurok* are seen as immoral in their actions while others are moral. Is this true? Are there good (*luajokak*) and bad (*luaronok*) *ngimurok*? If so, from your wisdom (*aouso*), what makes an *emuron* good or bad?"

Responses to this question from the *ngimurok* were fairly consistent. Good *ngimurok* were described first as hospitable, as "those who welcome visitors at their homes" (1.8); who "are known well for welcoming people, by the things he does, by his lifestyle, he has a good heart and he believes in God (*enupit Akuj*)" (2.3a). Furthermore, a good *emuron* does not just wait for people to arrive at his/her homestead; instead the good *emuron* calls people to come to their home when they know there a problem that has been revealed (2.22a). I was able to experience this hospitality throughout my research. While I initially feared that *ngimurok* would not be willing to talk with me at their homes, it soon became apparent that the success of this research would be due, in large part, to the overwhelming willingness of the *ngimurok* to have me stay at their homes, share in their food, and watch or participate in the rituals. It was not until the process of sorting through *ngimurok* descriptions, and especially the responses to the above questions, that I realized this was an important shared understanding of all *ngimurok*: to be an *emuron* is to be one who welcomes people at their home.

This type of hospitality comes at a cost for the *ngimurok*. On many occasions, at the homes of the more popular and active *ngimurok*, I would observe up to 20 clients at one time relying on the hospitality of the *emuron*. The wives of the *emuron* were constantly cooking for the guests; the *emuron* was visiting with guests and prescribing rituals from 6am until 9pm; new clients were arriving day and night. Each morning when we awoke and followed the *emuron* around the homestead, there were new people who had arrived during the night. The only time of rest for the *emuron* seemed to be during the middle of the day, a traditional time of rest in Turkana, when the equatorial sun and heat make it difficult to engage in much activity.[45] In the context of this amount of activity at the home of the *emuron*, one can see that an *emuron* who is considered hospitable would be someone specially gifted to make all feel welcome, giving up all of their time and days to respond to client needs. The break in *emuron* activity during the four days of the new moon could be seen as a much needed period of rest in the context of the requirements for *emuron* hospitality.

Another important characteristic of a good *emuron* is to be seen as effective, especially at calling down rain. Indeed, this was one of the key characteristics for the *ngimurok* who are considered great, even by other *ngimurok* today. There is no doubt in anyone's mind that the *emuron* who

---

45. The midday temperatures in Turkana range year round from 95-110F (35-44C).

can cause rain to fall is a good *emuron*. After hospitality, this was the most common description of good *emuron*: "A good emuron is the one that brings down rain" (i22.3); "The good emuron makes rain, heals sickness and kills the ariwo" (3.8b).

A good *emuron* is also seen as one who works in unity with other people, not keeping grudges and not envious of other *ngimurok* and their success. This is an important distinguishing marker in the morality of an *emuron*, because the evil practitioners, the *ekasuban* and the *ekapilan*, are most often identified by their jealous and envious motivations. Thus, the difference is that "the good *ngimurok* are those who move together in unity, whereas the bad *ngimurok* are those who compete with each other" (2.3b). When outperformed by another *emuron*, usually from within their own family, "the good *emuron* does not keep grudges" (2.22a).

Finally, good *ngimurok* are those who provide the services that people are seeking, effectively helping people in the right way, healing the sick and participating in the *ariwo* protection ritual. These are the services most sought after by their clients. Fulfilling the desires of their clients points to an *emuron* who is evaluated as morally good:

> A good *emuron* is one who, when a person comes to them and asks for something, they give it, whether is it food, or help in not being defeated at school, or help for not being defeated at work. Even if you cannot find work, the *emuron* says to you '*piu, piu*' [spitting sound], yes, go, and when you go you find work, that one is certainly good. If someone is plagued with continuous pain in their body, if this problem is sickness, he says '*piu, piu*' [spitting sound], brings water, and the person is healed, that *emuron* is certainly good. (i22:3)

A common desire of the people also includes protection for those preparing to embark on cattle raids or fighting enemies. It is the good *emuron* who "helps with the *ariwo* when people are going to fight the enemies" (3.8b).

Ngimurok are evaluated as morally bad, *naaronok*, when they don't fulfill the desires of the people and are seen as either ineffective or exclusively serving their own interests. There is doubt concerning whether or not the *emuron* who acts in this way is truly an *emuron* or has instead transitioned into the categories of either *ekapilan* or *ekasuban*. One *emuron* rejected the notion that there could be a bad *emuron* at all, exclaiming, "We are not familiar with evil!" (2.1b). But another explained the difference: "Yes, there are good and bad *ngimurok*; but the *emuron* who becomes bad is the *ekasuban*; we say that the one who curses the land (*esubi akwap*) is evil" (i15:5). "Cursing the land" is the opposite of sending down rain. Instead, rain is prevented, bringing drought and hunger. Just as the good *emuron* does not hold grudges, inversely, the "bad *ngimurok* are those who kill people, they curse (*irikarit*) people and they hold on to grudges. They will even finish your livestock" (2.22a); they "destroy many things" (3.11b). It is because of these grudges and jealousy that the bad *emuron* seeks to curse the land, which only results in "bringing hunger" (2.26a).

Bad *ngimurok* were commonly described by the *ngimurok* research participants as those who "kill people and curse people with words (*elami*)" (1.8b), who deceive and cheat people (*engalata ngitunga*), who cause people to faint (*kerakar ngitunga*), those who cause corruption (*akidem edeng*) (2.3a), and those who do not do the *ariwo* (3.8b). One particularly insidious activity was described:

> There are those who kill people who call themselves *emuron*. When they come and ask people for money, telling people they are an *emuron*, if you say, 'no.' they kill you. That one is very bad. (i22:3)

Again, it is questionable as to whether or not these ones are truly *ngimurok* or only those who falsely call themselves *ngimurok* in order to gain from the deception. Even so, there is the power or ability to kill if money is not received from the unwilling clients.

Can you curse or kill someone?

The descriptions of good and bad *ngimurok* occasionally led into a discussion that was more direct in approach regarding the abilities of the *ngimurok* research participants to curse or kill a person through their revelations or rituals. One such discussion is provided here:

> [If someone comes to you and wants you to kill a person who has stolen the animals, will you do it?] "No." [Does that mean that you are not able to do the things to curse someone?] "I am not able." [Do your not have the wisdom or the strength to do it? What if a very rich man came with ten camels to pay you to curse another man, are you not able to do it?] It is not possible for me; how could I kill a person? I refuse to kill a person. It's true; there are those who do, those who kill other people. But, from my heart/spirit (*etau*), it is not possible for me to kill another person, even if there happens to be people who kill other people. I am to help (*akingarakin*). The work of helping a person, helping, to help is my work. How could I then go to kill? If I killed a person, how could I then eat? (i15:5–6)

My understanding from this interview was not that the *emuron* is unable to curse someone or to even kill someone with *amuronut* or *akisub*, but that doing so would essentially change who they are, from *emuron* to one of the evil practitioners. If an *emuron* engaged in such practices, it would become difficult for them to continue to attract many clients. People would come to fear the *emuron*, and the *emuron* would be left asking themselves, 'How will I now eat?"

In discussing the question of *emuron* cursing, it was discovered that there are two different verbs used that can translate the action "cursing." One type of cursing is described as being practiced by all people, while the other is observed only by the malevolent ritual specialists:

> Cursing with words (*akilam*) is different than cursing with objects (*akisub*). The *ngikasubak* can kill people with *akisub*. But anyone can curse with words. If my animals are missing, I can curse the one who took the animals and he will get sick until he returns the animals (3.3a).

Thus, *akisub* cursing is very dangerous and requires ritual activity. The *akilam* are more general curses of everyday speech that need no specific rituals to make them effective.

The research did not simply clarify the moral positions of *ngimurok* as either those with evil or benevolent intent. Overwhelmingly, the *ngimurok* described themselves and their roles in the community as very positive and morally right. Yet, they did acknowledge that there are some who are willing to act immorally, but this is explained as being motivated by envy and jealousy or self-serving interests. Those who act in this way are in danger of no longer being part of the category *emuron* but are seen as transitioning into the categories of malevolent ritual specialist, *ekasuban* or *ekapilan*.

OTHER ROLES IN THE COMMUNITY

Apart from the ritual functions of the *ngimurok* at their homes, as observed in the research, *ngimurok* are also involved in some community-wide ritual events, specifically rituals of transformation. While I fully expected to find that the *ngimurok* were key participants in weddings and other public rituals, I discovered that they only voluntarily attended weddings and other rites of passage (such as the *asapan*), and even then attend as one of the elders in the community, not as the *emuron* to oversee or lead the ritual. Instead, *ngimurok* play a large role behind the scenes of these rituals, most often being paid by clients to perform rituals to "close the animals" (*akigol ngibaren*) or "close the young daughters" (*akigol ngide ngapesur*).

Weddings (akuuta)

The leadership roles of an *emuron* in the wedding are primarily due to being one of the elders in the community, not because an *emuron* is required for the ritual. Most *ngimurok*, when asked if they participated in leading the rituals of local weddings, did not understand the question. Responses ranged from, "yes, I go to the weddings and sit with the elders," to "I only go to weddings when I am invited." A few shared that they had a limited role in weddings: "At the weddings in our area on the day of the spearing of the bull, I throw the water on people as a blessing" (1.12b). The "spearing of the bull" is the final act of the wedding in which the final animal of the bride price, normally a bull (cattle or camel), is speared in the center of the wedding participants and then cooked for all to eat a great feast. It seems that at this time, some *ngimurok* will throw the water blessings on the crowd of people and the bride and groom. It does not appear to be a practice that is required or even consistently carried out at most weddings. The more common *emuron* practices surrounding weddings, but not part of the actual event, are *akigol ngibaren* and *akigol ngide ngapesur*.

Akigol Ngibaren "the closing of livestock"

During the times of weddings, people will visit their friends and extended families to ask for help in acquiring the large numbers of animals required to finish paying the bride price.[46] The father of the bride may worry that, because of a recent influx of animals into his herd from his son-in-law, others may quickly come to borrow or ask for animals from him for their own weddings. In an effort to prevent this from occurring, people will come to the *emuron* for their animals to be "closed" and protected from being used for weddings. The *emuron* applies ochre (*emunyen*) to the animals and declares them closed. If someone eats a closed animal or demands payment of closed animals they could become sick and even die. Only the *emuron* can officially "open" the animals. The "closing" of animals can occur for other reasons also: "I close the animals when there is sickness, when a debt is owed (*amicha*), and when there is a wedding" (2.4a). "When it is time for the wedding, I will go to the man's goat pen and have him take out the animals that are to be used for the wedding; then the remaining animals, I close by putting ochre on them; I put the *akolit* (whip) at the gate of the goat pen. I am not paid for that work until the wedding." (2.12b).

---

46. Bride prices in Turkana, depending on the wealth of the individuals involved, include payments as low as 20 animals, up to 500 animals, that are agreed upon by the parents of the bride and groom and are exchanged from the groom to his new father-in-law and the brothers of his father-in-law.

Akigol Ngide Ngapesur "the closing of young girls"

In a similar fashion to the ritual closing of the animals, fathers can call an *emuron* to the homestead to "close the daughters" in order to protect them, for a time, from men who may seek to steal the girls away from her family, either with the intention of marriage or solely for sexual activity. The *emuron* applies ochre to the young girls and declares them "closed." The specific markings of the ochre on the girls should be enough for men to identify that these girls have been set apart and that there are serious consequences if any man sleeps with a girl who has been closed: they will get sick, leading to death, unless they agree to marry the girl and pay a penalty to the *emuron* of 10 goats, one camel, and one fat sheep, along with sugar and tobacco. If this payment is brought to the *emuron* he can take away the problems from the man (3.18b, elsewhere). If an *emuron* has an older uncle or brother who is an *emuron*, an *emuron* does not do this ritual. Only the most senior *ngimurok* in a family or geographic area can perform these "closing" rituals.

Asapan

Again similar to weddings, the *emuron* does not have a regular required role in transformation rituals like the *asapan*. At least one *emuron* said that his role is to apply the chyme to the initiates (*kiwosakin ngikujit*) (2.2b); but again, most said that they participate only in the calling of the initiates alongside the other elders of the community, not as someone who has an officially separate role. One *emuron* who does regularly attend the *asapan* in his community, shared his role in the ritual: "I apply the chyme on the men; I also receive a fat sheep and goats from the families of the *asapan*" (2.12b).

These findings on the roles of the *ngimurok* in their communities display a more limited role than I originally suspected at the beginning of the research. My hypothesis was that the *ngimurok* would be central figures in all Turkana ritual ceremonies. But this is not the case. While the *ngimurok* do have specific roles in the community, their presence is not required at weddings and other rites of transformation, although they are often present and participate as one of the elders in the community.

Operating as one of the elders in the community, the *emuron* at times will help provide leadership for legal cases in the community. On one occasion I was able to witness a case being held regarding animals that had been stolen at the homestead of an *emuron* of the head. At times, such cases are held and rulings made at the home of the *emuron* to give the decisions more weight. Although the *emuron* does not lead the case (the oldest elder in the community leads), he is very influential as all believe that the *emuron*, especially at his home, has the power to make, coerce, or ensure that the testimony of all the witnesses are true. No one would dare give false testimony at the home of an *emuron* for fear that they might become ill or even die.

CHAPTER CONCLUSION

Who do the *ngimurok*, themselves, say that they are? This is a question that has rarely been asked in Turkana, especially by Western missionaries and other cultural outsiders. It is my hope that the descriptions provided here, from the words of the *ngimurok*, from their own homes, shared over Kenyan *chai* and the roasted meat of ritual sacrifices, with clients waiting at the fence for answers to their problems, are closer to the ways that the *ngimurok* describe themselves than any other description previously provided.

"We are the ritual specialists (*ngimurok*) who do rituals (*amuronut*)." Beyond this initial generic description, I found a depth of complexity throughout the process of the research, that I was not expecting. While I gradually came to suspect that the broadly negative, even demonized, descriptions of *ngimurok* I received as I first entered Turkana in 1994 were not a complete assessment of these men and women who had been such an important part of Turkana history, I did not expect to find as much complexity as was presented during my research.

While the *ngimurok* are certainly connected to each other by many of their rituals (see chapter 5), they are not identical. They are multifaceted in ways that even my attempt at categorization lacks the ability to capture. Table 1 in this chapter provides a beginning at understanding the different types of religious specialists who may be included within the term *emuron*. Still, the question remains, for each of these categories of Turkana ritual specialists, which ones can be called *emuron*? In many ways, the answer is dependent on the perspective of the one who is answering.

There are four categories of *ngimurok* that were self-identified and self-described: the *emuron* of the head, the *emuron* of the sandals and intestines, the *emuron* who reads (tobacco and money), and the *emuron akatuwan* who exorcises foreign objects from the body. Although the *emuron akatuwan* interviewed preferred to use the term *akatuwan* in her own description of herself, she did also describe herself as an *emuron*, and every other ritual specialist in this research described the *akatuwan* using the word *emuron* or the feminine form, *amuron*.

For these four categories, there is no uncertainty regarding the use of the term *emuron*. The research has clearly displayed that, from their own perspectives and the perspectives of others in Turkana, both Christian and non-Christian, these four categories of ritual specialists are *ngimurok* who provide the answers to everyday questions, from individuals to entire communities. Although each of them are differentiated by the ways they are validated as an *emuron*, the ways they receive knowledge as an *emuron*, the specific problems in which they specialize, and the specific ritual practices employed, all four types are *ngimurok*. In attempting to answer the question: "Who are the *ngimurok*?" these four categories of ritual specialists are the ones who provided the best answer and have provided the bulk of the data in this research project.

The second column in Table 1 lists five contested categories of *ngimurok*: the *ekasuban* and the *ekapilan*—both considered to be feared and malevolent ritual specialists—the *emuron a akomwa*, the *ekadwaran*, and the *dakitari*. Are these five categories also *ngimurok*? Again, the answer depends on the perspective of the one asking. From the perspective of Western missionaries and Turkana church teachings, these two evil practitioners and three other practitioners are generally grouped together in the same category as the four self-described *ngimurok*. From this perspective, all of them are traditional ritual practitioners, and all of them are working against the purposes of God in Turkana. From the perspective of the four types of uncontested *ngimurok*, these five are not in the category *emuron*. It is possible that the two evil ritual specialists were at one time *ngimurok*, but they are no longer considered *ngimurok*. For the self-described *ngimurok*, these evil practitioners are more akin to the traditional anthropological understandings of "sorcerer," in regard to the *ekasuban*, and "witch," in regard to the *ekapilan*. This is the perspective that has not been heard recently, even though my research indicates that this is the understanding of the majority of the people in Turkana.

The third column in Table 1 lists five more potential types that need to be considered within (or contrasted against) the category *emuron*. Two are related to the introduction of outside religions in Turkana: the leaders, or *emalaikat*, of the new religious movement Legio Maria; and the church leaders, *ngikarikok a ngikanisae*, of various Protestant and Catholic mission-initiated churches. The final three are those who play specific roles in the community: the *akariton* who helps with childbirth; the elders of the villages, *ngikasikou a ngadakarin*; and those who have imported or invented ritual practices unfamiliar to the Turkana, *lu nyeyenete*. While it is agreed by the majority of my research participants that these final three types are not part of the category *emuron*, many described them as being similar to the *ngimurok*. This similarity may be nothing more than the practice of rituals or a leadership role in the community, but there is enough of a connection that the types are mentioned in the research when asking the question: Who are Turkana *ngimurok*?

The case of the first two types in the third column of Table 1 is more complicated. While those who define themselves as being of the types in the first column do not acknowledge that the leaders from the *Legio Maria* Church or other Protestant churches, like the Community Christian Church, are *ngimurok*, they see these religious leaders as beginning to take on the role of the *emuron* in their communities. And likewise, even as the leaders of these churches are denouncing the traditional *ngimurok* of the first column as evil and of the same types as the *ekapilan* and *ekasuban*, and would abhor the thought that they are themselves beginning to be understood through the local cultural perspective as *ngimurok*, that is exactly what is happening in the Turkana context. From my perspective as the researcher, I would argue that the *Legio Maria* and other church leaders in Turkana are becoming *ngimurok*; that is, as various forms of Christianity push many of the different types of Turkana religious specialists into a single category of evil religious specialists, the leaders of the churches are beginning to fill the traditional *emuron* roles in the Christian communities. This argument is carried further in the conclusion of the study.

Through the data provided in this chapter, I have explored the complexities of the term *emuron*. Hopefully my analysis of the data provided by those who themselves experience the phenomenon of being the *ngimurok* helps to provide some clarity. Certainly it provides a description that has been missing in the literature regarding Turkana *ngimurok*. To be an *emuron* in Turkana is not one single type of specialist. To be an *emuron* in Turkana can include multiple types of specialists, and the words of these specialists themselves have been the primary guide in this project's presentation of the *emuron*. The next chapter will now provide more details on the rituals used by those who define themselves as *ngimurok*.

5

Specific Observed and Described Rituals and Ritual Objects of the *Ngimurok*

THIS CHAPTER PROVIDES DESCRIPTIVE and narrative summaries of Turkana *emuron* rituals and ritual objects that were encountered during the research. The researcher observed some rituals, while the *ngimurok* research participants described others. The researcher observed all ritual objects. The purpose of these descriptions is to provide further data on rituals regularly performed and ritual objects regularly used by Turkana *ngimurok* that may have been mentioned in the previous chapter. Turkana ritual specialists in all the uncontested categories of *emuron* presented in the research and by some of the specialists in the more contested categories of *emuron* presented here use these rituals and ritual objects. These rituals descriptions are not provided in any other known literature concerning Turkana *ngimurok*.

OBSERVED AND DESCRIBED RITUALS

Ariwo

The *ariwo* ritual is known as both the "obstruction" or "protection" ritual. It can be employed as an obstruction to the plans of enemies. For example, an *ariwo* can cause a group of enemy bandits to become confused and lose their way as they approach a village to steal animals. It can also obstruct the efforts of enemies to pursue a raiding party. Similarly, the *ariwo* can protect those going on cattle raids or more generally traveling for other purposes. Apart from raiding, the *ariwo* is seen as a powerful ritual that can effectively protect individuals or groups from evil ritual specialists, illnesses, or even repeated unwanted visits from ancestors.

The *ariwo* is normally a specific animal sacrifice that has been revealed to the *emuron*. This sacrifice can be from a variety of animal types, and the method of ritual sacrifice can also vary according to the situation and the specific revelation of the *emuron*. The sacrificial animal is normally a goat or a sheep, but can be any animal. The method of sacrifice also varies between traditional spearing (*akichum*), suffocating (see *kititik* ritual below), and disemboweling while alive (see *tongeere* ritual below). Occasionally, the word *ariwo* is used as a description of how *emunyen* (ritual ochre) works as another form of protection ritual, but this is uncommon.

Ariwo for cattle raiding

> "The *ngimurok* kill the *ariwo* for the young men who are going away so that they won't be killed in that place" (i24:6).

The *ariwo* that obstructs enemies and protects the community provides the most variations in the animal and type of sacrifice. A common form of *ariwo* during times of raiding bandits (*ngingoroko*) includes cutting the sacrificed animal transversely in half and then either walking between the halves for protection, or placing the sacrifice where the enemy might walk between the halves without initially knowing they had done so. The meat from the *ariwo* ritual, when dealing with enemies, is rarely eaten (2.2a).

The variety and the extreme nature of some of the *ariwo* rituals were described during a time of raiding in one of the villages where I was conducting research. The raiding had led to the killing of multiple people in the village over a period of more than one week. All of the village residents had moved about 2–3 kilometers from the main village. In such a dire situation the *emuron* performed multiple *ariwo* rituals:

> There have been three *ariwo* rituals done around Kangirisae because of the bandits who have been coming. The first was an *ekoroe langor* (a tan/brown he-goat) that was cut in half (on a horizontal plane in the lower thorax) and left where the bandits would walk between the two halves. The second was a yellow dog that had the eyes removed and then was tied, still alive, to a tree near the path. This was so the enemies won't be able to see like this dog. The third was a brown-marked she-goat that was cut in half and the people of the village passed between [for protection]. (2.3b)

The *ariwo* involving the dog is particularly unique for the situation, not only in the type of animal revealed, but the manner of the sacrifice that both efficiently paralleled the desires of those performing the *ariwo* and likely intimidated the approaching bandits.

For those who are going to other places to raid, the *ariwo* ritual performed by the local *emuron* can help to save many lives. Revelations received by the *emuron* will identify the specific animal required for the sacrifice and any specific instructions, including how or where to avoid an evil ritual specialist who would work to undue the effectiveness of the *ariwo*. One *emuron a akou* narrates the process when asked how he helps the raiders near Pokot land:

> Those who come like that, I spread *emunyen* on them here and then tell them there is an *ariwo* at a person's home that they should take with them. I tell them that when they reach a certain place (*Lomunyenkupurat*), kill the goat there, but watch out for a person there who would come to take away this protection from them by their practices, like those called *ngikapilak* or like *ngikasubak*. Be careful, that person is coming. [How do you know that a person would want to destroy the *ariwo*?] I find these things when I am sleeping. Then I tell those people to go. (i22:4)

This reiterates the research findings that there is rarely a set ritual formula that *ngimurok* follow for problems. For each *ariwo* there is a specific revelation.

> The *ariwo* is shown to me so that I know its body. I even know which goat pen it is in. It is taken from here and I tell the people, 'go and kill it there.' That *ariwo* will close (*togol*) all the things that came from that sickness. (i24:6)

If there is no revelation, the true *emuron* does not perform the *ariwo* ritual. "If the *ariwo* comes to my head, I kill it; if one does not come to my head, I don't kill it" (i15:6). One day's revelation from God or the *emuron* fathers may disclose a different animal to be used for the sacrifice with a different specific method used for killing the animal than may be revealed the very next day for an identical situation.

Additional Protection for Cattle Raiding

One *amuron* of the head described an additional ritual she performs in order to protect cattle raiders in conjunction with the *ariwo* sacrifice:

> When the group of men come to me before they go to take animals from the enemies, there is a thing I can do to protect them. I have a large milking container (*akurum*). I will take sand from

> the footprint of the leader of the men, add *engeso* [a type of stick, see below] and water and put them into the *akurum*. I will keep the *akurum* in my hut and I will not leave my home until they return. If I stay near the *akurum* and protect it then the men will return. (3.19a)

This is a ritual that I did not hear about from other *ngimurok* but was unique to this *amuron*. It provided added protection for the men as they traveled in addition to the *ariwo* sacrifice.

How do the *ngimurok* describe the way the *ariwo* sacrifice provides protection, not only from raiders, but from illness and even death? Another *emuron* provided an explanation:

> When you kill the *ariwo* it protects against those problems that happen when a spirit (*ekipe*) comes to a person. The person has death (*atingit akitu*), but the *ariwo* protects against it. Those problems don't come again. [So, is the *ariwo* protection or does the *ariwo* takes the death of that person who was going to die, instead of that person dying?] That *ariwo* takes those problems when that goat dies, the death of the *ariwo* raises up the person who had death. That person remains and is still living. That goat takes the death and the person remains to live. It removes all that death. (i15:6)

From this description we find the understanding that the *ariwo* is not just a protective barrier from evil and illness, but is a substitution sacrifice in which the "death" facing the individual is taken on by the *ariwo* sacrifice.

Ariwo for Ngipean and Ngikaram

In addition to obstruction and protection from bandits and sickness, more specific *ariwo* rituals were described for those afflicted with spirits or ancestors. These rituals are also connected to the application of ritual ochre (*emunyen*):

> When a person has problems with *ngipean* or *ngikaram*, I take ochre and smear it on head that the *ngikaram* are holding. I take the ochre and tap the head and the hair on the head. White ochre, or even yellow if that drives the *ngikaram* away." [Before you do this, do you know what to do on your own or does something tell you what needs to be done?] "Who else could bring me this but my father? He tells me saying, 'change to this ochre.' I do not lie by using even a few of my own words." [Do you kill anything like an *ariwo* for these problems, or do you only use ochre?] "A goat is also killed, if a word is brought to me saying 'use this goat

> like this,' or 'kill a goat like this,' I certainly kill it. When the goat is killed the person is healed. I eat a little of the goat here [at my home] with the people who are saved (*ngitunga lu ayarete*) and cover them with the skin from the goat. It is killed in the middle of the homestead in the morning." (i22:5)

While the previous *emuron* suggests a morning sacrifice for the *ngikaram*, others suggest that an *ariwo* ritual for *ngikaram* should happen at night (2.27a, i50). Another *emuron* also prescribed a night sacrifice with more specific parameters:

> For the one who has *ngipean* an animal is killed at night. The *ngipean* normally prefer a blue animal. The meat is thrown outside the home for the *ngipean* to eat and the chyme (*ngikujit*) is rubbed on the bodies of the people at that home. (3.3a)

During the research I was able to observe one evening *ariwo* ritual as described above, that was timed right at sunset so that the meat could be thrown outside the home after dark. In that ritual, the sacrifice was killed utilizing the *tongeere* ritual method.

Tongeere Ritual Method

This ritual sacrificial method, often used for the *ariwo*, is accomplished by cutting open the animal from the chest to the lower abdomen in a straight sagittal line with the tip of a spear while the animal, still alive, lays on its left side. The viscera are removed. The chyme (stomach contents, *ngikujit*) is immediately spread (*akiwosakin*) on the skin of the people receiving the benefit of the ritual. If the animal refuses to die during the ritual, then the heart is speared directly from the inside of the chest cavity (i15:6). An alternate ritual is to remove and use the heart while it is still beating (see *eutoro etau* below).

When observing this ritual method, I was surprised by how seemingly compliant the sacrificed animal was during the sacrifice. The animal, not sedated in any way, is held down on the ground while its entire abdomen and chest cavity is opened with a spear. It is difficult to imagine that the animal would remain quiet during such an ordeal as it did during this instance of the ritual. When asking the *emuron* about this after the ritual, he said that this was always the case. In fact, a compliant sacrifice helps to confirm not only that the instructions of the revelation were correctly followed, but also confirms the effectiveness of the ritual.

Kititik Ritual Method

There were two forms of *kititik* ("lay upon or press upon") ritual methods observed and described during the research. These are also methods prescribed by *ngimurok* for some *ariwo* rituals. The first is when the *emuron* instructs the clients with problems to sit on the animal until it can no longer breathe. After the animal dies from suffocation it is then butchered and cooked for all present at the ritual to eat. This ritual is done at the home of an *emuron*.

During the research I observed this ritual method multiple times at the home of an *emuron* who reads. In one instance, the *ariwo* ritual was being done to affect three people (one man and two women) from the same family. Ritual *emunyen* had been applied to their chests and backs. Before the sacrifice, each of the three participants knelt down and grabbed the head of the live goat, rubbing the top of the head of the goat four times from their face to their chest as prescribed by the *emuron*. The goat was then placed on its side on the ground and all three sat side by side on the sacrifice. Each sat with their legs outstretched in front of them placing all their weight on the goat. Within five minutes the goat had stopped breathing and the wife and daughters of the *emuron* took the goat body to the cooking area. Butchering and cooking of the goat began immediately, for everyone who was present at the ritual would share in the meat from the *ariwo* sacrifice.

A second *kititik* ritual method was described as being done in the wilderness away from homes and is killed and eaten in that place. Instead of the goat being pressed upon, the person for whom the *ariwo* is to protect or heal is pressed upon. With the person laying down on the ground the goat is placed above him or her. Then, a companion cuts the throat of the goat (*tongol*) and it is also speared with a knife, causing it to die. "Thus, the blood is poured out over the person, it is poured out on them and they are completely healed" (i24:4). This *kititik* ritual method was only described once, but is a very powerful image of the sacrificed animal taking on the illness or even death of the person.

Eutoro Etau/Ewatakin Etau lo Eyeri

A third ritual method is occasionally added to the *tongeere* ritual. Called the *eutoro etau* (the taking of the heart) or the *ewatakin etau lo eyari* (the beating with the living heart). In this ritual the *emuron* takes out the heart of the animal while it is still alive. The heart is then immediately used to beat the head, sides, back and chest of the person for whom the ritual is being done. When this is done with "the heart, the person will be completely healed (*ejoker jik*)" (2.2b). The *emuron* described, "I kill the goat like this [*tongeere*] and pull out the heart. Then I take it while it is still living and beating and pound the child with it, hitting repeatedly" (i15:6). This ritual is most often performed for children who are weak or sick and are diagnosed as having deficiencies in their blood. The beating heart is understood as working to increase the strength and quantity of the client's blood.

Amook Rituals

When a person has recovered from a sickness, has given birth, or has paid the penalty for sexual uncleanliness, such as committing adultery, they are in need of ritual cleansing; an *amook* ritual (*mook*, "cleanse, purge, purify"). When healing comes after an *emuron* prescribed *ariwo*, an *amook* ritual should also be performed at the home of the *emuron*. Sometimes the *amook* ritual is carried out at the home of an elder and not necessarily overseen by an *emuron*, especially when the *amook* is not following an *ariwo*, but follows a homestead situation like childbirth. I witnessed one such very common *amook* ritual in Turkana. When a woman gives birth she is considered ritually unclean and unable to even visit her father's home until she participates in an *amook* ritual. This ritual is carried out for her at her father's home.

The *amook* ritual I participated in was specifically for a woman who had given birth to twins, with one of the twins dying at birth. It was at the home of her father. The men of her father's household had speared two goats for the ritual. Skins were laid out on the ground. One skin was used for receiving offerings from the participants of any miscellaneous item and for the grinding of white sorghum that all family members and visitors participated in. Another skin was used for the butchering of the animals, prepared by the older women in the family. The old women cooked the meat in two pots while the men sat separate at the other side of the homestead.

The woman for whom the ritual was being carried out sat by herself on the east side of the homestead, near to the offering skin. As visitors arrived they were expected to place an offering on the offering skin. Offerings included beads, pens, and small amounts of money (20 KSH (about $0.25) was the largest coin I noticed). A wooden bowl of white sorghum had already been given by the father's family and sat on the offering skin next to two smooth grinding stones. Each visitor, after placing his or her own offering on the skin, was expected to grind some of the sorghum into a powder. At the time of eating meat after the ritual, the sorghum powder would be cooked and given to the woman to eat. The offerings were also given to the woman.

After a visitor gave their offering and ground some sorghum they were then required to greet all the women by shaking their hands, beginning with the woman benefiting from the ritual, then the woman overseeing the offering skin and lastly the women cooking the meat. After the eating of the meal the woman was considered clean and able to freely visit at her father's homestead.

While the *ariwo* ritual takes away sickness and death, the *amook* ritual cleanses a person so they may be fully reintegrated into society. One *emuron* explained the consequences for not following up with the *amook* ritual:

> Once a sickness goes away, after the *ariwo*, one does the *amook*. The person is made good (*ejoker itwaan*) at the *amook*. The *ariwo* is performed when the person is still sick; the *amook* is done once they are healed. The person offers a sheep, small goat, sugar and tobacco to the *emuron*. The sheep is then killed. This is the *amook*. It ends the sickness. If the *amook* is not done then even the *emuron* can get sick. (3.2b)

Thus, the *amook* ritual is necessary for complete healing and restoration, even after an effective *ariwo* ritual. If this ritual is neglected, the sickness or uncleanness is not completely gone, and can potentially even find its way back to the *emuron* who should have prescribed the *amook*.

Ewosakin/Etujukok Emunyen

An ever-present ritual that all the types of *ngimurok* research participants perform is *ewosakin emunyen*, the spreading of ochre on the body of clients; commonly applied to the head, chest, abdomen, back and face. Ochre is defined by archeologists and chemists in varying ways, but most commonly, ochre is a general term used for any rock or clay containing a significant amount of different forms of iron oxide that allows the substance to leave a residue that ranges in color from light yellow, bright red, to dark purple.[1] Archeologists have found evidence of ochre use among Homo sapiens in Africa as early 200,000 years ago, with recent evidence dating ochre use even earlier among Neanderthals.[2]

In Turkana, ochre is obtained by *ngimurok* from the exposed sides of hills in specific locations that differ for each *emuron*. Ochre is not normally purchased in town, but is collected by each *emuron* in their local area. The rocks or clay are then ground into a powder to which water is added, making

---

1. Popelka-Filcoff et al., "Trace Element Characterization," 17; Watts, "Red Ochre, Body Painting, and Language," 63–64.
2. Roebroeks et al., "Use of Red Ochre," 1889.

a paint-like substance in the colors white, yellow, red, blue and black. Often, the powder from special sticks (*ngikito*, "medicine;" see below) are also added to the ochre, including the traditional medicines: *ekeriau*, *ebata*, *engeso* (i22:4). Each color of ochre is stored in a wooden bowl (*atubwa*) and saved for when the revelation dictates a certain color of *emunyen*. The water in the ochre will evaporate within a day, so water is added to make a fresh mix each day (i15:4).

There are three methods for the application of the *emunyen* onto the body of others: with the hands, with leaves, or with an *athante* (a large fibrous brush made with a large animal tendon). How does the *emuron* decide which method to use when spreading *emunyen* on his or her clients? An *emuron* response is that "this is your work, the work that God has given to some people, whether it is *edome* leaves or not . . . God is the one who tells you. If God tells you then you use *edome* tree leaves" (i15:5). Still, other *ngimurok* are strict in believing the correct way to spread *emunyen* is with the hands, unless there is some extenuating circumstance:

> Certainly using the hand is the true way. An *athante* is used for a man who is initiated (*asapanit*) and is returning home after having been away from home for at least four days. Water is thrown on him with the *athante* to welcome him home. For the *ngimurok*, the hand is what should be used. (i22:4)

From this description, it seems the *athante* is only used in times when the *emuron* him/herself has questionable connections to uncleanness.

The effectiveness of *emunyen* is described as similar to medicine, and also as a type of *ariwo*. Seen as similar to Western medicine, the *emunyen* brings about the healing of sickness. An *emuron* described the ochre as his medicine, "so that if someone should come I spread it on that person to rectify the problem of sickness right there. It's just like when you drink [Western] medicine and it takes care of the problem" (i15:5). For other *ngimurok*, the *emunyen* acts to protect the community when a revelation from the father or *Akuj* (God) is received of an impending sickness. In that situation, before the revealed sickness arrives, another revelation will provide the details, "'take this certain *emunyen* and spread it on the people;' then I tell the people in the area to have that *emunyen* put on them, it is like an *ariwo*" (i22:3). In addition to healing and *ariwo*, *emunyen* was also observed being used to motivate and prepare people for the planting of crops. One *amuron* would call all the people to her house for the "opening up of crops" or the official start of the sorghum-planting season in the gardens. Once the community was at her house, she used white *emunyen* on the entire right arm and hand of each who would be involved in planting. The planting in the gardens would begin on that very day.

The research revealed that the most common practice in selecting the color of *emunyen* to be used in a ritual is to wait for revelation, especially among the *ngimurok a akou* and the *ngimurok* of the intestines. An *emuron a akou* explained, "I don't spread emunyen of one color or another on a person unless my father tells me. Even if I know one color is normally used for a certain sickness, I do not do it unless my father tells me" (3.10a). Even though this is normally the case when selecting different colors of *emunyen* for rituals, some *ngimurok* preferred to use certain colors over another, as was the tradition in their line of *ngimurok*. Other *ngimurok* were also able to describe some general ways that each of the different colors of *emunyen* matched up with certain illnesses or problems. In some cases, the colors of *emunyen* used were simply contingent upon which type of ochre was available in the local area; for others, symbolic meaning is already assigned to certain colors because of their family traditions. As an *emuron* in the line of Lokorijem described, "Our family only uses white and yellow ochre, we do not use the blue, red, or the black" (i22:4).

Ewatakin ngakipi

> "When I am throwing water (*ewatakin ngakipi*) on people I am calling on God (*tanyarae Akuj*) to give help to these people" (2.12a).

The *ewatakin ngakipi* (throwing water) ritual is the most common of all the rituals among all the categories of *ngimurok*, except for the *ekasuban* and the *ekapilan*. The ritual is accomplished by filling an *elipet* (tall, narrow wooden container for water or milking) with water that has been set aside for the ritual. The water is often mixed with a small amount of ground powder from medicinal sticks (*ngikito*) and/or a small amount of ochre (*emunyen*). The *emuron* stands about 1 meter from those being blessed and forcefully throws water at their heads, faces and chests. Some only throw with hands, some use the leaves of the *edome* (more common among Lokerio descendants), and some (only a few) use a tool called an *athante* made from the tendon of a large animal and has been beaten on one end to resemble a brush. One *amuron* (f.) described minor variations in the ritual depending on whether the *emuron* and the client are male or female:

> I throw water on people from the *atubwa* (wooden bowl). The *elipet* (tall milking container) is for men to use. I throw the water using my hand. If it is a man who has returned from driving

animals from far away and he is a member of our family, then I use the *athante* to throw water, but other than that, I always use my hand. (i23:5)

Again, we find the *athante* being used as a ritual object instead of the hands when either the *emuron* or the client are ritually unclean because of a specific circumstance.

The throwing of water by the *emuron* is a blessing on those receiving the water. It can also be like an *ariwo* (protection ritual), or even "like medicine when you add sticks (*ngikito*) or ochre (*emunyen*) . . . the water is all of those things" (10/23/11 030.mov). The water is meant to cool (*tolimer*) a hot (*emona*) person—a common colloquialism in Turkana for someone who is angry or beset with problems, or even ill. For others, the ritual is also seen as a prayer of supplication for God (*Akuj*) to give help to the people (2.12a).

Throwing/jumping (akilamlam) Sandals and Reading (akisemeere) Intestines

As practiced by the *emuron* of sandals and intestines, the throwing of sandals precedes the reading of intestines, but the two rituals work together in a cycle. The sandals reveal which animal should be killed for the intestine reading; the intestine reading reveals the problem and what should be done to either prevent or solve the problem. If this process does not sufficiently answer the question or problem then it is repeated; sandals are thrown again to select another animal and intestines are read again until the intestines reveal that there are no problems.

THROWING (AKILAMLAM) SANDALS

The first part of the ritual cycle is the throwing of the sandals. This ritual was observed multiple times and also video recorded. Special sandals are used for throwing that have been made from the skin of a large animal, preferably a hippopotamus or bull or camel. These sandals are not worn by the *emuron*, but are used only for sandal throwing. As described in the *emuron* of sandals and intestines section of the previous chapter, before throwing the sandals an offering of tobacco is made for the *ngipean* in the sandals by sprinkling a small amount of tobacco directly on the sandals.

The sandals are then initially thrown a few times to see if they are willing to talk; if they will answer any questions. The bottoms of the sandals are placed together and the *emuron*, seated on his short wooden stool (*ekicholong*), holds both of the sandals together, the top of the left sandal facing him and the top of the right sandal facing away, with the toes of the sandals pointing to the left and the heels to the right. Raising them about 6 inches off the ground, the *emuron* quickly taps the side of the sandals down on the ground. Then raising them up again about two feet, the *emuron* throws the sandals down to the ground while opening the fingers of the right hand that was holding the sandals.

The sandals land in various ways, upside down, right-side up, overlapping, barely touching, toes touching, heels touching, toes touching heels, or even not touching at all. Most of the time a specific question is asked of the sandals that can be answered with a yes or a no. When interpreting the configuration of the sandals, special attention is paid to the right sandal and whether or not it is closer or farther way from the *emuron* when the sandals land on the ground.

The configurations of the sandals provide either positive or negative feedback to the question being asked. The questions could be related to a sickness, but especially concerning whether or not an *ariwo* sacrifice should be killed. Once that is established, the sandals will help to determine which specific animal should be killed. "The sandals are asked which goat. When the shoes have space between them that is the one to be killed. If they are touching the answer is 'no'" (3.1b). The basic sandal configurations are shown in Figure 3 below.

In Figure 3, there are nine basic sandal throwing configurations representing the placement of the sandals once they have rested on the ground. Configurations either provide a negative or positive response to whatever the question is at hand. The configurations should be understood as lying on the ground directly in front of the *emuron*. That is, each configuration is a top view, in which the *emuron* is seated just below the configuration.

Configurations 1 (both sandals facing up and next to each other) and 2 (both sandals upside down and next to each other) are both negative configurations because the right sandal has moved beyond the left sandal, farther away from the *emuron*. Configurations 3, 4 and 5 are all positive configurations of the sandals. Configuration 4 is the most positive because the sandals are additionally pointed in the same direction. Configurations 6 and 7 are also very positive configurations of the sandals. Both of these configurations, with the right sandal covering the heel of the left sandal, represent the closing of bad things (*togol niaronok*) and are positive responses to any questions. Finally, configurations 8 and 9 are very negative representations. Configuration 8, in which the end of the sandals are touching each other, are said to be telling each other secrets; they are talking but the *emuron* doesn't know what they are saying. Configuration 9 again has the right sandal slightly farther away from the *emuron*, but the left sandal is also concealing it.

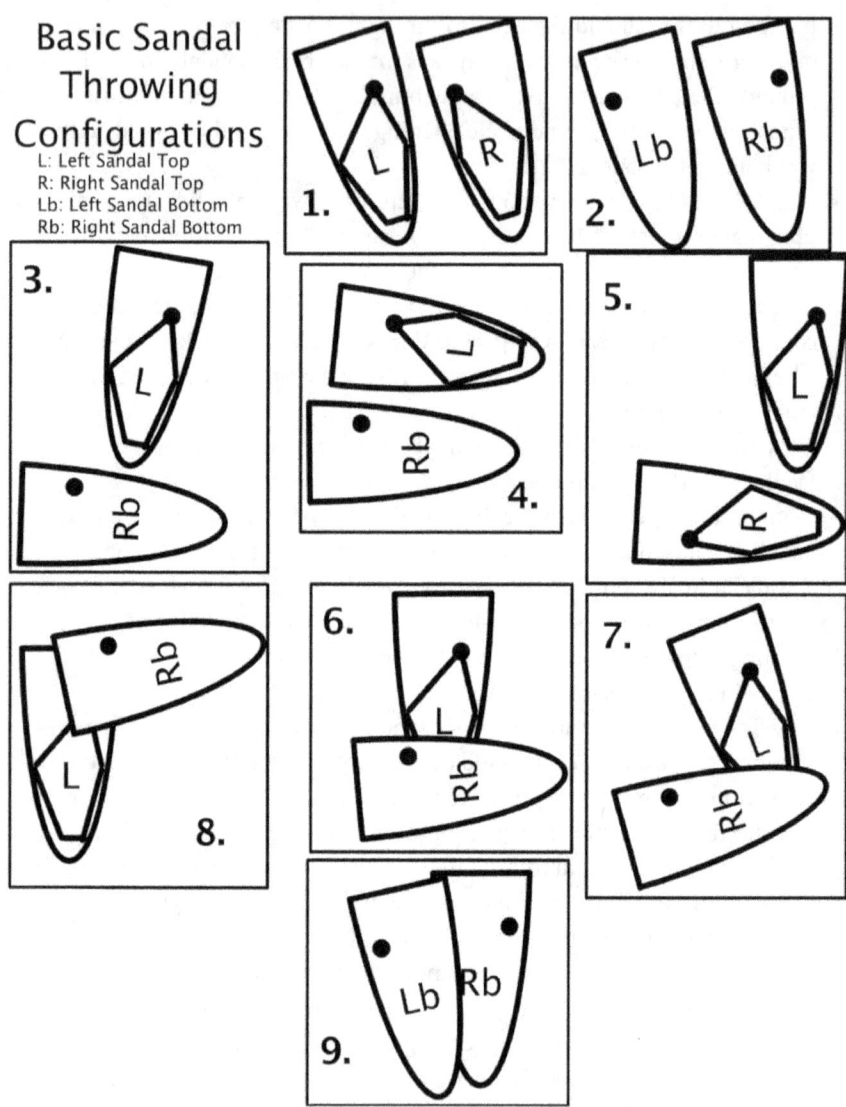

Figure 3. Basic Sandal Throwing Configurations

Reading Intestines (Extispicy)

Once the sandal throwing has confirmed that an *ariwo* is required and has specified which animal must be brought for the sacrifice and the intestine reading, the client will go to search for the animal. Once the animal is brought to the home of the *emuron*, preparations are made for a traditional *akipeyos* (sacrifice). Immediately after spearing the animal, normally a goat, the intestines are removed and placed on top of the side of the animal a few feet in front of the makeshift leaf table.

Old men gather around with the *emuron* to assist in the extispicic reading (*akisemeere*) of the intestines (3.7b). The intestines provide a map of the local geographic area extending out to the surrounding rivers, mountains and plains. There is a main doorway or gate (*ekidor*). "If there is a gland or a tumor near to the *ekidor*, it is bad. The color of the gland reveals what goat should be killed to prevent the problem from happening" (3.1b). If a person is clearly identified by the group as one of the spots in the intestines, and it is confirmed by the *emuron*, then an *ariwo* must be sought out. This reading is a group process, but it was made clear that the *emuron* always has the final say concerning the interpretation of what is seen in the intestines:

> When I am reading the intestines there are always other people sitting around the intestines also looking. Some people agree with what I see and some disagree. But I am the doctor (*dakitari*) of the intestines and I have the last word. They don't disagree after I have spoken last. (3.5b)

The new goat selected for the *ariwo* should match the person seen in the intestines and the *ariwo* is done differently depending on the color of the identified spot:

Red: Both the person and the goat lay down on their side with the person facing the east and the goat facing the west. Then the goat is killed and the intestines are read again to see if the problem has been resolved.

Black: This is an *ariwo* in which the person takes the new goat away and kills it in the place identified in the intestines, then the potential problem is finished.

Brown-red (*mugerengan*): This is when a person is sick or will become sick. The new goat is speared with a long spear (*akwaara*) and then released to the west of the home. Non-family members can eat the goat and the *emuron* is called to read the intestines. Sometimes this color reveals that the unripened clusters of palm nuts (*nangole ngicherikoi*) are to be used. Sometimes the palm nuts are burned or the person who may become sick sleeps with the *ngicherikoi* and then they are thrown out of the homestead the next day. This is an *ariwo* that is described as "washing the intestines (*akipak ngamaliteny*)" (3.4b).

Dark-brown (*mugkirion*): A man goes in a hut (*etem*) with a large dark-brown he-goat that is tied to the *eipa* tree in the *etem*. The man sleeps with the goat tied there for four nights, then another goat is killed. The one that has been tied for four days is not killed but released. If this does not work then the man does a *kititik* and lays on a goat until it is dead" (3.4b-3.5a). The different colors found on the spots in the intestines also show the color of the ochre (*emunyen*) that should be used (3.5b).

Solving problems through the sandal throwing/extispicy cycle can require as many as five goats for one problem. The intestines of one goat will point to another goat until no problems are found; "until the intestines say that all is well (*ejoker*)" (3.5a). This can be a very expensive proposition. While the sandal throwing ritual is inexpensive, "costing only 20, 40 or 50 [Kenyan Shillings] and some tobacco for the sandals," payment for the intestine readings often requires more than just the sacrificed animals. Payment can be creative, but it must be paid or else the client could face dire circumstances: "They either pay me a goat or something else, whatever there is. If they don't pay me, they get sick" (3.5b).

Extispicy: *Akisemere Ngamaliteny*

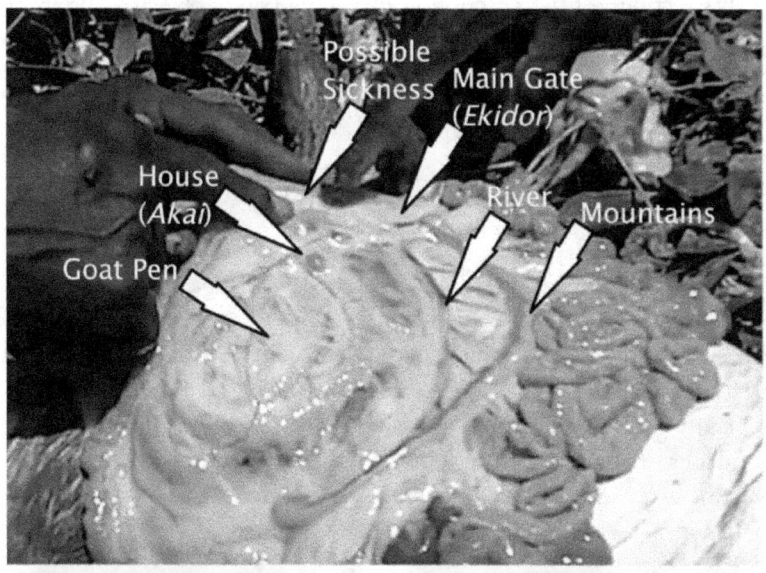

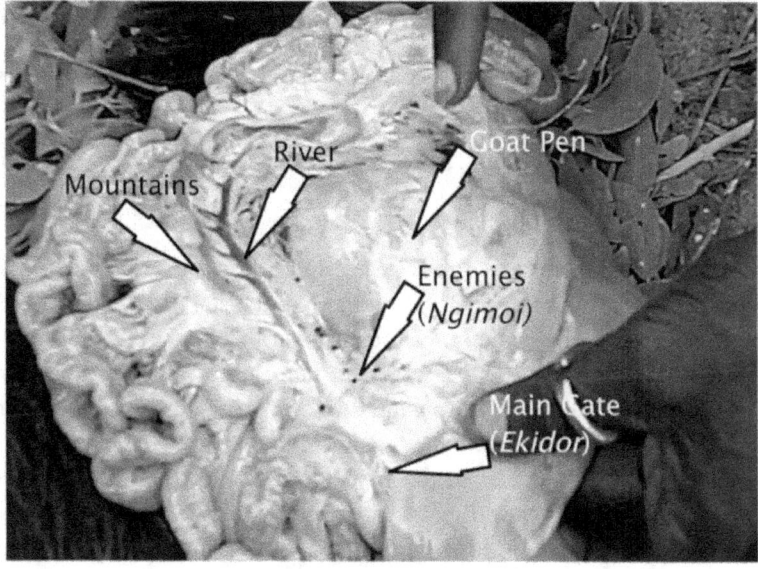

Figure 4. Extispicy Maps

EMURON RITUAL OBJECTS

In this section, a brief description of *emuron* ritual objects is provided, specifically, the types of ritual ochre and special medicinal sticks that are employed in rituals. Most of the objects were observed during the research while some were described by the *ngimurok*.

Ritual Ochre (emunyen)

WHITE (LOAKWAN)

This ochre is "for general sickness" (1.9a). When "opening" the time for planting sorghum in the gardens, the *emuron* was observed using white ochre. The *emunyen* was applied to the right arm and hand (the hand used for planting the seeds). "I mix the dried ochre with water in this wood bowl (a plain wood bowl used for eating food) and I blow dust from the *ebata* wood four times, then I smear it onto the person on the arm, even the face, even the stomach" (i15:5). On *emuron* also explained "this one is also good to use for malaria" (3.10a).

YELLOW (LONYANG)

This ochre is generally "for sickness, especially when the body is swollen" (1.9a). One *emuron* shared that it is often used for healing *arukum* (congestion of the head and lungs)" (3.10a).

RED (LOARENGAN, LOKOPRIAT)

This color ochre is limited in its usage to within the ancestral line of Lokerio, calling the color *lokopriat* more than the standard term for red, *loarengan* (2.3b). The *ngimurok* descendants of Lokorijem only occasionally use red ochre, "Yes, this is used for animals and for putting on the young unmarried women for making them red" (i15:4). But most *ngimurok* from the line of Lokorijem made statements about red ochre similar to the following: "Red? That is for the family of Lokerio" (2.15b); "I don't use red, only white and yellow. Red is mixed with *ekeriau* (the stick), which I do not accept" (2.21b). Even the descendent of Lokedongan explained, "I refuse red, red is evil" (2.27b, i50).

BLUE (LOPUS)

Blue ochre is often seen as connected to the healing of spirit or ancestor possessions: "Yes, this one is also used (blue *emunyen*), but it is for the *ekipe* (spirit), that is, it is used for the person who has problems with *ngikaram*.

First you feed the *ngipean* (with the meat from an *ariwo*), then, after you use the blue *emunyen*, that person is healed" (2.15b). Another *emuron* explained that there was a common perception among young people concerning blue ochre that he was willing to go along with, but not completely validate: "*Lopus* is for *arukum* (congestion/head or chest cold), or that's what the young people think. They buy it in town and bring it to me to smear on them. I will smear it on them, there is nothing wrong with it" (i23:6).

Black (*lotumkol, lokirion*)

The black ochre is very rare. One *emuron* explained: "This one comes from a stream near the village of Kalikol and helps women if they are about to miscarry their child; it quiets the womb (*Aberu na irimokini achakun ikoku kitamatae, kidatak akook*). It is more like a salt, or even the smoke that comes from a vehicle, it's very black (*lokirion chuch*)" (2.24b, i24:3–4).

Sticks (edawa/ngikitoi)

> "These are the things that God has given to the ngimurok that
> go along with saliva; the sticks: *engeso, ebata,* yes, and *ekeriau*"
> (I15:1–2).

Along with the use of ritual ochre, most of the *ngimurok* also collect and use sticks (*ngikitoi*) from very specific trees and plants. These sticks are often ground into a fine powder and mixed in with water used for water blessings (*ewatakin ngkipi*) or even mixed in with the ritual ochre. Sometimes a small piece of stick is attached to a necklace or bracelet for either medicinal or protection properties. The following information was found during the research pertaining to each type of *ekitoi*. The first three, the *Ekeriau, Ebata,* and the *Engeso* were observed on many occasions and seemingly used by all types of *ngimurok*, while the remaining four *ngikito*: *Lokapilak, Akamuja, Kumukwa,* and *Lomanang* were only briefly described by a few *ngimurok*.

Ekeriau

Ekeriau is a tuber from the grass family commonly known in Europe and North America as "nutsedge," *Cyperus articulatus* (Morgan 1981). Because of its pleasant smell, the most popular use for *ekeriau* is for the person who has *arukum* (head/chest congestion); "they will wear the *ekeriau* normally on a necklace" (3.10a). For many, it is also effective for more than congestion. People also wear *ekeriau* "to prohibit the return of problems" (2.12b), or even to treat the spirit caused problem in the body (*ekipe a nakwaan*) (2.27b).

Ebata

Ebata, Terminalia spinosa[3] is the most commonly mentioned of the *ngikito*. *Ebata* is regularly mixed into the ritual ochre, put in water for the *ewatakin* ritual, and is also worn by people to keep problems away (*akibatar ngichen*), or is even able to help in the complications of childbirth (3.10a). *Ebata* is also described as a powerful defense against your enemies:

> Ebata turns evil things away from you; if something is coming or an enemy is coming to attack you (*akinges*), he's coming to kill you. You turn your knife (*kipirpirak*) in the *ebata* like this and then you blow it with small puffs of air (*tokuta, tokuta, tokuta*) toward the thing or person you want to turn away and they will return to where they came from. Even for the government or police, if they are coming to take you away in their truck, you use the ebata this way and it turns them away. Or, if they make it to your house and you have used the ebata, they arrive and are empty-headed and talk to you completely forgetting the evil thing they came to do to you. (i15:2)

Another *emuron* described the ways he was able to use *ebata* to help people with the problems of *ngipean* and *ngikaram*:

> I helped people who had these problems [*ngipean* and *ngikaram*] in days past, but I am old these days. A long time ago I healed many people who had ngipean. I would throw water on them the same way and also grind *ebata*. I would put the ground *ebata* into the head through the nostrils. I grind and soak the *ebata* and put it into the head until mucous comes out, different mucous, then it opens. I grind the *ebata*, I soak it in water, it turns yellow then I separate the water from its solute. The wet solute remains, I put it in the nostrils and they start fighting. That is the person of *ngipean* the one that *Akuj* possesses. I would do this and they would be healed. It always worked. (i24:5)

Engeso

Engeso is a bitter stick that is used in powerful ways. It is so powerful that no one actually ingests this stick or even wears it on their body (as compared to *ebata* and *ekeriau*) (2.12b). *Ngimurok* will chew on *engeso* when they are speaking against evil (2.1b). Found near the Loima mountains, it is said that *engeso* grows on the same tree that milking gourds come from.

---

3. Morgan, "Ethnobotany of the Turkana."

Chewing the *engeso* is thought to be good for the body, but it should not be swallowed. (i15.2)

Engeso is also used to help women giving birth:

> . . . she bites the *engeso* between her teeth and chews it. When she spits it out she gives birth. The woman who is in birth pangs, who is completely refusing, engeso makes her vomit right away if she has engeso. We spread [ochre] on her back then she chews and spits it out. Then she gives birth. This even works for the camels and other animals refusing to give birth. (i24:4)

Other Ngikito

Four other *ngikito* were briefly described during the research, but were not observed. They include:

> *Lokapilak*: "This one is used help with the problem of the evil eye (*akong*) of the *ekapilan*" (2.27b).

> *Akamuja*: This one puts a person to sleep (2.1b).

> *Kumukwa*: "Used when there is a thief (*ekokolan*) or to tie up (*tokud*) an ekapilan" (2.27b).

> *Lomanang*: "Drink this for sickness, pressure in the stomach" [this is a local grass, *Seddera hirsuta*] (3.10a).

CONCLUSION OF THE CHAPTER

This chapter has provided descriptions of key rituals, ritual methods, and ritual objects that have never before been described. It was an honor to be allowed to participate in these many local Turkana traditions as an outsider. All of the *ngimurok* displayed greater hospitality and openness regarding their rituals than I ever imagined it would be possible to observe. As I reviewed my notes, interview transcripts and video recordings concerning these rituals, I cannot help but feel overwhelmed by the immense amount of symbolism yet to be explored. This chapter of ritual descriptions has merely set the foundation for what could easily be a lifetime of work. Now that this chapter has provided further resources regarding Turkana rituals that were not covered in the proceeding chapter, we next move to the final piece of data in this study of the phenomenon of Turkana ritual specialists; a survey of Turkana Christians regarding their thoughts and interactions with Turkana *ngimurok*.

6

What Turkana Ngimurok Say about Christians and
What Turkana Christians say about Ngimurok

Ngimurok statements and a Turkana Christian Survey

THE PRIMARY PURPOSE OF this research project is to provide a clearer understanding of the persistent and changing roles and practices of *ngimurok* in Turkana communities. In order to accomplish this purpose, my primary objective was a description of Turkana *ngimurok* through their own words, which were provided in chapters four and five. This chapter helps to accomplish my secondary objective: to gain understanding in the ways that the roles and practices of the *ngimurok* continue to persist in Turkana Christian communities and shape indigenous understandings of Christianity.

Additional questions that need to be answered by the research include: Do Turkana Christians still continue to visit the *ngimurok*? If so, to what extent and for what purposes do they visit the *ngimurok*? What are the types of problems that would encourage a Turkana Christian to go against the teachings of their church concerning *ngimurok* and seek the help of an *emuron*? Before answering these questions, can we even establish what some of the standard teachings concerning *ngimurok* are among Christian churches in Turkana?

In this chapter, I present a summary of the findings of a small sample survey of Turkana Christians in order to quantify some of the data concerning the persistence of the *emuron* phenomenon in Turkana, Kenya. While my experience and qualitative hypothesis is that the role of the *emuron* in Turkana is persistent, yet changing, this survey was intended to provide quantitative evidence of that persistence. The survey did reveal that even among Christians, answering the questions of the survey immediately following a worship service, there were those who disclosed that either they still visited an *emuron* or that someone they knew in their church had visited an *emuron*.

Before discussing the Turkana Christian perceptions of the *ngimurok* revealed in the survey, I have decided to preface with a brief summary of the various ways that *ngimurok* described Christians in Turkana during my research. I believe this contrast will help in further understandings of the ways both the *ngimurok* and Turkana Christians not only view each other, but also the ways in which Christians in Turkana often operate within both Christian faith and the traditions of the *ngimurok*.

NGIMUROK STATEMENTS ABOUT CHRISTIANS

Even the Christians Come (but they want modifications)

Most of the *ngimurok* were very quick to point out that many of their clients were Christians, regardless of what church leaders and pastors taught about *ngimurok*. Christians visit the *ngimurok* when there are problems, just like everyone else, especially "when they are hungry, when they are looking for work, and when they are sick" (2.13b).

Sometimes when there are churches nearby, the *emuron* is still asked to solve difficult problems:

> Even though many of the Christians reject me, they still come. There was recently a Christian woman who came to my home because of spirits making her crazy (*ngikerep*). She stayed here for many days and was healed. I say, let the church leaders teach and help in the community, but they should not say bad things against me (3.11a).

Yet, even though it was commonly stated that Christians do come to the *ngimurok*, they were often described as refusing to participate in the ritual ochre (*emunyen*), choosing instead to only receive the water blessing (*ngakipi*).

Even when Turkana Christians were willing to go as far as seeking "the *ariwo* sacrifice . . . they don't take the smearing of *emunyen*" (2.1b). While non-Christians have no problem accepting the *emunyen*, Christians seem to only accept the throwing of water. Of course, there were also exceptions that included the throwing of sandals and the reading of intestines as ritual activities in which Christians would allow themselves to participate (i19,

44:00–45:20). For whatever reason, the Christians in Turkana seem have the freedom to participate in many of the *ngimurok* rituals (although often in hiding), except for the ubiquitous ritual of spreading ochre on the body.

While it may at first seem unusual that this ritual practice, the smearing of *emunyen* on the body of the client, would be the ritual singled out as unacceptable to Christians, it became very clear through observing the ritual what the reasoning was behind their selectivity: a Christian client who has come to visit the *emuron* cannot hide the fact that they have visited the *emuron* when the ochre has been applied to their body. Their visit and willingness to participate in *ngimurok* rituals could no longer be kept secret. The *ngimurok* accommodate the Christians in accepting them as clients and allowing them to leave without the ritual *emunyen* so that they do not have to publicly display that they have visited the *emuron*.

God (Akuj) is the Same God

One way that *ngimurok* describe their work in relation to the Christianity that is now also in many of their villages, is that there is only one God; that the God of the *ngimurok* and the God of Christianity is one and the same. This causes the *ngimurok* to wonder why the Christian leaders speak negatively against them:

> I hear them [the church leaders] say these things, that people should not visit the *ngimurok*; they even say the *ngimurok* are of the evil spirits (*ngipean*); they say these things because they believe that the traditions (*etal*) of the *ngimurok* do not go along with the traditions of the church; but I believe that that God, the God they worship, is the one that also created me. Even me, I entreat (*akilip*) the same God, these same entreaties that God gave my father and my grandfather long ago. Even when I entreat my father instead of God it is the same as God because God is the same God of my fathers long ago. (2.13a)

For the *ngimurok*, this means there is no inconsistency between the work of the church and the *emuron*. On the side of the *emuron*, syncretism is acceptable and "there is no problem for people to be in the church and to visit the *ngimurok*; for there is only one God" (2.13a).

This monotheistic view provides some of the *ngimurok* with a more open position in regard to the church. Even though many *ngimurok* do not attend the churches in their area, some have no problem simultaneously working as an *emuron* and attending church. One *emuron* explained, while "many *ngimurok* don't enter the church, for me, God is great, so I have entered the church. We all [inclusive, *ngoni*] pray to the God who made everything, the one God" (2.22b). Because of this perspective, many *ngimurok* do not understand Christian condemnation of their practices. The Christians are equally seen as "calling out to God (*Akuj*)," just as the *ngimurok* "are also calling out to God (*Akuj*)" (i19).

The Church is Causing the Problems

If the *ngimurok* do not view themselves in opposition to the church, how do they explain the strong divisions that occasionally arise between the church and the traditional ritual specialists? For most of the *ngimurok* interviewed, the problem is to be found on the side of the church. It is the "Christians who say that *ngimurok* are evil, those ones, they have hatred in their hearts (*arem*)" (3.18a).

This perspective of the church causing the division led quickly to suspicion for one *emuron*:

> "It is the people of the church who are digging into, undermining, speaking ill (*ebokete*) of the *ngimurok*. The *ngimurok* are not speaking ill of the church. The church wants to snatch/steal (*ademar*) the traditions from very long ago and teach their own traditions" (2.13a).

Yet, even though the church is seen as the one creating the divisions in the community, one *emuron* humorously shared his response to the negative comments of church leaders by comparing them to the annoyance of ravens. "Those things they say about me are like the call of a raven, '*kwak, kwak*' that you want to be quiet. I hear it, but those words are nothing" (i22:7). Here we find that the *ngimurok* not only find fault in the church for causing the division in villages between Christians and traditional practices, but go even further in identifying church leaders as either thieves of traditions or the squawking of annoying birds that make sounds for no reason.

Observed relationship with Christianity

Through my interviews and visits at the homes of the *ngimurok*, it became clear that there is a close relationship between the *ngimurok* and the church in most of the rural areas I visited in Turkana. I found that many of the wives and children of the *ngimurok* were active members of the church. Immediately following a discussion concerning the tense relationship between Christians and the *emuron* at one homestead, in which the *emuron* made it clear that Christians do not accept all the *emuron's* practices, his wife appeared with *chai* for us to drink. As the tea was poured into our cups, the *emuron* told his wife to pray for the *chai* before we drank. The words she spoke and the ease with which she prayed in the name of *Yesu Krisito* (Jesus Christ) revealed that she was more than merely imitating Christian forms because I was present, but was a Christian who has spent significant time in connection with the church.

In some situations, the relationship between the *emuron* and the church is even closer, with some *ngimurok* serving as leaders in the church or even adjusting their practices because they have become Christians. As one *emuron a akou* reported; "There is no problem with the church, I am even an Elder in the Baptist church over there" (3.22a). At the home of another *emuron* who reads tobacco, the *emuron* explained:

> We are believers (*ngikanupak*) [Christians]. We pray first when there is sickness. We take medicine [western medicine from the clinics and hospitals]. Then we bring in tobacco and spread ochre on the bodies. (3.3b)

Some of the *ngimurok* even reported that they have adjusted their own practices since they have become Christians:

> Now that my family and I have entered (*alomarere*) the church, I don't even like to touch some of those things [the sticks, *ngikito*]. I refuse to use them and only throw water. I don't want people to see what I am doing, so I also refuse the ritual ochre. When white or yellow ochre is applied it becomes problems when people go away [and are seen]. I have stopped doing that (*atapalik*) now that God has set me apart (*epaku*) I don't touch those things. Only throwing water is acceptable. (i23:5)

Thus, we find a variety of responses to Christianity from the *ngimurok*. These responses range from disregard for what the church leaders say about the *ngimurok*, to full integration as an *emuron* leader in the church. In between these extremes we find those who add Christian practices to their own ritual activities and those who are adjusting their practices in response to their newfound Christian faith. These varied responses are in contrast to the standard Christian response to the *ngimurok*: one of rejection and denunciation.

Clearly, the perspective of the *ngimurok* is that many Turkana Christians, even those considered pastors or church leaders, continue to visit the *ngimurok* in times of need. There is also a lack of understanding on the part of the *ngimurok* as to why their activities cannot be accepted by the church leaders; they serve the same God, they are taking care of the same problems in the community. Finally, the *ngimurok* are astute in pointing out the correlations between their own roles in communities and those of the

Christian pastors of churches. Both act in prophetic ways, seeking God's help for healings and problems. From the perspective of the *ngimurok*, it may even be jealousy and greed on the part of the church pastors that causes them to publically speak so boldly against *ngimurok*, while privately filling the role of the *emuron* for their congregations.

I will now turn to the perspectives of Turkana Christians regarding the *ngimurok* in their communities as revealed through the use of a sample survey tool during the research period.

A TURKANA CHRISTIAN SURVEY

As already noted, the main purpose of the sample survey in my research design was to contrast the differences in the ways that *ngimurok* describe themselves and their practices and the ways that Turkana Christians describe *ngimurok* and their practices. The survey was meant to reveal the general ways that Christians in Turkana describe the *ngimurok* and their descriptions of official church teachings concerning the *ngimurok* and acceptable Christian interaction.

In addition to this descriptive contrasting purpose, another purpose of this survey was to quantitatively verify the qualitative descriptions I was receiving from the *ngimurok*, specifically concerning whether or not Turkana Christians were continuing to visit and consult the *ngimurok*. While I met Christian clients at *ngimurok* homes and *ngimurok* repeatedly confirmed that Turkana Christians visited them, I was interested in knowing if Turkana Christians would admit to their continued consultations with the *ngimurok*.

The Survey Methodology and Statistics

A two-page survey was designed first in English and then a version with both English and Turkana was created in consultation with my research assistant and other Turkana assistants in Lodwar at the beginning of the research. Each survey was printed on the front and back of one sheet of paper. A sample of one of the anonymously filled out surveys, along with the complete responses of all the survey questions, can be found in Appendix G.

Once the surveys were printed, we brought them with us when we attended worship services in churches in the villages where we were conducting *ngimurok* interviews. With the permission of the church leaders, after the end of the service I would stand up and describe the research and the purpose of the survey instrument. One of the major difficulties is that the majority of people who willingly responded to the survey were not literate and could not take the survey and respond on their own. This meant that my research assistant and I were required to sit with each respondent who was unable to read and write their own answers, asking them the questions and writing their answers on the survey paper. In most situations, this greatly limited the number of people who could respond to the survey.

While my hope was to receive at least 100 usable survey responses, by the end of the research 71 surveys had been received that were useable. While this presents a relatively small sample size, and consequently a larger than ideal confidence interval, this is not a major problem for this type of instrument, and is common in ethnographic research (Bernard 2006:184). For a confidence level of 95 percent, standard sampling theory for a relatively small population and sample size would place the results of this survey within a margin of error of 11.5 percent-11.67 percent depending on how the estimated population size of Turkana Christians is calculated. These estimates are based on either the population size of Turkana Christians in the congregations surveyed, approximately 1,500, and the estimated total Turkana Christian population size in the region surveyed, approximately 15,000.

Table 2. Confidence Levels of Turkana Christian Small Sample Survey

Approximate Population Size	Approximate Number of Christians in the Survey Area: 15,000	Approximate Number of Christians in the Churches Surveyed: 1,500
Sample Size	71	71
Confidence Level	95 percent	95 percent
Margin of Error	11.67 percent	11.5 percent

While this larger than desired confidence interval will not allow for precise quantitative predictions regarding Turkana Christian *emuron* interactions, the confidence level does not negate the results of the survey. This is especially true for the qualitative perspectives gleaned from the open-ended survey questions regarding Turkana Christian descriptions of both *ngimurok* and *ngikapilak*.

Demographics of Respondents

Gender, Age, Clan

Despite being a sample survey with a relatively small sample size, there was a wide demographic spread in regard to gender, age, clan identity, and home location. Participants were 58 percent male (n=41) and 42 percent female (n=30). A majority, 63 percent, were between the ages of 16–30 (n=45); 22 percent (n=16) aged 31–45; 13 percent (n=9) aged 46–60; and

1 participant 61 or older. This is a normal age range in Turkana with an estimated life expectancy in 2009 of 56 years and the majority of the population under 30 years of age (Oxfam 2009). Twelve different clans were self-identified in the survey, with an additional one participant identifying herself generally as "Turkana."

Table 3. Gender of Survey Participants

Female	n=30	42 percent
Male	n=41	58 percent

Table 4. Ages of Survey Participants

0–15	n=0	0 percent
16–30	n=45	63 percent
31–45	n=16	22 percent
46–60	n=9	13 percent
61–	n=1	1 percent

Table 5. Clan (*Emachar*) Identification of Survey Participants:

(Open-Ended Question)

Emeturanait	n=20	28 percent
Emosorokoit	n=9	13 percent
Epuchoit	n=9	13 percent
Esigerit	n=7	10 percent
Epongait	n=6	9 percent
Eduyait	n=4	6 percent
Ebilait	n=3	4 percent

Emacharkotait	n=3	4 percent
Ekatekit	n=2	3 percent
Ngikemoroki	n=2	3 percent
Edochait	n=1	1 percent
Ngitaparokolong	n=1	1 percent
"Turkana"	n=1	1 percent

Christian Identity

One way to identify whether or not the survey participant was a Christian was to ask them to mark the rites of passage in which they had participated. Participants first identified the traditional Turkana rituals they had completed. A significant number, 49 percent of the men (n=20) indicated that had participated in male initiation (*asapan*); 31 percent (n=22) of all respondents had "speared the bull" in a traditional Turkana wedding; 59 percent (n=17) of the women had participated in the *akinyonyo* ritual that is used to initiate a women into the clan of her husband. The respondents then indicated whether or not they had been baptized into a church. Baptism into Christian faith, and a church, was indicated by 99 percent (n=69) of the respondents. This response overwhelmingly indicates that the respondents of this survey identify themselves as members of churches in Turkana. However, almost all the respondents are church members, the practice of church weddings, as opposed to, or in addition to traditional Turkana weddings (*akuuta*), had only been completed by 9 percent (n=6) of all respondents. This last statistic indicates that a traditional Turkana wedding is still preferred to a church wedding in the areas where the research was conducted.

Nearly all the respondents identified themselves as members of the mission-initiated church denomination "Community Christian Church" (CCC). This Kenyan denomination has more churches and Christians in the research area of this study than any other denomination and is affiliated with the American mission organization, CMF International.[1]

1. This is the mission organization and Kenyan church denomination my wife and I worked with in Turkana from 1999–2008. In 2012 there were approximately 42 CCC churches in Turkana County, mostly in rural villages to the east and south of Lodwar town. The approximate baptized church membership of the CCC in these 42 churches is 6,500.

Respondents also identified the number of years they had been believers (*ngikanupak*) in Jesus Christ. With CMF International missionaries first arriving in Turkana in 1978, it was not surprising to find a wide range of responses regarding years of belief in Jesus.

Table 6. How Long Have You Been a Believer in Jesus Christ?

(Open-Ended Question)

1–5 years	n=3	4 percent
6–10 years	n=18	26 percent
11–15 years	n=22	31 percent
16–20 years	n=13	19 percent
More than 20 years	n=14	20 percent

Additionally, a significant number of survey respondents, 61 percent (n=43), identified themselves as church leaders (*ngikarikok a ekanisa*) in their churches. In the current structure of CCC churches, only church pastors (*epastait*) and church elders (*ekasikout a ekanisa*) are ordained positions in the church, but there are no paid leadership positions. With a high value placed on the concept of "the priesthood of all believers," many church members take on leadership roles in the congregation. The following chart lists the roles identified by the 43 respondents who described themselves as church leaders in an open-ended response to question 4b of the survey:

Table 7. If a Church Leader (n=43), What is Your Position in the Church?

(Open-Ended Question)

Pastor (*epastait*)	n=8	19 percent
Deacon (*akingarakinan*)	n=5	12 percent
Choir Director	n=4	9 percent
Elder (*ekasikout a ekanisa*)	n=4	9 percent

Secretary	n=3	7 percent
Teacher	n=3	7 percent
Treasurer	n=3	7 percent
Women's Leader	n=3	7 percent
Youth Leader	n=3	7 percent
Church Leader (unspecified)	n=2	5 percent
Choir Member	n=2	5 percent
Bible Study Leader	n=1	2 percent
Healer (*eketedekan*)	n=1	2 percent
Usher	n=1	2 percent

From these responses regarding the Christian identity of the respondents, it is clear that 99 percent of the respondents are identified as Christians and members of churches through baptism. Furthermore, 61 percent of the respondents consider themselves to be leaders in their churches. Without a doubt, the responses to this survey concerning Turkana *ngimurok* are the responses of Turkana Christians who are actively involved in their churches. A possible limitation of the survey is that it was overwhelmingly responded to by Christians from within one Kenyan denomination, the Community Christian Church. In this regard, even though the CCC churches are the most common and prolific in the research area, it must be made explicit that the "Christian" perspective on *ngimurok* in the survey findings are limited to the CCC denomination of churches.

Major Findings of the Survey Regarding Ngimurok

The major findings of the survey are provided here regarding Turkana Christian knowledge and perspectives of *ngimurok*, specific teachings of the church regarding *ngimurok*, whether a missionary or a pastor could be an *emuron*, and the differences between an *emuron* and an *ekapilan*.

Persistence of Visiting the Emuron

The level of acknowledgement of *ngimurok* in the respondent's home area, knowledge of their homestead locations, and knowledge of people who visit the *ngimurok* was quite high among the survey respondents. A full 93 percent acknowledged that there are *ngimurok* in their home areas. Of these 66 respondents, 60 asserted that they know where the *ngimurok* in their home area live. Of all the respondents, 87 percent (n=62), personally know people who continue to visit the *ngimurok*.

Of those who identified themselves as church leaders, 100 percent (n=43) admitted to knowing people who still visit the *ngimurok*. These numbers indicate that the *ngimurok* are still very active in the communities where there are Christians, and that Christians are not unaware of their presence and activities. Furthermore, a 100 percent response from those self-identified as church leaders would seem to indicate either a greater awareness of *ngimurok* activity or increased honesty in responding to the questions.

In an attempt to avoid social desirability bias, before asking directly if the respondents still visit the *ngimurok*, I asked a few open-ended questions that helps understand Turkana Christian perspectives regarding why people visit the *ngimurok* today. Seven responses were the most common, comprising 84 percent of all the answers. These can be seen in the table below:

Table 8. What Do You Think Are Reasons People Still Visit The *Ngimurok*?

(Open-Ended Question)

Sickness	n=46	65 percent
Rain/Drought	n=22	31 percent
Wealth/Job	n=11	16 percent
To Solve Problems	n=9	13 percent
Ariwo Protection Ritual	n=8	11 percent
Children/Barrenness	n=5	7 percent
Cursing Others	n=5	7 percent
They Are Crazy	n=4	6 percent
Power/Strength	n=2	3 percent
I Don't Know	n=2	3 percent

It is intriguing that there were very few negative responses, other than the four responses that explain that the people who still visit the *ngimurok* are "crazy." Overwhelmingly, the responses were positive aspects of what the *ngimurok* do for clients. This list is seen as consistent with the descriptions of the *ngimurok* themselves from chapter 4. This positive perspective gradually disappears in the survey results as the questions move from more general to more specific, concerning the practices of the survey respondents.

While 87 percent of all respondents admitted to knowing someone who still visits the *ngimurok*, the percentage of admissions steadily decreased as the questions moved closer to the homestead of the respondent. 71 percent (n=50) of respondents stated that yes, they knew someone in their church who still visited the *ngimurok*. This number decreased to 54 percent (n=37) when asked if someone in their immediate family still visits the *ngimurok*. The numbers likewise declined for church leaders as the questions moved closer to home, with 100 percent (n=43) of church leaders admitting to knowing someone who still visits the *ngimurok*, 79 percent (n=34) stating that yes, they knew someone in their church who still visited the *ngimurok*. This number decreased to 61 percent (n=26) when asked if someone in their immediate family still visits the *ngimurok*.

Table 9. Do You Personally Know Someone That Still Visits the *Ngimurok*?

	All Respondents answering "Yes"		All Church Leaders answering "Yes"	
Anyone?	n=62	87 percent	n=43	100 percent
In Your Church?	n=50	71 percent	n=34	79 percent
In Your Family/Home?	n=37	64 percent	n=26	61 percent

Finally, the survey questions centered on the activity of the survey respondents themselves. Respondents were given a range of choices regarding how often they had visited the home of an *emuron* both before they had become a Christian and after they had become a Christian.

Table 10. Before You Were A Christian, How Many Times Did You Visit An *Emuron*?

0	n=23	36 percent
1–5	n=24	35 percent
6–10	n=1	2 percent
more than 10	n=18	27 percent

Table 11. After Becoming A Christian, How Many Times Did You Visit An *Emuron*?

0	n=54	93 percent
1–5	n=4	7 percent
6–10	n=0	0 percent
more than 10	n=0	0 percent

While only 4 people taking the survey admitted to having visited an *emuron* after becoming a Christian, this does not completely negate the fact that Christians do still continue to visit the *ngimurok*. It seems difficult to reconcile the 71 percent of all respondents and 79 percent of church leader respondents state that they know someone in the church who still visits the *emuron*, while only 7 percent of all respondents state that they personally have visited an *emuron* after becoming a Christian.

It might be suggested that especially because the surveys were administered immediately following Sunday morning worship services in the presence of other people, and often administered orally by my research assistant, or myself, that social desirability bias has come into play in this situation. That is, within the church, visiting the *emuron* is considered a negative activity, or is not a socially desirable norm; therefore, people are reluctant to respond affirmatively regarding current visits to the *emuron*.

This suggests that the survey instrument does not provide significant quantitative evidence as to the specific percentage of Christians who continue to visit the *ngimurok*, but the survey results do point to the continued use of the *ngimurok* by Christians in the respondents' churches, just not for the respondents themselves.

I will now move on to the Turkana Christian appraisals and understandings of Turkana *ngimurok*.

Positive and Negative Appraisals of Ngimurok

Turkana Christians emphatically display a negative perspective on the work of the *ngimurok*, even when asked to respond to the question: What are the good things *ngimurok* have done in your area in the past and now? The number one response displays Christian commitment to the teachings of the missionaries and the church leaders: "No, there is nothing good." After this negative evaluation, the rest of the responses look similar to the above list of reasons for why people still visit the *ngimurok*.

Table 12. What Are Good Things *Ngimurok* Have Done In Your Area In The Past And Now?

(Open-Ended Question)

Nothing Good	n=27	39 percent
Bring Rain	n=23	33 percent
Heal Sickness	n=13	19 percent
Protect the Animals from Raiding	n=5	7 percent
Blessings	n=4	6 percent
Help With Childbirth	n=3	4 percent

When answering the next question on bad things that *ngimurok* have done, the answers become even more specific, but can be grouped together into 3 main categories:

Table 13. What Are Bad Things *Ngimurok* Have Done
In Your Area In The Past And Now?

(Open-Ended Question)

They Kill People Through Cursing	n=30	43 percent
They Lie to People and Take Their Wealth	n=30	43 percent
They are Opposed to God	n=6	9 percent

From these responses we can see the negative appraisals of the *ngimurok* coming from within the church. There is a focus on the supposed ability of the *emuron* to curse and kill individuals and on the *emuron* profiting from and taking advantage of the people who come to him or her with problems. The final complaint is that *ngimurok* are working in opposition to the efforts of God (*Akuj*) in Turkana.

What Do Churches Teach Concerning Ngimurok?

What do the churches of the respondents teach concerning the *ngimurok*? Respondents provided answers to this open-ended question, which I have placed into 7 categories:

Table 14. What Does Your Church Teach About The *Ngimurok*?

(Open-Ended Question)

They are False Prophets	n=30	43 percent
Do Not Visit Them	n=19	28 percent
They Need To Be Saved	n=12	17 percent
Believe Only in God/Jesus as the Great *Emuron*	n=9	13 percent
They Destroy People	n=7	10 percent
They Are Evil	n=7	10 percent
They Are Opposed to God and Don't Know Jesus	n=4	6 percent

From these responses we see a fourfold approach in the teachings of the church in regarding to the *ngimurok*. First, the church attacks the validity and moral character of the *ngimurok*. They are not viewed as true prophets of God and in the long-run, their evil practices end up destroying people. They are opposed to the will and purposes of God. Second, the church provides Christians with a warning: Do not visit the *ngimurok*. Don't consult with them when you have problems. Third, we see in the teachings a genuine concern for the *ngimurok*. Even the *ngimurok* need to be, and can be, saved by acknowledging Jesus as Lord. Fourth, the church offers a proper way to view the term *emuron*: through redemption. Jesus is the true *emuron*, the one who is our intermediary with God. If you need an *emuron* to solve your problems, Jesus is the great *emuron* who has the power to deal with any problem.

Sources of Power/Wisdom

Other key differences in the way the *ngimurok* describe themselves and the ways in which Turkana Christians understand the *ngimurok* has to do with the understood source of *emuron* wisdom and power. This is a significant difference revealed by the survey. While the *ngimurok* of different types give exclusive credit to God or their fathers for the wisdom and power they have received, 53 percent of the Turkana Christians surveyed attributed *emuron* wisdom and power to evil spiritual forces. These are the very same spiritual forces that the *ngimurok* describe they are working against.

Table 15. Where Do *Ngimurok* Power And Wisdom Come From? Turkana Christian Responses

(Open-Ended Question)

From Evil Spiritual Forces	n=32	53 percent
Ngipean	n=11	18 percent
Ngikaram	n=7	12 percent
Lokipe (Satan)	n=6	10 percent
Ngakujo (gods)	n=6	10 percent

Idols	n=2	3 percent
From Their Fathers	n=20	33 percent
From God (*Akuj*)	n=13	21 percent
From Their Own Strength	n=7	12 percent
From Dreams	n=4	7 percent
From Other *Ngimurok*	n=2	3 percent
From Curses	n=2	3 percent
From Rituals	n=2	3 percent
From Their Clan	n=1	2 percent
Throwing Sandals	n=1	2 percent
They Buy Power From Others	n=1	2 percent

Practices of the Ngimurok

While *emuron* descriptions by the churches and Turkana Christians vary widely in regard to purported evil actions in the community and the sources of power and wisdom, the listing of *emuron* practices by the Christian survey respondents are strikingly similar to the list of practices provided by the *ngimurok* themselves and described in chapter 5. Although there is an emphasis on cursing, an answer provided by 28 percent of survey respondents that was not emphasized by the *ngimurok*, most of the *emuron* self-described practices are present. The rituals missing from this list include the *Tongeere, Kititik, Eutoro Etau* rituals, all three of which are rituals that are rarely discussed apart from their actual practice.

Table 16. From Your Understanding, What Are
The Specific Practices That *Ngimurok* Do?

(Open-Ended Question)

Apply *Emunyen*/Ochre	n=28	33 percent
Cursing People	n=19	28 percent
Ariwo Protection Ritual	n=6	9 percent
Togol Ngide and *Ngibaren*	n=3	5 percent
Reading Sandals	n=3	5 percent
Healing the Sick	n=2	3 percent
Blessing People	n=2	3 percent
Amook Cleansing Ritual	n=2	3 percent
Feed Spirits (*ngikaram*)	n=2	3 percent
Reading Tobacco	n=1	2 percent
Reading Intestines	n=1	2 percent

Christian Ngimurok?

In an intriguing final section of the Turkana Christian Survey, I included questions to test Christian perceptions of those *ngimurok* who continue to practice as *ngimurok* and simultaneously identify themselves as Christians. I was surprised to find that 32 percent (n=22) of Turkana Christian respondents stated that they believed it was possible for a pastor or a missionary to be an *emuron*. In addition, 42 percent (n=30) stated that they personally knew an *emuron* who was also a follower of Jesus.

Table 17. Is It Possible For A Pastor Or A Missionary To Be An *Emuron*?

(Open-Ended Question)

Yes, it is possible	n=22	32 percent
Yes, if dependent on the direction of the Holy Spirit	n=1	1 percent
Yes, if the *amuronut* comes from God	n=1	1 percent

Yes, with strong faith in God he can see things and pray for them	n=1	1 percent
No, it is not possible	n=36	52 percent
No, unless he is God's *emuron*	n=5	7 percent
No, unless his faith is weak	n=1	1 percent
No, unless his heart is divided	n=1	1 percent
No, an *emuron* can't be saved	n=1	1 percent
No, unless it is a false prophet hiding in the church	n=1	1 percent

Table 18. Do You Know Any *Ngimurok* Who Are Followers of Jesus Who Still Do The Work Of An *Emuron*?

(Open-Ended Question)

Yes	n=30	42 percent
Yes, but they have stopped the work of the *emuron*	n=14	20 percent
No	n=20	28 percent
No Answer	n=7	10 percent

These responses indicate that for at least one third of all Turkana Christian respondents, Christianity and the practices of the *ngimurok* are not mutually exclusive. While this perspective would not be acceptable according to the current church teaching regarding *ngimurok*, a significant number of Christians believe that it is possible to be an *emuron* and a Christian. In fact, it seems that there is a way that a Church pastor or even a missionary (*emeanara*), a word normally reserved for Western missionaries in Turkana, could be an *emuron*. Based on Turkana church teachings already revealed in this survey, one might expect every Turkana Christian to respond that there is no way for this to be possible, yet this was the response of only half the respondents. These responses unmistakably reveal a persistence of the positive roles of Turkana *ngimurok*, even in the minds of Turkana Christians.

Various Understandings of Emuron and Ekapilan

What are the differences between an *emuron* and an *ekapilan*? While there is clearly a distinction between the terms *emuron* and *ekapilan* for most Turkana Christian respondents, and the differences are similar to the ways that the *ngimurok* both describe themselves and the *ekapilan*, there are responses that seem to merge the two terms together. A full 19 percent (n=13) of the respondents commented that, "there is no difference between them." And again, 9 percent (n=6) of the respondents stated that "the *emuron* is an *ekasuban*." These two statements point to the extent of the differences between Turkana Christian and *ngimurok* understandings of Turkana ritual specialist categories.

Summary of Survey Findings

This small sample survey has served to both quantitatively and qualitatively describe the differences between the *emuron* descriptions provided by the *ngimurok* and the common views held among a group of Turkana Christians. These revealed differences include a significant difference in the perceived source of power and wisdom for the *ngimurok* by the survey respondents and the earlier *emuron* descriptions provided in chapter 4. While the different types of Turkana *ngimurok* normally attribute their wisdom and power to their fathers, God or their clan, a significant number of respondents to the survey attributed the wisdom and power of *ngimurok* to evil spiritual forces. An understanding of this significant difference will be discussed in the concluding chapter of this study.

In addition to this significant finding, the survey revealed that there is some flexibility in Turkana Christian thinking in regard to the *ngimurok*. This was particularly displayed in the result of the questions regarding the ability of a person to simultaneously be both a Christian and a practicing *emuron*. This reveals a persistence, even among Turkana Christians, in understanding some *ngimurok* as having very positive roles in their communities. While the official teaching of the church may denounce the *ngimurok* and equate them with evil ritual specialists who receive power from evil spiritual forces, this survey has revealed that this general perspective is not the complete perspective of all Turkana Christians.

Another important contribution from the survey is a documentation of church teaching regarding the *ngimurok*. The fourfold response that came out of my analyzing the results helps elaborate nuances in the Church's teaching. First, the church attacks the validity and moral character of the *ngimurok*. They are not viewed as true prophets of God and Christians are cautioned against the destructive nature of their practices. Second, the church provides Christians with a very clear warning: Christians should not visit the *ngimurok*. Third, the church displays a genuine concern for the *ngimurok*. Even the *ngimurok* need to be, and can be, saved by acknowledging Jesus as Lord. Fourth, the church offers a view of the true understanding of *emuron*: Jesus is the true *emuron*.

Finally, the survey succeeds in providing additional evidence, apart from the descriptions of the *ngimurok*, of the fact that Turkana Christians continue to visit the *ngimurok* in spite of the teachings of their churches. While the survey did not provide a clear predictive quantitative statement regarding how many Turkana Christians continue to visit the *ngimurok*, it does provide further reliable qualitative and quantitative evidence that some Christians do continue to continue to participate in *ngimurok* rituals.

7

Conclusions: Toward a New Approach to Turkana Religious Specialists Today

AS I REFLECT BACK on the tension I often felt as a missionary, traveling with church leaders to these very same villages and homesteads where this research project was conducted, seeing the *ngimurok* in complete opposition to the work I was trying to accomplish, I wonder what could have happened, years ago, If I had simply sat down with these men and asked them to tell me who they are in their own words and to show me what it is that they do to help their clients. Did I limit the growth of the indigenous Turkana church by continuing on in the ways of demonization and fear? What mixed messages might have been received by the churches if I had spent the night at the home of an *emuron*? Did I encourage the growth of a syncretistic dual-allegiance church by the words I spoke against the *ngimurok*?

Maybe it was the lack of official affiliation with a mission agency, but the tension I felt as a missionary in Turkana from 1999–2008 only briefly resurfaced at the beginning of my research in 2011. Sitting with my research assistant, James "Lopeyok" Ibei Eipa, we pondered how such a research project would be received by the *ngimurok*. Would anyone even talk to us? Would we be seen as agents of the Kenyan Government helping in a witchhunt? Would people react violently toward our investigations into secret knowledge and rituals? Would we be condemned by the very churches or the missionaries we were trying to assist? The answers to my research questions were certainly not the only unknowns!

After agreeing to our research plan, it took a great deal of energy that first morning to pack up our rented vehicle and head out past villages in which I had spent years ministering, in order to arrive at the homestead

Conclusions: Toward a New Approach to Turkana Religious Specialists

of a well known *emuron*—one that I had confronted with church leaders years before—and ask for his permission to be a guest at his home. But the tension was quickly relieved when the *emuron* welcomed me with open arms, inviting us to stay at his home as long as we wanted. He even spent time recounting the good things I done for the area in front of the other guests staying at his home. His hospitality in regard to my research was overwhelming. The initial tension that James and I felt was gone. We began to not only see a way forward with the research, but to grasp a genuine desire on the part of both *ngimurok* and Christians to openly dialogue about traditional Turkana religious practices.

This is my personal desire for this research, that open discussions regarding the practices of *ngimurok*, beginning with their own perspectives, combined with a more careful understanding of how best to understand the category *emuron* and the way it is used in the church, will serve to empower those who seek the best for the people of Turkana. Instead of fear that I might have opened the door to further syncretism and hidden practices among Turkana Christians, I have joy and hope: joy that the *ngimurok* are beginning to see God's love from Christians, and hope that Churches in Turkana will use this research to begin a more explicit process of critical reconciliation of their faith in Jesus Christ with their Turkana culture.

In this concluding chapter, I will review some of the major accomplishments of the research, evaluate the research objectives in each of the three interdisciplinary realms of the initial research design, suggest a way forward in understanding the current tensions between Christian teaching and the *ngimurok*, provide missiological implications and recommendations for the Turkana context based on the phenomenological data, propose a new religious studies category for Nilotic ritual specialist in East Africa, and finally, suggest potential areas for further study that have come out of the research.

OVERVIEW OF ACCOMPLISHMENTS

There were many accomplishments that I view as significant that have come out of this research project. Three of the major accomplishments are noted here. The first was the willingness of so many *ngimurok* to talk to me and show me their rituals. It is difficult to fathom that in 50 interviews I was able to visit with 33 self-described *ngimurok* and experience only one outright rejection. The hospitality of the *ngimurok* was so great that I will certainly have many years of research ahead of me. I was given permission to video record at least 10 separate types of *ngimurok* rituals, including the ritual of the *akatuwan*; the *ariwo, amok, tongeere,* and *kititik* sacrifices;

sandal-throwing, extispicy, water-throwing, ritual ochre smearing, and even a sun-staring ritual.

Second, I am honored to have identified a third ancestral lineage of *ngimurok* that has yet to be documented in the literature. For this I am grateful to my research assistant, James, his own personal interest in the research, and his vast connection of contacts. While it is always significant to uncover something that those who have studied a topic have not known existed, for me the major accomplishment is in regard to what this says about the ancestral *ngimurok* system. This third ancestral line indicates that there is still the possibility of uncovering the histories of other *ngimurok* ancestries, and indicates the possibility that new lines of *ngimurok* may still be in the process of being created.

Third, this study has provided an opening for greater discussion between Western missionaries and Turkana Christian church leaders regarding the persistence of the role of *ngimurok* in their communities. There are now many possible starting points from which both Turkana Christians and missionaries can discuss traditional religious specialists in Turkana without using generalized statements regarding *ngimurok*. It is now possible for greater differentiation and accuracy regarding these ritual specialists.

EVALUATING THE RESEARCH OBJECTIVES

The primary goal of this study was to seek a clearer understanding of Turkana *ngimurok* through an ethnographic-phenomenological approach. While this phenomenological study was the priority, there are multiple research questions and objectives that the data from this phenomenological study ultimately seeks to answer and achieve. Since each of these research objectives is supported by a theoretical framework that fits the multidisciplinary nature of Intercultural Studies, I will evaluate the objectives through each discipline.

Primary Phenomenological Objectives

The goal of a phenomenological study such as this one is to provide a description based on the lived experience of a phenomenon shared by a group of people; in this case, the shared phenomenon of the research participants is identifying as a Turkana ritual specialist within the broad category of *emuron*. This description comes out of the self-descriptions and the perspectives of those experiencing the phenomenon. The researcher *attempts* to not challenge the perspectives of the research participants, but brackets his or her own belief system concerning the phenomenon in order to present

Conclusions: Toward a New Approach to Turkana Religious Specialists 199

the phenomenon more accurately and to contrast the self-descriptions with the perspectives of others. This contrasting analysis has the opportunity to challenge biased or even unjust perspectives.

The phenomenological description provided in chapter 4 provides answers to all of the primary phenomenological research questions proposed in chapter 2. These include:

- How do Turkana *ngimurok* perceive and self-describe their roles in Turkana communities?
- What are the specific practices of the *ngimurok*?
- Where and how do *ngimurok* receive the knowledge of these practices? Are they learned from other *ngimurok*, received from a spiritual realm, transmitted through the *ngimurok*, or learned in some other way?
- Are there different types of *ngimurok*, or a hierarchy of *ngimurok* as suggested by previous researchers?

At the end of the research, it can be said that this phenomenological approach, employing multiple ethnographic research methods, has successfully fulfilled the phenomenological research objectives outlined in the research design:

- To articulate an exhaustive, non-evaluative, bracketed, interpretive understanding of Turkana *ngimurok*.
- To evaluate prior descriptions of Turkana *ngimurok* in the literature.

First, an "exhaustive" description of Turkana *ngimurok* has been provided in chapters 4 and 5. Second, this research provides vastly more data and descriptive material concerning Turkana *ngimurok* than any previous study, which allows for a more complex understanding than the more simplified models presented by Barrett. While *ngimurok* are certainly engaged in forms of divination, they do not strictly follow the limited models of previous descriptions for "diviner." Instead, the complex descriptions presented here are more in-line with Curry's recent understanding that models of divination are infinitely varied and require description in each context (Curry 2010).

Toward East African Religious Specialist Terminology: The Case for Muronism

Additionally, one of the challenges in the literature has been deciding which English religious specialist word should be used in the translation of Nilotic religious specialists. While Gulliver (1951) set the pattern for the usage of "diviner" throughout East Africa, and specifically Turkana, the current research does not compel me to use the term "diviner" for the *emuron*. Instead, the research provides confirmation of both Waller's[1] and Fratkin's[2] research concerning a separate type of religious specialist among Nilotic groups that exhibits the characteristics of diviner, prophet and priest, with "more attention being paid to emic typologies."[3] The research has confirmed for me that I need to continue to use either "Turkana religious specialist" or be as specific as possible and use the local name for the type: *emuron*. There are no other traditional religious specialists in Turkana that fill the role of the diviner, the prophet or the priest. The *emuron* encompasses all three roles. In fact, in much the same way that "shaman" has been used as a recognized category of religious specialist, I will suggest the term "muron" as a title for the category of diviner, prophet, priest religious specialists in East Africa. This category of religious specialist is not possessed by spirits and does not travel in the spirit world.

Secondary Anthropological Objectives

The anthropological questions asked throughout the research sought to achieve the following research objectives within the scope of this study:

- To describe the ways that Turkana *ngimurok* are a persistent, integral part of Turkana identity, religious understanding and foundational epistemology.
- To produce quantitative and qualitative evidence of the persistence of *emuron* consultation from among self-ascribed Christians in Turkana.

Research participants confirmed throughout the study, both qualitatively and quantitatively that the roles of traditional Turkana religious specialists have persisted in Turkana. Both non-Christian and Christian Turkana visit the *ngimurok* of different types and there is evidence that the *ngimurok* have accommodated some of their practices for Turkana Christians by not requiring the smearing of the ritual ochre, which has generally been rejected by Christians. This accommodation allows for Christians to continue to seek the rituals of the *ngimurok* without the consequence of bearing the evidence of having visited an *emuron*. Turkana Christians continue to seek ritual answers to everyday problems, especially those problems

---

1. Waller, "Kidongoi's Kin."
2. Cited in Winkelman and Peek, *Divination and Healing*.
3. Peek, *African Divination Systems*, 13.

for which the church does not provide answers. This reality will be further discussed in the concluding section on missiological implications and suggestions for the Turkana church.

Yet, the tensions of the problem of discrepancy between the Christian and non-Christian moral evaluation of the *ngimurok* remain. Clearly, there is a difference between the common Turkana religious understandings of different ritual specialists—with some being extremely helpful in dire situations while others evaluated as acting with malevolent intent in the community—with the common Turkana Christian understanding in which Turkana church leaders and Western missionaries have moved all the category types that used to be understood in differentiated terms to be understood today under the one unifying term "*emuron*" with exclusively negative moral and spiritual implications.

Having participated in the ongoing witchcraft discussions at both the American Society of Missiology meetings and the Evangelical Missiological Society, I have participated with the study group headed up by Dr. Robert Priest that is working to help explain this shift in traditional religious specialist evaluation in contexts where Christianity has entered and is growing. Specifically, the study group is often frustrated by attempts to define the term "witchcraft" in various cultures. Pre-Christian and non-Christian understandings are more likely to differentiate between "witches" as sources of evil causal ontologies in the community, and ritual specialists of different types as positive, beneficial "socially approved" forces in the society.[4] Christian understandings tend to shift all the traditional religious types into the category of an evil practitioner, or "witch." While "witch" may have stood alone in the negative category before the introduction of Christianity, the positive traditional religious specialists are now in the same category, causing great confusion.

In a paper presented to both of the working groups in 2012, Priest illustrated the shift with these two images that are helpful for understanding the situation in Turkana regarding not only *ngimurok*, but the roles of Turkana church leaders, pastors and missionaries as well:

---

4. Priest, "On the Meaning."

202   Who Do the Ngimurok Say That They Are?

Figure 5. Separate Categories of Religious Specialists before the
Introduction of Christianity (Priest 2012)

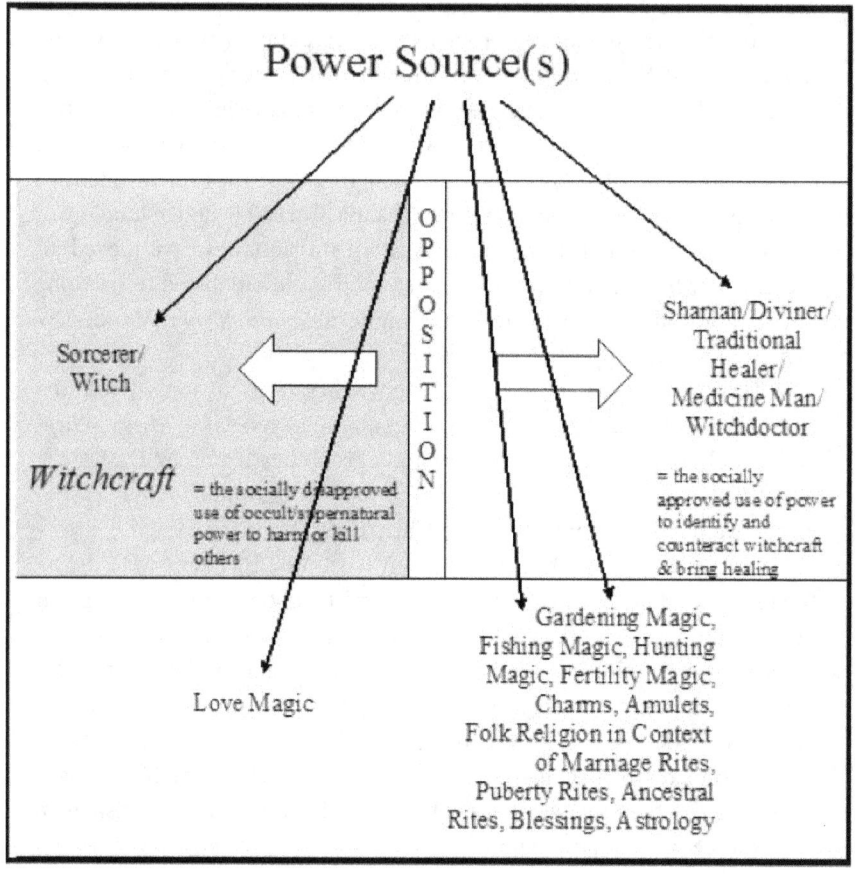

Figure 6. The Category Shift after Christianity (Priest 2012)

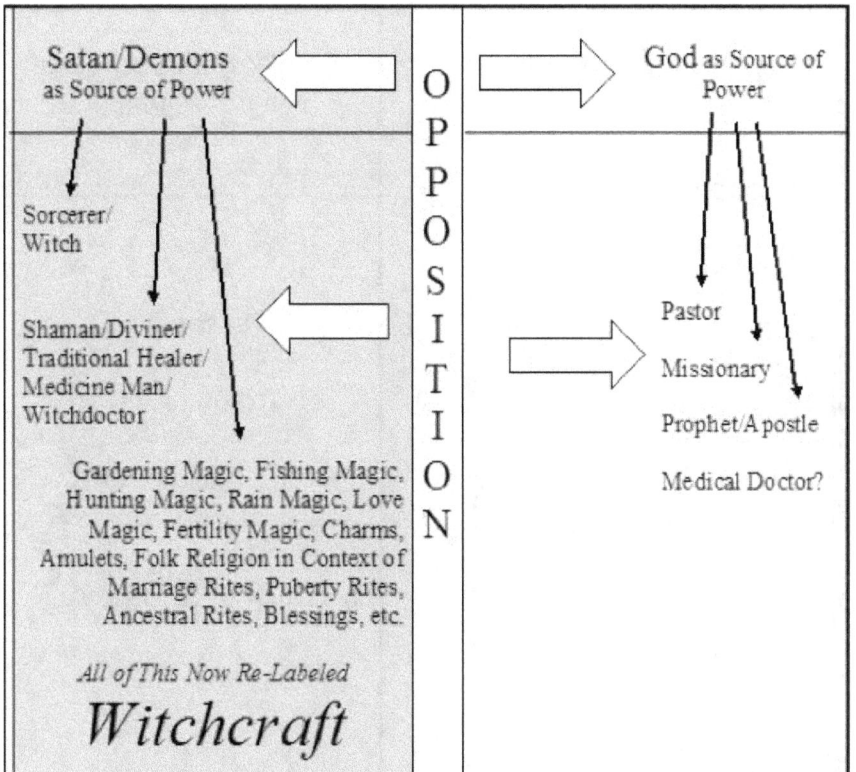

As visually described in Figure 5, "witchcraft" is a socially disapproved category that only includes the types "witch" and "sorcerer." Whereas "shaman, diviner, traditional healer, medicine man, witch doctor" are all types of religious specialists that are considered "socially approved to bring healing" and protection from evil. Figure 6 demonstrates the shift that has occurred with the advent of Christianity in many societies. The official socially approved religious specialists are now exclusively those in the church, "pastor, missionary, prophet, and perhaps medical doctor." The formerly socially accepted practitioners have all been relegated together under the category "witchcraft" and re-evaluated as exclusively evil and in opposition to the church and the ways of God.

I have reimagined Figure 6 for the Turkana context:

204   Who Do the Ngimurok Say That They Are?

Figure 7. The Religious Specialist Category Shift in Turkana

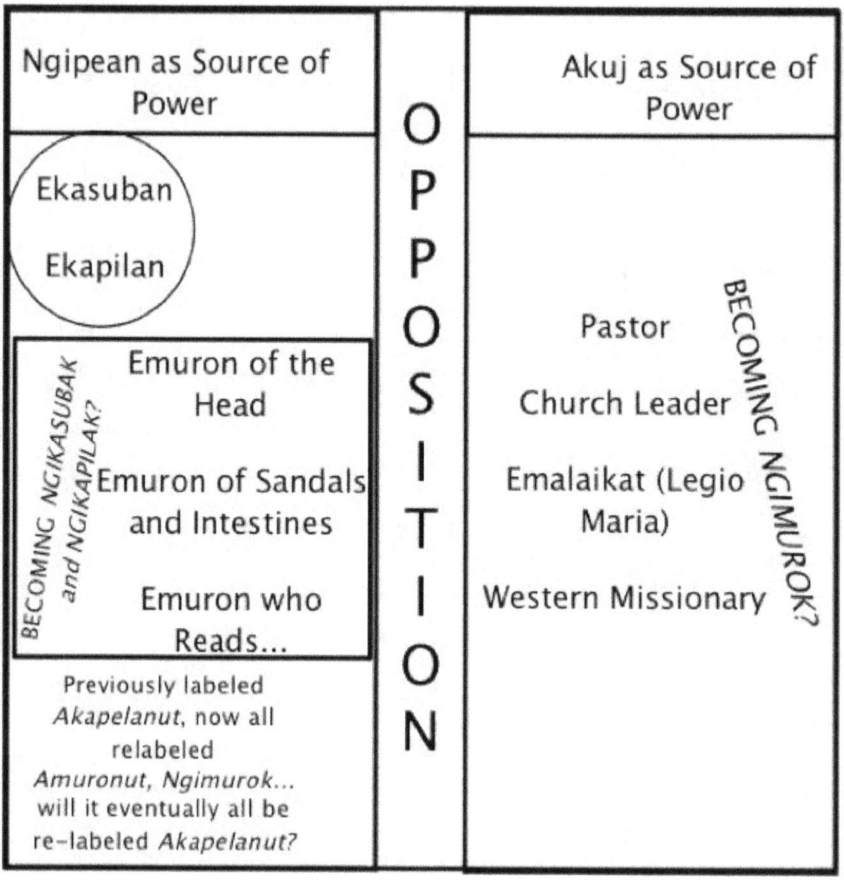

Ngipean as Source of Power	O P P O S I T I O N	Akuj as Source of Power
Ekasuban Ekapilan		
BECOMING NGIKASUBAK and NGIKAPILAK? Emuron of the Head Emuron of Sandals and Intestines Emuron who Reads...		Pastor Church Leader Emalaikat (Legio Maria) Western Missionary *BECOMING NGIMUROK?*
Previously labeled *Akapelanut*, now all relabeled *Amuronut, Ngimurok*... will it eventually all be re-labeled *Akapelanut*?		

Following Priest's theory, Figure 7 demonstrates the religious specialist category shift that is still occurring in Turkana. I would propose that because the shift has more recently occurred in Turkana, with the first introduction of Christianity in very small numbers in the 1970s, a complete shift as described by Priest in Figure 6 has not yet occurred. All the types of religious specialists on the left side of the figure are still generally grouped together under the category *emuron*. If Priest's model is predictive, it may be that eventually all the types in the left column will be under the category of *akapilanut*.

It is also possible that in this context, Priest's model is not predictive. The data from my research in Turkana clearly demonstrates the opposite of what Priest suggests. Instead of the socially accepted traditional religious specialist category *emuron* being subsumed under the socially disapproved

Conclusions: Toward a New Approach to Turkana Religious Specialists

category equivalent for "witch," both of the categories are being incorporated into the positive *emuron* terminology. Additionally, my research displays that in the local understanding, people still view these broad categories as being differentiated in much more specific subcategories of socially approved specialists. It seems that it is mainly the missionaries who are contributing to a category shift in which the *ngimurok* are "witches."

My questions in the APM and EMS witchcraft group discussions have centered on the reconfigured right side of the figure. Are church leaders and missionaries becoming "witches" or are they becoming *ngimurok*? While that question might horrify some missionaries who have helped to create the category shift illustrated here, I believe there are ways in which they do exhibit the characteristics of socially accepted roles of *ngimurok* in Turkana, especially through the Turkana religo-cultural interpretive lens. While I have argued that this causes unexpected problems in the community for missionaries, I have simultaneously suggested that this could potentially be a positive aspect for missionaries.[5] I will return to that discussion in the missiological implications.

Figure 7 represents the ways that Western missionaries and Turkana church leaders have included the Turkana morally unacceptable categories of *ekasuban* and *ekapilan* within the general, undifferentiated category, *emuron*. This error in generalization concerning all traditional religious specialists in Turkana continues to create a gap in Turkana Christian understandings on how to deal with problems for which morally acceptable religious specialists provide answers.

Clearly, we (starting with missionaries, missiologists, anthropologists, religious studies scholars) need to do a much more careful job of studying and describing the contextually specific phenomena of traditional religious specialists before relying on meta-categories that come out of our dualistic Western theology or older overly simplified ethnographies. The research from this current study of *ngimurok* could help to begin that process in the Turkana context and offers a possible alternative to Priest's model.

Tertiary Theological Objectives

Although the theological objectives were important for the missiological aspects of this research, the acquisition of data through the phenomenological study was primary during the research period. Chapter 6, in contrasting *emuron* statements concerning Christians and presenting the findings of a Turkana Christian survey concerning the *ngimurok*, served to answer many of the theological questions originally raised by the research. In general, the

---

5. See Lines, "Neoliberal Witches, Christian Diviners."

theological research objectives for this project centered on the concept of religious continuity from Turkana *ngimurok* religious concepts to faith in Jesus Christ. I have reworded each of the four theological objectives of the study into a question that I will briefly answer through the theoretical lens of each objective.

In what ways can Christianity be seen as the fulfillment of Turkana traditional religion? This question seeks to not only know if God is working through the Turkana *ngimurok*, but whether or not Christianity could be viewed as the fulfilment of the Turkana traditional religion. This is a very difficult question to answer and would require the examination of the Turkana religious system as a whole. Such an examination though, of the whole of Turkana religion, seems less likely to me after this research. It would seem overly optimistic to think that there is one religious system in Turkana; in fact, we would be placing our own Western conceptions of religion upon a very complex, varied and clan-based system.

In what ways can we see that *ngimurok* have been part of the *missio Dei*? This question is more accessible through the present research. If we bracket the recent lens of Western Christianity in Turkana and look to the positive roles of the *ngimurok* in their community, we can certainly see the possibility that God has been at work through the *ngimurok*. The difficulty is seeing the positive roles of the *ngimurok* through the denunciation of the church. The positive roles most commonly associated with the *ngimurok*, even by Christians, include healing sickness, bringing rain when needed, and protecting the community from bandits. The concept of *missio Dei* would allow for these positive activities of even the *ngimurok* to be incorporated into God's mission in Turkana.

Can the category *emuron* serve as ontological expansion of our Christology? The phrase, "Jesus is the great *emuron*," is commonly used in the Turkana church and is seen as acceptable by Western missionaries mostly because the phrase is used in the Turkana translation of the Bible in passages, particularly in the epistle to the Hebrews, that describe Jesus as the High Priest. The translators used *emuron* for the translation of priest. This translation and the suitability of the christological statement, "Jesus is the great *emuron*," will increasingly become problematic as the church continues to denounce the traditional *ngimurok*. Another christological statement I heard during the research is, "Jesus is my *ariwo*." Can the church think of Jesus as a preemptive sacrifice to keep us safe from danger?

What can we reflexively learn about ourselves and our own faith from *ngimurok* understandings? This is a personal question through which I can offer my own experience through interaction with the *ngimurok*. In general, I was most impressed by the hospitality displayed to me by the *ngimurok*.

It was a rare occasion when I felt as if the *emuron* was not genuine in his or her hospitality. Missionaries and church leaders in Turkana could learn from the hospitality of the *ngimurok*. Reflexively, another thing I learned from the *ngimurok* was the ability to start with the ontological perspective that there is only one God when faced with a belief system that is different than my own. While Turkana Christians pray to the same God as the *ngimurok* by name (*Akuj*), the general sense in the church is that the *ngimurok* do not acknowledge God, which is not a valid conclusion, according to the research.

Theological Difficulties

While seeking a theological perspective on the *ngimurok* informed by *missio Dei*, ontic expansion and fulfilment theology, there were some theological difficulties encountered during the research that should be discussed and evaluated by the Turkana church. Briefly, these include: 1) The ambiguity among the *ngimurok* of the head in their usage of God or father in describing who provides them with revelatory information. Is this a form of ancestor worship? 2) Sacrifices are regularly made to ancestor spirits to keep them from bothering people. 3) Again, sacrifices are commonly made to appease spirits, from throwing tobacco on the ground to sacrificing a large animal. 4) Many people seemed trapped in a very expensive never-ending cycle of sacrifices that is not effective for very long. Some people in dire need might return multiple times in one month. When bringing two animals to every session, this becomes very expensive for the clients. 5) *Ngimurok* are admittedly involved in blessing the groups of young men who go on cattle raids among neighboring ethnic groups. The *ngimurok* receive huge profits for successful raids that they have blessed and protected. This type of activity, seen as socially acceptable from within Turkana, is illegal by the laws of Kenya, and complicates the ability to use the *emuron* concept theologically.

FURTHER MISSIOLOGICAL IMPLICATIONS

Both the anthropological and theological research objective reviews have already brought up a number of missiological implications. In this section I provide even more reflections on the implications of this study for mission.

First and foremost is that the descriptions of *ngimurok*, provided by the *ngimurok* themselves, provides many new options for the church and missionaries in Turkana to relate to the *ngimurok*. Turkana Christians can now engage in discussions regarding specific practices of the *ngimurok* revealed through this study. Connected to that is the potential for the easing of the tensions that have built up through demonization of the *ngimurok* by

Christians. This would mean that new relationships between Christians and *ngimurok* could be built based on something other than distrust.

In general, the study should allow for more open discussion in the church concerning the reasons people still visit the *ngimurok*. This is a discussion that is needed in order to begin evaluating 1) whether or not the church can provide answers to the problems people are bringing to the *ngimurok*, and 2) Whether or not new practices and symbols should be included into the Turkana Christian community for more effective discipleship. If people are seeking powerful rituals to connect themselves to God's power, can the church provide some new forms of powerful rituals?

Particularly, this study should encourage the church to consider the ways that the church can participate in these specific activities:

- The blessing of people with water similar to *ewatakin ngakipi*
- The opening of the planting of gardens
- Recognizing the spiritual and relational aspects of healing the sick
- Prayers for those who are barren
- Prayers for rain
- Prayers and guidance for those seeking employment or going to school
- Help for those who are mentally disturbed
- Help for those who are possessed/bothered by spirits

Although not a "critical contextualization" study itself, this study should also help to provide more data for critical contextualization studies that may be incorporated into the above considerations. This current research could certainly provide a phenomenological study as the first step in a critical contextualization project. While missionaries and missiologists continue to recognize the need for use of critical contextualization as a method for discerning the acceptability of cultural practices in light of Christian faith, the phenomenological step is rarely completed at the level I have been able to accomplish in this study. Phenomenology helps to reveal local understandings of the moral roles of traditional religious specialists.

Finally, it is my desire to suggest a phenomenological approach for missiological research in the future. While I have rarely seen this approach employed in missiology or in mission strategy field research, I believe the approach of seeking to understand who people are from their own perspectives is an important first step to sharing the good news of the Kingdom of God with others, incarnationally. It is an approach that I have now seen work in its ability to generate more open discussion regarding issues that have been kept secret for many years. For most of my research participants, the approach was very non-threatening as I engaged them with no other agenda other than to learn who they were, from them.

SUGGESTIONS FOR FUTURE RESEARCH

My research findings have opened up new opportunities for continued missiological research in Turkana. Upon returning to Turkana, I hope to use this research in order to continue the discussion regarding the specific roles of *ngimurok* today and their relationship to the church. In addition, I believe this research project has provided a basis for studying the ways that church leaders, pastors, and missionaries of both mission-initiated and African-initiated churches are replacing or filling the roles of the traditional religious specialists in Turkana and many other contexts, at least in Africa.

Another area where additional research is needed is in relation to cattle raiding and ethnic conflict in the Turkana region. The current research project revealed direct relationships between the blessings of the *ngimurok* and cattle raiding in the wider regions. Yet, peace efforts in the area have ignored the role of the *ngimurok*. Incorporating *ngimurok* involvement in region wide peace plans could have tremendous impact on the raiding.

Finally, it would be a joy to continue this research and gradually create an even larger and more accurate description of religious specialists throughout Turkana County and all the southern Nilotic groups. Research is still needed on the *emuron* perspectives of many other church groups beyond the Community Christian Church in Turkana.

Postscript

And how much that goes into the notebooks should go into print? Ideally, I suppose, everything, because what is not published may be, and generally is, forever lost—the picture of a people's way of life at a point of time goes down into the dark unfathomed caves. And one cannot know how valuable what may appear to one at the time to be a trifle may be to a student in the future who may be asking questions which one did not ask oneself . . . One is burdened for the rest of one's life with what one has recorded, imprisoned in the prison one has built for oneself, but one owes a debt to posterity.

E. E. Evans-Pritchard, 1937.

I ENTERED INTO THIS project not exactly certain where it would end up. Everyone hopes for significant research findings that will change the course of something or other. But, as I studied, interviewed and visited with the *ngimurok*, I found that there was significance in merely listening and recording their words. The *ngimurok* see that times are changing, even in Turkana, and part of their willingness to share seemed motivated by a desire for people to know who they are and what they do. And not necessarily people far away. My sense was that they wanted their words written down in a book that they can't read so that their grandchildren who are all going to school and reading books in English might someday be able to read and know about the *ngimurok*. I'm happy to be part of that documentation of a way of thinking and living and connecting with God that might not be part of Turkana identity in the near future; especially as the use of the Turkana language diminishes.

I'm even more excited about the implications of this research for the Turkana church and the Western missionaries who still live and work in Turkana. This project has started an open and honest dialogue about the continued role of *ngimurok* ritual traditions in the church. If the Turkana church can move a little further in the direction of learning what it means to be Turkana Christians instead of imitating Western Christians (or even other Kenyan Christians), this will have all been worth it for me. If Western missionaries can use this study to begin to more carefully study the Turkana culture and traditional understandings instead of employing broad denunciations, I believe their message will be even more effective, Turkana Christians will stop hiding practices, and more of the *ngimurok* will be open to following the way of Jesus because of their willingness to learn.

Finally, I look forward to unpacking what feels like a lifetime of information to study from this research project. I pray for the opportunities to continue to return to Turkana to learn together with my brothers and sisters in that place. In between those opportunities, I look forward to helping others work out their calling to serve as intercultural servants in the *missio Dei* of helping to bring reconciliation between all the world and God. May these efforts be even one small piece in God's expanding kingdom.

APPENDIX A

Maps

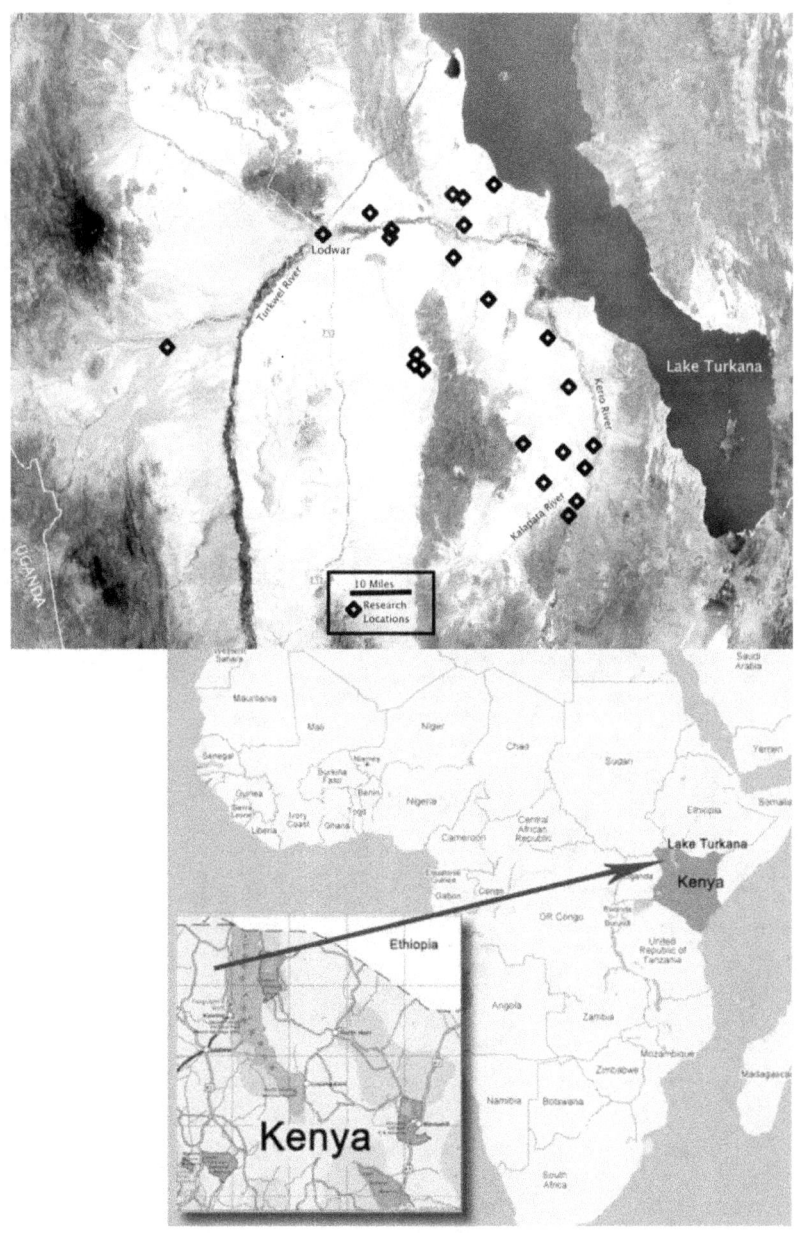

APPENDIX B

List of Interviews

Interview	Date	Name	Self-ascribed	Clan/Brand	Location of Interview	Ancestor
1	10/21/11	Male Emuron #1	emuron	Esigerit	Kalochan	No
2	10/22/11	Male Emuron #1	emuron		Kalochan	
3	10/23/11	Female Amuron #1	akatwan		Kalochan	
4	10/23/11	Male Emuron #2	emuron a akou	Emeturanait	Nakaalei	Lokerio
5	10/24/11	Male Emuron #2			Nakaalei	
6	10/24/11	Male Emuron #3	emuron a akou	Ebilait	Katir	Lokorijem
7	10/24/11	Male Emuron #3				
8	10/25/11	Male Emuron #4	emuron a akou		Natome	Lokerio
9	10/26/11	Male Emuron #5	emuron	Ebilait	Lokwarnakalesio	Lokorijem
10	10/26/11	Male Emuron #5				
11	10/26/11	Male Emuron #6		Emeturanait	Lokwarnakaleso	Lokerio
12	10/27/11	Male Emuron #6	emuron	Emeturanait	Nakurio	Lokerio
13	10/27/11	Male Emuron #7	emuron a akou	Ebilait	Katapakin	Lokorijem
14	11/1/11	Male Emuron #8	emuron a akou	Ebilait	Nakalale	Lokorijem
15	11/1/11	Female Amuron #2	amuron a akou	Ameturanait	Kakimat	Lokorijem
16	11/1/11	Male Emuron #9	emuron a akou	Ebilait	Nangorecheto	Lokorijem
17	11/2/11	Male Emuron #9				
18	11/2/11	Legio Maria (3 Men)	emuron a ngimalaikae		Nangorecheto	
19	11/2/11	Male Emuron #10	emuron a ngamaliteny	Emosorokoit	Nangorecheto	No
20	11/2/11	ME#10 (intestine reading)				
21	11/2/11	ME#10 (Sandal Throwing)				
22	11/2/11	Male Emuron #11	emuron a akou	Ebilait	Loriamatet	Lokorijem
23	11/3/11	Male Emuron #12	amuron a akou	Asigerit	Loriamatet	Akilerio (Lokorijem)
24	11/3/11	Male Emuron #13	emuron a akou	Ebilait	Lokitela	Lodip, Lokorijem
25	11/4/11	Male Emuron #14	emuron a akou	Ebilait	Emong Kirion	Lodip, Lokorijem
26	11/19/11	Male Emuron #15	emuron a akou		Nakaititi	Lodip (through Mother)
27	11/20/11	Male Emuron #15				
28	11/21/11	Male Emuron #16	emuron a ngamaliteny	Esigerit	Napusimor	
29	11/21/11	ME#16 (Sandal Throwing)				
30	11/21/11	Female Amuron #3	Legio Maria		Napusimoru	
31	11/21/11	Male Emuron #17	emuron a ngamaliteny	Epuchait	b/t Napus and Kaekorsigol	
32	11/22/11	Male Emuron #18	emuron a akou	Ngiblait	Napusimoru	Lokorijem
33	11/22/11	Male Emuron #19	emuron a ngamaliteny	Meturonait	Nakipi	
34	11/22/11	ME#19 (intestine reading)				
35	11/23/11	Male Emuron #19				
36	11/23/11	Male Church Leader	church leader	Esigerit	Napusimoru	
37	11/23/11	ME#16 (intestine readi	emuron a ngamaliteny			
38	11/28/11	Female Amuron #4	Akatuwan		Ile Springs (Eliye)	
39	11/29/11	Female Amuron #4	Akatuwan		Ile Springs (Eliye)	
40	11/30/11	Female Amuron #5	Amuron a Akou	Ebilait	Nachuan	Lodip, Lokorijem
41	11/30/11	Female Amuron #6	Amuron a Akou	Epongait	Nachuan	Lodip, Lokorijem
42	11/30/11	Male Bandit	Itwaan (interview about	Emosorokoit	Nachuan	
43	12/5/11	Male Emuron #20	emuron a ngamaliteny		Narengo	
44	12/6/11	Male Emuron #21	emuron a ngamaliteny	Esigerit	Natagilae	
45	12/6/11	Male Emuron #22	emuron a akou	Ebilait	Lomopus	Lodip, Lokorijem
46	12/6/11	Male Emuron #23	emuron a akou	Ebilait	Kalotim	Lodip, Lokorijem
47	12/7/11	Male Emuron #24	emuron a ngamaliteny	Emosorokoit	Chokchok	
48	12/8/11	Male Emuron Son		Ebilait	Lodwar	Lokedongan
49	12/8/11	Female Amuron #7	amuron a akou		Lodwar	Lokedongan
50	12/9/11	Male Emuron #25	emuron a akou	Ngitongor	Lorugumu	Lokedongan

OTHER VIDEO INTERVIEWS IN KANGARISAE RELATED TO RECENT RAIDING (See video index)

APPENDIX C

An *Emuron* Interview Model

ONE-PAGE GUIDE FOR INFORMAL INTERVIEWS WITH TURKANA *NGIMUROK*

I am very happy to be at your home today. I bring greetings from [name villages and Elders you have recently visited]. Some people may have told you what I am doing in Turkana these days. I am trying to learn as much as I can about being a righteous Turkana from the Elders and the *Ngimurok*. Many people do not understand who the *ngimurok* are and are even saying terrible things about the *ngimurok*. I am coming to visit the *ngimurok* to hear their own words. I want to share the words of the *ngimurok* to help others understand, so that people will not tell lies or rumors about the *ngimurok*.

Can I talk to you today? I know that many *ngimurok* do not want to talk about the things they do because the government wants *ngimurok* to stop their practices. I am not connected to the government and am here as a learner connected to my school in America.

Some people have said that you are an *emuron* who has blessed many people through your rituals. What are some of the blessings that come from the *ngimurok*? Which blessings do you use most often?

I have heard that when people need help with many problems, they come to see you. What problems do people bring to you? How do you find answers to those problems?

[At this point, depending on the answers, the interviewer should be able to tell if the person is indeed an *emuron*. If so, we want to try and find any special name used to describe them or their work by others, and any special terminology used to describe their practices]

Tell me a story of someone who came to you that you have recently helped.

Do you serve as the *emuron* in area weddings? Do you help with the *asapan* (male initiation)?

Tell me about God. Does God ever send you dreams? What things are revealed in these dreams? (How do you know the color of an animal that is supposed to be sacrificed?)

How did God make you an *emuron*? Was your father an *emuron*? Are your sons or daughters *ngimurok*? Which of the great *ngimurok* is your ancestor?

Are there *ngimurok* in Turkana that are hidden and people are afraid of? Why are people afraid of them?

Do the *ngimurok* ever come together for a big gathering?
Are some *ngimurok* more powerful than other *ngimurok*? In what ways?

Since the church has come to ["Turkana" or village name], is there any conflict between the church and *ngimurok*? What is that conflict about? Would you ever go to the church? Have you ever heard the church teach bad things about you or other *ngimurok*? What bad things do they teach about *ngimurok*?

APPENDIX D

Rituals and Interviews Recorded on Video

Video Date	Video File .MOV	Date	Type (R, I, O, M)	Length (time)	Description
10/22/11	062	Oct 21, 2011	M	0:01:24	Entering House
	063		M	0:00:16	House
	064		M	:28	Kids in Nakor
	065		M	1:12	Nakor food distribution
	066		M	:11	Chief with Emuron
	067		M	:31	Emuron Gestures
	068		M	:25	Kangirisae Chief
	069		M	:29	Man with AK-47 and Emuron
	070			:05	Deleted
	071		O	:55	Morning at Emuron house through the tent
	072		M	:53	James and Kip walking back to Emuron home in morning
	073		O	:16	Emuron homes
	074		O	:07	Emuron homes
	075		O	:17	Entering Emuron home with chickens
	076	Oct 22, 2011		:06	Delete
	077			:18	Delete
	078			:03	Delete
	080			:03	Delete
	081		O	:50	Emuron receiving sugar and tobacco
	082		O	:22	Goat and Sheep brought for ariwo and payment
	083		O	:40	Preparing the fire and cooking pot for cooking meat
	084		O	:26	Sick woman with problems has come for help
	085		I	1:02	Other people describe the sick woman's problems
	086		R	5:53	Taar Ariwo a nawi Emuron. Aboikin ngitunga kidiama
	087		R	4:17	Awatakin ngkipi ngitunga daang (tani erot)
	088		R	9:15	Ewasakin emunyen following emunyen into the house
	089		R	:19	The emunyen turns white when it dries.
	090		R	:32	More Dried Emunyen
	091		O	:39	Butchering the ariwo goat from 086.MOV
	092		R, I	10:44	Two tobacco readings and instructions: 0-2:50 and 2:50-6:50, then I interview Emuron 6:50-10:44
	093		R	1:03	Ewatakin Ngakipi and another man receives instructions
	094		O	:41	2 cooking pots for ariwo goat, upper parts and lower parts
	095		O	3:52	Carrying the cooked meat into the house and the dividing of the meat
	096		O	2:37	Further dividing of meat, a bowl for boys, Kip gets a piece of liver.
	097		O	:54	Dividing meat, handed to girls
	098		O	:48	More Meat
	099		O	:22	Men receive meat, wake up
	100		O	:03	Woman with child and meat
	101		O	:06	Boy eats meat
	102		O	:44	Children of emuron and emuron eat meat
	103		O	:21	Echom, sitting, then men (homeguards) eat meat while lounging
	104		M	1:09	World Vision Adicho distribution in Kangirisae, Jane Ngasike helping
	105		M	:26	World Vision Adicho distribution one large cup and one small cup
	106		I	3:36	Pele talks (ngaturkana) about the problems caused by the recent raids in Kangirisae
	107			:11	Delete
	108			:01	Delete
	109		I	3:13	Simon Lobei talks (kiswahili) about the problems caused by the recent raids in Kangirisae
	110		I	1:50	James' English explanation of what Simon Lobei said.
	111		I	2:19	Man in Kangirisae describes the problems
	112		I	2:30	Achukwa from across the river describes the problems (Ngaturkana)
	113		I	1:29	Margret Esinyen Ekwee, whose husband was killed, describes the problems
	114		O	:09	The group who came to describe problems
	115		M	:29	People at the World Vision adicho distribution in Kangirisae
	116		O	:10	The group who came to describe problems
	117			:04	Delete
	118		I	4:42	Joseph Esekon describing the problems (English) in Kangirisae because of raiding
	119		R, I	4:32	Emuron Tongere Akine kisimuj Ngikaram, 3:13 interview woman with sick children
	120		R	:40	Placing tobacco on the back of the ariwo for ngikaram
2011-10-23	001	Oct 23, 2011	O	:36	Emuron house from the tent at sunrise
	002		M	:32	Sunrise through fence
	003		M	:30	Kip walking opening truck door
	004		R	9:00	Ariwo for 4 people at Emuron home, sitting on top
	005		R, I	3:30	Ewatakin Ngakipi for ariwo then description of sun ritual
	011		R	3:34	Sun Ritual
	014		M	1:05	Woman at Lomunyen Akwaan School/Church (DISTORTED AUDIO)
	015		M	:28	Diff stuck in Kalapata loose sand
	016		M	:23	Diff stuck in Kalapata loose sand
	017		M	:05	Diff stuck in Kalapata loose sand
	018		M	:07	Diff stuck in Kalapata loose sand
	019		M	:16	Nakaalei Church
	020		M	:24	Kangirisae Church
	021		O	1:29	Epapeton leading "Yesu ngesi arai ariwo" song in Kangirisae church
	022		O	1:03	Ekapeton finishes song with some teaching
	023		O	:14	Filling out questionaires
	024		O	:11	Filling out questionaires
	025		O	:47	Filling out questionaires
	026		M	:44	"Obama" at Lorunye's home
	027		M	:24	Echom and James resting at Lorunye's house
	028		M	1:50	Kip jokes with Lorunye "brainwashed by Western Medicine"
	029		I	1:55	Kip interviews Emuron (audio recording is better for audio)
	030		I	1:30	Kip interviews Salalei (audio recording is better for audio)
	031		I	1:12	Kip interviews Emuron (audio recording is better for audio)
	032		I	:11	Kip interviews Emuron (audio recording is better for audio)
	033		I	:32	Kip interviews Emuron (audio recording is better for audio)
	034		I	:43	Kip interviews Emuron (audio recording is better for audio)
	035		I	:45	Kip interviews Emuron (audio recording is better for audio)
	036		I	1:52	Kip interviews Emuron (audio recording is better for audio)
	037		I	:37	Kip interviews Emuron (audio recording is better for audio)
	038		I	2:07	Kip interviews Emuron (audio recording is better for audio)
	039		I	:43	Kip interviews Emuron (audio recording is better for audio)
	040		I	:53	Kip interviews Emuron (audio recording is better for audio)
	041		I	2:17	Kip interviews Emuron (audio recording is better for audio)
	042		I	1:46	Kip interviews Emuron (audio recording is better for audio)
2011-10-24	001	Oct 24, 2011	M	:50	Lorunye home inside tent early morning James wrapped in blanket
	002		M	:38	Lorunye home inside tent early morning James wrapped in blanket
	003		M	:19	Lorunye home inside tent early morning James wrapped in blanket

Appendix D: Rituals and Interviews Recorded on Video

Date	#	Date	Type	Length	Description
	004		M	:15	Lorunye home inside tent early morning James wrapped in blanket
	005		M	:36	Lorunye home early morning boy eating rice before school
	006		M	:10	Nakalei walking to choo
	007		M	:17	Nakalei walking to choo
	008		M	1:11	Nakalei walking to choo
	009		M	:11	Nakalei walking to choo
	010		O	1:09	Kids at Lorunye, Lorunye filling out questionaire
	011		O	:55	Filling out questionaires
	012		O	:58	Filling out questionaires
	013		M	:41	Kids at Lorunye, Lorunye filling out questionaire
	014		M	1:16	Delivering food to school kids at Loupwala
	015		R	1:27	James, Echom, and me at Emuron home, watching ariwo being cooked
	016		O	:44	Hiding in Emuron hut because of rain
	017		M	:19	Kip in Emuron hut, ipaga
	018		I	2:10	Kip interviewing Emuron (MESSED UP AUDIO, AUDIO FILE IS BETTER)
	019		I	2:23	Kip interviewing Emuron(MESSED UP AUDIO, AUDIO FILE IS BETTER)
	020		I	1:38	Kip interviewing Emuron (MESSED UP AUDIO, AUDIO FILE IS BETTER)
	021		M	:06	Kip emerging from Emuron hut
	022		M	:10	Children at Emuron Home
	023		M	:08	Children at Emuron Home
	024		M	:21	Children at Emuron Home
	025		M	:07	Driving goats with James and Emuron
	026		I	:14	Emuron River interview
	027			:09	Delete
	028		O	:10	James and Emuron driving goats back to house
	029		O	:04	James and Emuron driving goats back to house
	030		M	:42	Emuron home
2011-10-25	001	Oct 25, 2011	M	:37	James and Kip looking for a choo and finding a strange Eipa tree
	002		M	:49	Strange Eipa Tree
	003		M	3:04	My description of how things are going and the huge rain/wind last night
	004		O	:21	Ritual tree at Emuron House
	005		O	:19	Etem at Emuron house
	006		O	1:24	Shadow of Eowe, ritual tree, wife walking into etem a Emuron
	007		O	:47	Inside akol of Emuron youngest wife
	008		M	:06	Nyalu Ngitunga?
	009		M	:15	Children at Natome River
	010		M	:49	People at Natome, Meeting Emuron
	011		M	2:28	Tour of our Natome campsite at the home of Emuron
2011-10-27	001	Oct 26, 2011	M	1:04	Morning at Natome campsite from inside tent
	002		M	:08	Drinking coffee with Emuron and Ngamasio at Natome
	007		M	:06	Filling out a questionaire in the morning at Natome
	008		M	:10	Filling out a questionaire in the morning at Natome
	011		M	:32	Broken Pump at Natome
	014		M	:14	House of Emuron and the mobile phone booth
	015		I	5:56	Kip explains to Emuron why I have come to ask him questions
	016		I	1:40	James rexplains what we are doing
	020		O	3:05	Government chief and emuron discuss when to do the ariwo to protect the people from bandits
	021		M	:44	Dancing Ngingoroko
	022		M	:15	Dancing Ngingoroko
	023		M	:25	Dancing Ngingoroko
	024		M	2:34	Singing Ngingoroko
	025		M	:55	Interrupting a goat roast to see the akisemere a ngimaliteny
	026		R	7:03	Intestine reading finds a women will get sick
	027		M	:14	Eating an orange in the visitor shade
	028		I	4:17	Interview with Emuron (Audio recording is better and complete)
	029		O	:10	Ngaberu ka ngide a Emuron
	030		M	:39	Ngide a Emuron sing a church song
	031		M	1:10	Ngide a Emuron sing a church song
	032		O	:42	The etem of Emuron
	033		O	1:09	The emunyen and other things in the etem of Emuron
	034		O	:56	Leaving the etem and seeing the tall "ngikeyokok" sticks
	035		O	:36	Closing the door of the inner etem
	036		O	:08	Red emunyen (lokupriat) on the fence post
	037		M	:11	Sitting with Emuron waiting for a goat
	038	Oct 27, 2011	R, I	5:25	Emuron kisimuj apakeng with tobacco and sugar then asks me for lots of money (then I left)
	039		I	1:23	Emuron tells me to come back when there is a moon
2011-10-31	001		M	:51	Rain at Morden House
	002		M	:38	Rain at Morden House
	003	Oct 30, 2011	M	:54	Youth Choir Lodwar CCC, Grace dancing
	004		M	:25	People at Lodwar CCC
	005		M	2:33	Adult Choir Lodwar CCC
	006		M	3:00	Adult Choir Lodwar CCC
	010		M	2:48	Adult Choir Lodwar CCC
2011-11-2	001	Oct 31, 2011	M	:45	Clasroom at Kaakimat built by LifeBridge CC
	002		M	1:31	Trying to cross Kaakimat river, very clear water
	003		M	:50	Sunset at Nakaalale
	004	Nov 1, 2011	I, O	1:09	Emuron shows the athante
	007		O	:32	People at Emuron House
	008		M	:31	James and Echome and closeup on the mountain I used to climb
	009		M	:52	Kids at Emuron Home
	012		M	:14	Bad Choice, Stuck in the River
	013		O	:10	Engeso Stick
	018		I, O	:16	Kimak engeso, tojoker
	019		I, O	1:05	Emuron describes how to use ebaata
	022		I	4:05	Interviewing Emuron about different types of ngimurok
	023		I	:35	Asking Emuron about emunyen
	024		I, O	3:30	Showing the ilepit, atubwa and emunyen
	028	Nov 2, 2011	M	:18	Goats leaving the pen at sunrise at Emuron home
	029		M	:21	Sunrise at Emuron home
	030		O	:5	Legio Maria at Emuron home
	033		M	:15	People at Emuron home
	034		M	:52	Eating lunch waiting for intestine reading
	035		R, I	7:01	Emuron intestine reading
	036		R	:09	Cooking the goat
	039		I, O	2:29	Emuron Sandal Throwing
	040		M	:04	Kip with Emuron Asbury Shirt
	041		I	:57	Kip thanks Emuron

Appendix D: Rituals and Interviews Recorded on Video

Date	No.	Date	Type	Duration	Description
	044		I	:13	Interviewing Emuron, left side paralyzed
2011-11-03	001	Nov 3, 2011	M	1:22	From inside tent eary morning at James' mother's home
	002		M	:52	Ayore inside tent
	006		O	1:01	Inside Emuron akol
	007		I	:53	James explaining why we are interviewing Emuron
	008		M	:09	Echom in truck with storm coming
	009		O	1:40	Spearing the camel at Emuron home
	010		M	:45	Wind on hill overlooking Emuron home
2011-11-23	001	Nov 22, 2011	M	:09	Children at Lokaliban's home
	005		O	:13	James looking at Elipet and atubwa at Emuron home
	006		M	:20	Children at Lokaliban's home
	007		M	:35	Children at Lokaliban's home
	010		R, I	13:27	Night aksemere ngamalibeny with Emuron
	011		O	:41	Nighttime Goat Roast at Emuron home
	012		O	:47	James grinding ngingonwa at amook ritual
	015		O	1:52	Chapman at amook, cooking pots (2)
	016		I, O	:25	About amook na
	017		I, O	10:50	Emuron reading intestines
2011-11-29	001	Nov 28, 2011	I, O	:49	Akatuwan in ile making a basket and instructing daughter to go get her elipet
	002		I, O	1:34	Akatuwan demonstrating how her mother ritually gave her the things to do her work and then letting her son demonstrate on her how it works.
	003	Nov 29, 2011	M	1:20	At the shore of Lake Turkana in the morning where we camped.
	005		M	:09	Children at the Chief's house in Ile Springs
	006		M	:10	Children at the Chief's house in Ile Springs
	007		O	5:05	Akatuwan doing her work on old woman, removes sticks from head near left eye. Says that stick resembles a person.
	008		M	:23	Children at the Chief's house in Ile Springs
	014		M	:11	River flowing across the road to Kangatosa
2011-11-30	001	Nov 30, 2011	M	:06	Children in Kangatosa
	002		M	:12	Children in Kangatosa
	003		M	:09	Children in Kangatosa
	004		M	:26	Children in Kangatosa
	005		O	:21	James holding the emunyen from Emuron (The Lokonjem Ancestor)
	006		O	:07	The Emuron daugter of Eperon, Akileu, showing her atubuo and elipet

APPENDIX E

Photographs

An *emuron* of the head, Lokorijem descendent with the author.

Research Assistant, James Ibei Eipa. Morning at the home of an *emuron*.

Appendix E: Photographs 221

Ngikito: *Engeso*

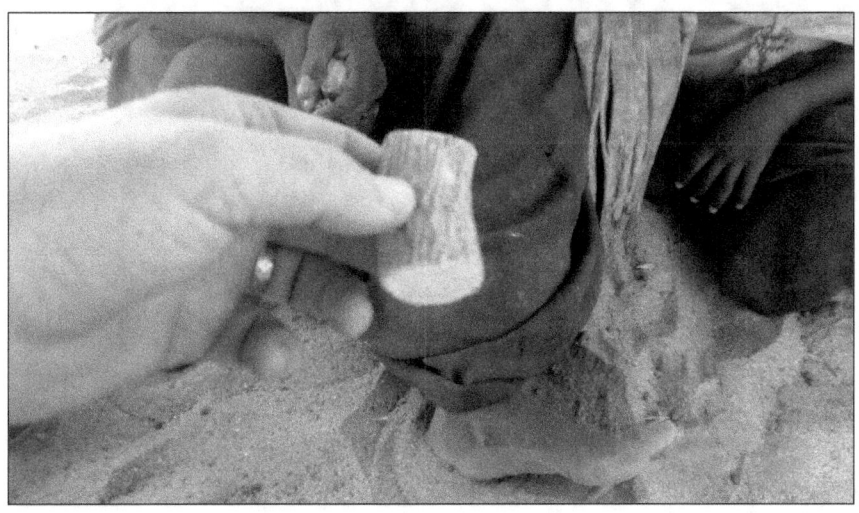

Ngikito: *Ebata*

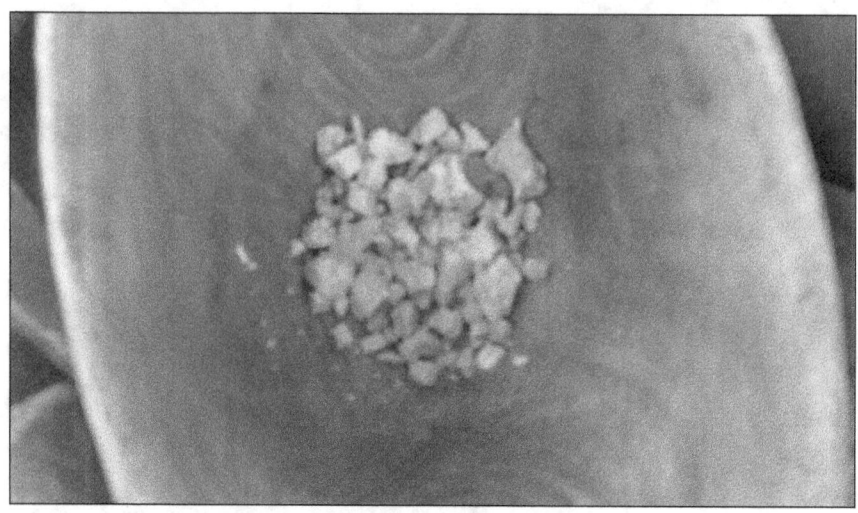

Dried Ritual Ochre (White): *Emunyen*

Emuron of the Sandals and Intestines

Appendix E: Photographs 223

Emuron a Akou

Emuron a Akou

Emuron of Sandals and Intestines

Recording Video of an *Emuron* Intestine Reading

Appendix E: Photographs 225

Grave of the *Emuron* Lokedongan

At the Home of an *Emuron a Akou*

APPENDIX F

Glossary of Common Turkana Terms Related to *Ngimurok* Used in this Study

aberu	woman/wife
abiblia (Ngakiro Naajokak)	Bible (Good News)
acham	I agree/accept
agata	blessing
akai	house structure
akamu	famine
akapel	curse to death
akapelanut	evil ritual magic
akariton/ekariton/ngikaritok	one who rubs/pulls (helps with childbirth)
akatuwan/ngikatuwak (pl)	one who ritually removes
akichum	traditional spearing
akidem edeng	one who causes corruption
akidoun	birth
akigol ngibaren	to "close" the animals
akigol ngide ngapesur	to "close" the young daughters
akilam/elami	cursing with words (not ritual)
akilamlam	throwing (sandals)
akingarakin	to help
akinyonyo	female initiation ceremony
akirikar	to violently & completely destroy
akirimrim	go round and round
akiru	rain
akisemeere	to read/interpret (exegete)
akongo	eye (aka evil eye)
Akuj	God
akuuta	marriage
akwap	land
amak/akimak (akimuak)	To spit upon and set apart for a task
amook	cleansing, purging, purifying ritual
anakanak	monitor lizard [*Varanus albigularis*]

Appendix F: Glossary of Common Turkana Terms Used in this Study

angajep; Ngaturkana	lit. the tongue; the Turkana language
anook	nighttime circular animal pen
Apa	father
Apaa	paternal grandfather
apiaret a awi	blessings of the house
apolon	one who is great
ariwo	protection sacrifice
arukum	congestion
asapan	male initiation ceremony
asub (akisub- to do)	to curse, manipulate, obstruct with objects
asubanut/asubes	ritual cursing and manipulation
atangaa ngamaniat	to open the garden planting
athante	fibrous brush made from animal tendon
atubwa	wooden bowl
dakitari	doctor; loan word from Swahili doctor
e/amuronut / amurote	ritual activity of the emuron
ebata	medicinal stick (*Terminalia spinosa*)
ebu	mad (crazy) hyena
echom	baboon
echoto	mud
edeke/ngidekesinei	sickness
edome	type of large bush
ejoker itwaan	a healed person
ekadwaran	the one with a bitter mouth/saliva
ekapilan (pl)	Evil hidden ritual specialist (witch)
ekapolon	lord, one who is great
ekasuban/ngikasubak	Evil ritual specialist, learns rituals (sorcerer)
ekayangan	one who skins (aka: *ekapilan*)
ekeriau	medicinal stick (tuber *Cyperus articulates*)
ekerujait	one who dreams
ekipe/ngipean	spirit, spirits (Christian: satan)
ekoroe	he-goat
elamlam ngamuk	sandals reading/throwing sandals
elepit	milking container/container to hold water
emachar/ngimacharin	brand/tribe/clan
emalaikat	sw. for "angel," term used for *Legio Maria*
emoit/ngimoe	enemy/enemies
emunyen	ritual ochre

Appendix F: Glossary of Common Turkana Terms Used in this Study

emuron a akomwa/ ngakomwae	emuron of the termite mound
emuron/amuron/ngimurok	Turkana traditional religious specialist m/f/pl
engalata ngitunga	to cheat people
engeso	medicinal stick (bitter, not swallowed)
enupit	believe
erujae	dreams
etaba	tobacco
etal/ngitalio	laws/traditions
etau	heart/spirit
eteem	separate sleeping place for *emuron*
etereku	greed/jealousy
etio/auono	hollow gourd
etuwae	exorcises
eutoro etau	removing animal heart while still beating
ewatakin ngakipi	blessing of water
ewosakin/etujukok emunyen	spreading ochre over body
ikwaan	the same
italiunitoe	sacred, holy
itwaan	person
kang (apakang)	my (as in "my father")
katuwa	ritual ability to remove something
kerakar ngitunga	cause people to faint
kipio	struggling
kititik	suffocating ritual
loakwan	white
loarengan/lokopriat	red
lonyang	yellow
lopaekeng, ekone	my friend, friend
lopus	blue
lotumkol/lokirion	black
luaiteni	that which is true
luajokak/naajokak	someone/something who is good
luaronok/naaronok	someone/something who is bad, evil
naju	sleep
nakamaran	sister in law
ngakiro naaronok	bad things
ngamaliteny	intestines
ngamaniat	gardens

Appendix F: Glossary of Common Turkana Terms Used in this Study

ngaropiae	money
ngesi	him/her/it (3rd person sing.)
ngibaren	livestock
ngichen	problems, troubles
ngikaram	ancestors
ngikarikok a ngikanisae	elders/leaders of the churches
ngikarikok/ngikasikou/ etategon/etetamen	leaders/elders in the community
ngikito	medicinal sticks
ngikujit	chyme (stomach contents)
ngimurok a akou (ngakeis pl)	emuron of the head
ngingomwa	sorghum
ngingoroko	bandits
ngitunga	people
ngitunga lu nyeyenete	people who do not know
Ngiturkana	the Turkana people
ngoomwon	number four (common symbolic number)
tongeere	disemboweling an animal while alive
tongol	to slaughter by cutting the throat

APPENDIX G

Turkana Christian Survey Results

G.A: A SAMPLE SURVEY RESPONSE (TWO PAGES)

> DO NOT WRITE YOUR NAME ON THIS PAPER
>
> Ngakiro ta anu ngadi naaronok asubakis ngimurok alore kon kolong a angorot ka ngirwa lu?
>
> *Itatamete ngituya akiwap erot kech toaribu ka akitusub ngitanga ngakiro narenak*
>
> 10. Do you have any family members (mothers, fathers, aunts, uncles, brothers, sisters, wives, husband, children) who still visit the ngimurok?
> Iyakasi ngiyenet kon ngidi: ngitunga a awi kus (itiokon, apakon, taeyakon, taamaekon, talokaatokon tanakaatokon, ngaberu, ngikiliok ta ngide kon) lu eringa eloseenete lomurok a?   *Mam*
>
> 11. Do you know of anyone in your church who still visits the ngimurok? Do NOT give any names.
> Eyakasi ngitunga ngidi alokanisa kon lu eringa eloseenete lomurok a? Nyimaru ngirora kech.   *Ee*
>
> 12. Before you were a Christian, how many times did you visit an emuron on your own or with family members?
> CIRCLE ONE: Ngalosiet: (0,)   1-5,   6-10,   more than 10 times?
> Kolong eringa iyong nyeliworo ekiristoit, ilosit iyong lomuron alowae kon kori ka ngitunga a awi kon?
>
> 13. What were the main reasons for visiting the ngimurok then?
> Ilosit iyong lomuron kotere nyo? Nyo ngakiro naapolok kiyarito iyong kori esi inaa?   *Ngalosene Jiik*
>
> 14. After becoming a Christian, how many times have you visited an emuron on your own or with other people?
> CIRCLE ONE: (0,)   1-5,   6-10,   more than 10 times?
> Arumoret a araun ekristoit, ilot iyong lomuron ngalosiet ngaik iyong bon ka ngitunga a awi kon dang?
>
> 15. What does your church teach about the ngimurok?
> Ngakiro anu itatami ekanisa kidiama ngimurok?   *Ngikalickek, kotere nyinusosi ngakiro na ekakasi ngaka akuj*
>
> 16. From your understanding, what are the specific practices that ngimurok do?
> Ngakiro anu esubeente ngimurok itemem ka ayenut kon?   *Esubete ngakiro na era ngaka njipean. nikataapakech*
>
> 17. How do the ngimurok learn these practices? Where does their power and wisdom come from?
> Itatamasi ngimurok ngakiro na esubete nu kwai? Aliwae itorunit agogongu ka aosou kech?   *Lokipe*
>
> 18. Are there any stories of great ngimurok that you know?
> Eyakasi ngikoyo ngidi a ngimurok aluapolok iyeni iyong a?   *Apupi kolong ngakiro alokenyo — bes atubl angeani kitunit ngikaltek neni*
>
> 19. Can a pastor or a missionary be an emuron?   *Ee*
> Epedori epastait kori emeanara aliwor emuron a?
>
> 20. Do you know any ngimurok who are followers of Jesus? Do they still do the work of an emuron?   *Mam*
> Iyeni iyong ngimurok ngidi lu eraakasi ngikewapak a Yesu a? Eringa kechi esubete etich a emuron a?
>
> 21. Are there any ngimurok who only do evil practices?   *Ee*
> Eyakasi ngimurok ngidi lu esubete ngakiro na aronok make, ikote akapel ka asuba?
>
> 22. What is the difference between emuron and ekapilan?   *Sinyae emuron Ekasuban ngesi etich keng. ebikinit eyuunes kiwapa Yesu*
> Nyoni etiakit akiroit be emuron ka ekapilan?
>
> 23. Are there any other stories about the ngimurok you would like to tell us? Would you be willing to let us record the story?
> Eyakasi ngikoyo ngidi a ngimurok lu isaki iyong akisisakin sua a? Ipedori iyong achamun sua kiwaakini ngakiro nakisisakinit iyong sua narediola?   *Ee*

230

Appendix G: Turkana Christian Survey Results   231

Questionnaire for Turkana Christians concerning *Ngimurok*
Ngakingiseta Kidiama Ngimurok – Kotere Ngikristoi Luturkana

DO NOT WRITE YOUR NAME ON THIS PAPER

1-27 7.36

These questions are to help us understand:
Who the Turkana *ngimurok* are today.
What influence they continue to have in Turkana communities. What the church teaches about *ngimurok*.
What types of problems Christians still take to the *ngimurok*.

Kingarakinete ngoni ngakingiseta nugu akiyen:
Ikokinite ngitunga eyenete itwaan ni erai emuron ai?
Ikokinete ngitunga eyenete kechi alokiding ngitunga luche ai?
Nyo ngakiro naapolok esubete ngimurok anadakarin a Ngiturkana? Ngakiro na itatami ekanisa kidiama ngimurok.
Ngichan ta alu eyanarete Ngikristoi lomurok.

All answers you provide will remain confidential. Your name will **not** be used when the results of this study are written. There are no wrong answers. Please be as honest as you can so that we can learn about the *ngimurok*. The only wrong answers are if you hide the truth. This is not a government of Kenya survey. This is not a church survey. This survey is for the research I, Kip "Erot" Lines, am doing in school at Asbury Theological Seminary.

Idongokinete ngakiro na kiruoro ngoni kane kiding kang ka iyong. Emam itwaan elimuni ekiro kon moi igirio ngakiro nu. Emam ngatachunet erakasei ngaka alioko. Tolimokinae kare ngakiro na iteni sodi atopedosi akitatama kidiama ngimurok. Meere nangolenyang a Kenya ingitanari ngakingiseta nu. Meere tani ngakingiseta nu ngaka ekanisa. Nakaneni erakasi ngakingiseta nu ngaka esukul kang, lo enyaritae Asbury Theological Seminary.

AGE / NGIKARU KON [40]   GENDER / EKILE KORI ABERU [Ekile]   CLAN / EMECHAR [Ngiduya]

HOME AREA / AKWAP KON [Napusimoru]

1. Mark all you have done:

   ASAPAN / ISAPANIT IYONG A? [Ee]   TURKANA AKUUTA? [ ]   AKINYONYO? [ ]

   KIBATISO ALOKANISA A? [Ee]   AKUUTA ALOKANISA? [Enye]

2. What church do you attend?
   Iloseene iyong lokanisa ali? [C.C.C. NAPUSIMORU]

3. How long have you been a believer in Jesus Christ?
   Irai iyong ekanupan a Yesu Kristo akisiakin ori? [1820 1982]

4. Are you a church leader? [Ee] If so, what is your position in the church?
   Irai iyong ekarikon a ekanisa a? Ani kikote neni, irai iyong nyo, kori nyo isubi iyong? [Etatami]

5. In your home area are there any ngimurok? [Ee] Do you know who they are and where they live?
   Eyakasi ngimurok ngidi lore lo ilomit iyong a? Iyeni iyong atamar tangae kechi anabo aliwae elomito kechi? [Napusimoru]

6. Do you know people who continue to visit the ngimurok?
   Iyeni iyong keyakasi ngiturkana ngidi eringa eloseenete lomurok a? [Ee]

7. What are some reasons you think people visit the ngimurok? [Kotere akitajoko]
   Itamit iyong atamar nyo eloseeneto ngitunga lomurok?

8. What are the good things the ngimurok have done in your area in the past and now?
   Ngakiro ta anu ngadi ajokak asubakis ngimurok alore kon kolong angorot ka ngirwa lu?

   [Etoweyete kolong aren angi turukana make, Abeyo ayaunite akitu]

9.

G.B

Complete Survey Responses

Which category below includes your age?

Answer Options	Response Percent	Response Count
15 or younger	0.0%	0
16-30	63.4%	45
31-45	22.5%	16
46-60	12.7%	9
61 or older	1.4%	1
answered question		71
skipped question		0

What is your gender?

Answer Options	Response Percent	Response Count
Male	57.7%	41
Female	42.3%	30
answered question		71
skipped question		0

What is your clan (emachar) name?

Answer Options	Response Percent	Response Count
Ebilait	4.2%	3
Edochait	1.4%	1
Eduyait	5.6%	4
Ekatekit	2.8%	2
Emacharkotait	4.2%	3
Emeturanait	28.2%	20
Emosorokoit	12.7%	9
Epongait	8.5%	6

What is your clan (emachar) name?

Answer Options	Response Percent	Response Count
Epuchoit	12.7%	9
Esigerit	9.9%	7
Ngikemoroki	2.8%	2
Ngitaparokolong	1.4%	1
Turkana	1.4%	1
No Answer	4.2%	3
answered question		71
skipped question		0

What is your home area?

Answer Options	Response Percent	Response Count
Kangirisae	18.3%	13
Kaitepi	4.2%	3
Napusimoru	32.4%	23
Nakaalei	1.4%	1
Kitale	1.4%	1
Natorube	1.4%	1
Kakimat	1.4%	1
Lodwar	12.7%	9
Nakor	4.2%	3
Nabulon	1.4%	1
Kalokol	1.4%	1
Kenam-Kemer	1.4%	1
Kangatosa	1.4%	1
Nakurio	1.4%	1
Lokwarangikaleso	5.6%	4
Natome	1.4%	1
Kodirin	1.4%	1
Kanaan	1.4%	1
Kosipir	1.4%	1
Lokori	1.4%	1
Nadoto	1.4%	1
Loupwala	1.4%	1
answered question		71
skipped question		0

Mark all that you have done:

Answer Options	Response Percent	Response Count
Asapan	30.0%	21
Turkana Akuuta	31.4%	22
Akinyonyo	47.1%	33
Kibatiso Alokanisa	98.6%	69
Akuuta Alokanisa	8.6%	6
answered question		70
skipped question		1

What church do you attend?

Answer Options	Response Percent	Response Count
Community Christian Church	94.3%	66
Anglican Church of Kenya	1.4%	1
Catholic Church	1.4%	1
AIC (Africa Inland Church)	1.4%	1
Miracle Revival Fellowship Pentecostal Church	1.4%	1
answered question		70
skipped question		1

How long have you been a believer in Jesus Christ?

Answer Options	Response Percent	Response Count
1-5 years	4.3%	3
6-10 years	25.7%	18
11-15 years	31.4%	22
16-20 years	18.6%	13
more than 20 years	20.0%	14
answered question		70
skipped question		1

Are you a church leader?

Answer Options	Response Percent	Response Count
Yes	60.6%	43
No	39.4%	28
answered question		71
skipped question		0

If yes, what is your position in the church?

Answer Options	Response Percent	Response Count
Deacon (akingarakinan) helper at church activities	11.6%	5
Pastor (epastait)	18.6%	8
Choir Director (Etatami Ekoya)	9.3%	4
Choir Member (Ekaeon)	4.7%	2
Treasurer (etingit esadak)	7.0%	3
Youth leader (chaiman, secretary)	7.0%	3
Healer (eketedekan)	2.3%	1
Woman leader (akimat ekanisa)	7.0%	3
Elder (overseer, ekasukout a ekanisa)	9.3%	4
Teacher (etatami)	7.0%	3
Secretary	7.0%	3
Bible Study Leader	2.3%	1
Usher	2.3%	1
Church Leader (general)	4.7%	2
answered question		43
skipped question		28

Are there any ngimurok in your home area?

Answer Options	Response Percent	Response Count
Yes	93.0%	66
No	7.0%	5
answered question		71
skipped question		0

Do you know where they live?

Answer Options	Response Percent	Response Count
Yes	78.9%	56
No	12.7%	9
Everywhere (wadang)	5.6%	4
Blank	2.8%	2
answered question		71
skipped question		0

Do you know people who continue to visit the ngimurok?

Answer Options	Response Percent	Response Count
Yes	87.3%	62
No	12.7%	9
answered question		71
skipped question		0

What are some reasons you think people still visit the ngimurok?

Answer Options	Response Percent	Response Count
Drought	4.2%	3
Rain (Akiru)	26.8%	19
Edeke (To be healed from sickness)	60.6%	43
Edeke a ngibaren	4.2%	3
Ngimoe	1.4%	1
Ariwoe (To protect themselves)	7.0%	5
Ariwoe a edeke	1.4%	1
Ariwo a emoit	1.4%	1
Wealth	9.9%	7
Tongop ikoku, Children (want)	7.0%	5
Garden blessing (planting time)	1.4%	1
Tosub itwaan niche (To witch others) (curses)	2.8%	2
Curse someone they hate	1.4%	1
Akiar ngitunga luche (to kill others)	2.8%	2
Revenge	0.0%	0

G.B: Complete Survey Responses

What are some reasons you think people still visit the ngimurok?

Answer Options	Response Percent	Response Count
To Appease their Gods	1.4%	1
To seek divine intervention	1.4%	1
Cleansing	1.4%	1
Blessings	2.8%	2
Job Seeking	5.6%	4
Abanganut Kech (They're Crazy)	5.6%	4
Amuronot (divination)	1.4%	1
Awoyakin Aurere	1.4%	1
Asakete Akiyar	1.4%	1
To worship them	1.4%	1
To worship unliving spirit	1.4%	1
Akuj nasubuna akingarakino (for help from idols)	1.4%	1
To solve problems	12.7%	9
I don't know	2.8%	2
Power	2.8%	2
Akinup (Because they believe)	2.8%	2
answered question		71
skipped question		0

What are the good things the ngimurok have done in your area in the past and now?

Answer Options	Response Percent	Response Count
Bring rain	33.3%	23
Togol edeke kotere ariwo (end sickness with ritual)	4.3%	3
Heal sickness	11.6%	8
Akisidoun itwaan (help with birth)	1.4%	1
Help a woman have a child	2.9%	2
Take sickness from the animals	2.9%	2
Protect from enemies	4.3%	3
Long ago they heard from God, but not now	5.8%	4
Help people take the livestock of their enemies	1.4%	1
Protect against raiding	1.4%	1
Keep people from doing wrong in an area through fear of revealing secrets	1.4%	1

G.B: Complete Survey Responses

What are the good things the ngimurok have done in your area in the past and now?

Answer Options	Response Percent	Response Count
Go against God's commands	1.4%	1
Destroy people's plans and their houses	1.4%	1
They destroy people	1.4%	1
Akidwar (prophesy in general)	5.8%	4
Amuronot (divination in general)	1.4%	1
They solve problems	2.9%	2
Blessed for jobs and people got jobs	1.4%	1
Bless the young to be vibrant	1.4%	1
Prophesy as a business for earning a living and enrich their families	1.4%	1
Reveal problems through sandals and intestines	1.4%	1
Nothing Good, No	34.8%	24
They are false	4.3%	3
I don't know	2.9%	2
No answer	13.0%	9
answered question		69
skipped question		2

What are the BAD things the ngimurok have done in your area in the past and now?

Answer Options	Response Percent	Response Count
Ngilam (cursing with words)	13.0%	9
Akisub (cursing/sorcery with objects)	10.1%	7
Esubete ngitunga taara (killed people with akisub)	2.9%	2
Dream things that were going to happen	1.4%	1
Rob people of their animals through emunyen rituals (edmete ngitunga ngibaren kech)	11.6%	8
Erikasi ngibaren (finish/destroy/eat people's animals)	7.2%	5
Abused people's wealth	5.8%	4
Engalate ngitunga (deceive people, lie to people)	11.6%	8
Iratanakinete kechi ngitunga alokanisa (fool people in the church)	1.4%	1
Akiwas ngide (takes the first share of bride-wealth)	1.4%	1
Corrupt, unjust, even when client dies they still take payment	2.9%	2

G.B: Complete Survey Responses

What are the BAD things the ngimurok have done in your area in the past and now?

Answer Options	Response Percent	Response Count
They teach people to follow their dark path	1.4%	1
They have magic and power from the devil	0.0%	0
Make people do bad things	1.4%	1
Made it rain	1.4%	1
Say it's going to rain but it is false	1.4%	1
Itooliyarito ngitunga (poison/kill people)	1.4%	1
Aara ngitunga (kill people)	10.1%	7
Cause people to become sick/die through magic	5.8%	4
Bewitch people and their property	2.9%	2
Opposing community development, ie education, water	1.4%	1
The land is cursed due to their activities	1.4%	1
They compete with God	2.9%	2
They kill children for rain	1.4%	1
Interfere with livelihood and lifestyle of the people	2.9%	2
They overcharge their clients	1.4%	1
They accuse people who believe the Word of God	1.4%	1
They predict bad things so people will come and pay them for protection	1.4%	1
Yes	1.4%	1
No	7.2%	5
I don't know	4.3%	3
No Answer	18.8%	13
answered question		69
skipped question		2

Do you have any family members who still visit the ngimurok?

Answer Options	Response Percent	Response Count
Yes	54.4%	37
No	39.7%	27
No Answer	5.9%	4
answered question		68
skipped question		3

G.B: Complete Survey Responses

Do you know of anyone in your church who still visits the ngimurok?

Answer Options	Response Percent	Response Count
Yes	71.4%	50
No	28.6%	20
No Answer	0.0%	0
answered question		70
skipped question		1

Before you were a Christian, how many times did you visit an emuron on your own or with family members?

Answer Options	Response Percent	Response Count
0	36.4%	24
1-5	34.8%	23
6-10	1.5%	1
more than 10 times	27.3%	18
answered question		66
skipped question		5

What were the main reasons for visiting the ngimurok then?

Answer Options	Response Percent	Response Count
sickness (healing)	52.3%	34
blessing	6.2%	4
seeking wealth	3.1%	2
because of poverty	1.5%	1
break a curse	1.5%	1
dig out a curse	1.5%	1
to solve a problem (reveal a secret)	4.6%	3
rain	4.6%	3
protection from enemies (ariwo a emoit)	3.1%	2
protect from danger	3.1%	2
my parents took me because I had eye problems	1.5%	1
sickness in my teeth	1.5%	1
sickness of my family	1.5%	1
sickness of children	1.5%	1

G.B: Complete Survey Responses

What were the main reasons for visiting the ngimurok then?

Answer Options	Response Percent	Response Count
sickness of my father	1.5%	1
ekuutan (scorpion bite/sting)	1.5%	1
business, job	1.5%	1
to find help	1.5%	1
I went with my father	1.5%	1
problems of drought (akamu)	3.1%	2
to be made clean (cleansing, purification, amook)	1.5%	1
I never went to the home of an emuron	0.0%	0
I was sick for a long time (edeke loapolon)	1.5%	1
I wanted a child	1.5%	1
I don't know	3.1%	2
N/A	23.1%	15
answered question		65
skipped question		6

After becoming a Christian, how many times did you visit an emuron on your own or with family members?

Answer Options	Response Percent	Response Count
0	93.1%	54
1-5	6.9%	4
6-10	0.0%	0
more than 10 times	0.0%	0
answered question		58
skipped question		13

What does your church teach about the ngimurok?

Answer Options	Response Percent	Response Count
Toyunos (be saved)	7.2%	5
Believe in God	1.4%	1
Only pray to God	2.9%	2
It's good for them to come know the true God	4.3%	3
That people should not visit ngimurok (kimiekisi)	20.3%	14

G.B: Complete Survey Responses

What does your church teach about the ngimurok?

Answer Options	Response Percent	Response Count
They destroy people	7.2%	5
They cannot help	1.4%	1
To be against their law	1.4%	1
Do not follow them	5.8%	4
Going to the emuron is worshiping man-made gods (ngakujo nasubuna)	1.4%	1
Akuj bon erai emuron loapolon (Only God is the great emuron)	1.4%	1
Jesus is the true, great emuron	4.3%	3
Their blessings are seasonal	1.4%	1
They are false prophets	15.9%	11
They are false teachers	1.4%	1
They are evil witches (ngikapalak)	1.4%	1
The church teaches the goodness and badness of ngimurok	1.4%	1
To love them	1.4%	1
Try to teach and save them from being lost	4.3%	3
Pray against their gods	1.4%	1
They lie to people	26.1%	18
They do not know God or Jesus	1.4%	1
They don't follow the ways of Jesus (ngitalio a Kristo)	1.4%	1
They want to turn people away from God	1.4%	1
They are against God	1.4%	1
Be against them	2.9%	2
They usurp the praise intended for God	1.4%	1
Go to church, not to the ngimurok	0.0%	0
They turn people away from coming to God	1.4%	1
They lead to darkness	1.4%	1
The church refuses what the ngimurok tell them to do	1.4%	1
Watch out for divination (amuronot) because it brings many problems to the body	1.4%	1
They are pagans	1.4%	1
They are business people	1.4%	1
They are not the emuron of God that we should pray to	1.4%	1
Eroko (evil, bad)	10.1%	7

G.B: Complete Survey Responses

What does your church teach about the ngimurok?

Answer Options	Response Percent	Response Count
The word of God keeps them away (ibatarito anakiroit Akuj)	1.4%	1
Don't go to them "itemem ka aberu na alelete ngaakot"	2.9%	2
answered question		69
skipped question		2

From your understanding, what are the specific practices that ngimurok do?

Answer Options	Response Percent	Response Count
Iosee ngitunga (akiwos)	7.5%	5
Akiwos ngide	1.5%	1
Ilamlamete (ngilam, cursing)	13.4%	9
emuronot	16.4%	11
ngamunyin (akiwos emunyen)	10.4%	7
Apiar ngitunga	4.5%	3
Akisub (esubete, ngikasubak)	13.4%	9
Akigol ngibaren	3.0%	2
Akisimuj ngikaram	1.5%	1
Akiar itwaan	13.4%	9
Amook	1.5%	1
Bless bandits (warriors, war)	4.5%	3
Curse people and the land	1.5%	1
Instruct to kill ariwo	1.5%	1
They kill ariwo	7.5%	5
Akiru	11.9%	8
They treat people using herbs	0.0%	0
They stop outbreak of disease	1.5%	1
They treat the sick	6.0%	4
They tie a symbol on your body	1.5%	1
They are false	7.5%	5
They bewitch people	1.5%	1
They foretell the future	1.5%	1
They read shoes	4.5%	3
They read tobacco	1.5%	1

From your understanding, what are the specific practices that ngimurok do?

Answer Options	Response Percent	Response Count
They read intestines	1.5%	1
They direct rituals to be performed	3.0%	2
They deceive people (mislead)	11.9%	8
They pretend to do rituals that bring rain	1.5%	1
They are false blessing to people	1.5%	1
They pray to false Gods	1.5%	1
They akisub akwaan with water and sticks (ngikito)	1.5%	1
They walk at night hours	3.0%	2
They do the things of evil spirits (ngipean)	1.5%	1
Destroy people's plan	1.5%	1
They use red ocher (emunyen)	4.5%	3
Use white mud	1.5%	1
Use yellow mud	1.5%	1
They use ngikujit	3.0%	2
They are medicine men	1.5%	1
They are mediators	1.5%	1
They enter graves and speak to spirits (ngikaram)	1.5%	1
I don't know	0.0%	0
No Answer	7.5%	5

How do the ngimurok learn these practices? Where does their power and wisdom come from?

Answer Options	Response Percent	Response Count
Lokipe (ekipe, biblical satan, devil, evil one)	9.8%	6
Lopean (ngipean, spirits/ancestors)	18.0%	11
Ngikaram (spirits/ancestors)	11.5%	7
Ngakujo (gods)	9.8%	6
From their fathers (ancestors)	32.8%	20
From their dreams	6.6%	4
From their clan	1.6%	1
From other ngimurok	3.3%	2
Given by God	13.1%	8
God called them (Akuj alimokinit)	4.9%	3
It was a gift of God but ngimurok use it wrongly	3.3%	2
Through practices (naesubete)	3.3%	2

How do the ngimurok learn these practices? Where does their power and wisdom come from?

Answer Options	Response Percent	Response Count
I don't know	1.6%	1
From their divination (namuroe)	3.3%	2
From throwing sandals and receiving food	1.6%	1
From praying to idols	3.3%	2
From themselves (nakesi)	4.9%	3
From their strength (agogong)	3.3%	2
From their fame/greatness (anapolosio)	1.6%	1
From their own wisdom (aosou)	1.6%	1
They pay a fee to a person having powers and then receive	1.6%	1
answered question		61
skipped question		10

Are there any stories of great ngimurok that you know?

Answer Options	Response Percent	Response Count
Atorongimoe (emoit)	1.5%	1
Lokinee (emoit)	1.5%	1
Anangakinoi (akine)	2.9%	2
Kamarakwaan/Nguupe (Chaama's Father- akinei)	2.9%	2
Kuwom (rain)	1.5%	1
Lokinei (rain, sickness)	1.5%	1
Eperon (ariwo against ngimoe)	2.9%	2
Lokerio (totub anam)	2.9%	2
Lokerio (totub ngesi aberu, tolem ikoku yau nawi keng)	1.5%	1
Apasogol (protected land, killed ariwo to keep ngimoe away)	1.5%	1
Lokorijem	2.9%	2
Akilerio	1.5%	1
Lodip	1.5%	1
Yes	36.8%	25
No	32.4%	22
No Answer	17.6%	12
answered question		68
skipped question		3

Can a pastor or a missionary be an emuron?

Answer Options	Response Percent	Response Count
Yes (Ee, epedori)	31.9%	22
No (mam, nyepedori)	52.2%	36
Yes they are Emuron a Akuj (ngimurok a akai a Akuj, God's prophet)	7.2%	5
No, unless he is not strong in his faith	1.4%	1
No, nyeliwor loyuun (ngimurok can't become those saved)	1.4%	1
Yes, some carry out simultaneously	0.0%	0
Yes, if dependent on the direction of the Holy Spirit	1.4%	1
Yes, if only God has given him that amuronot	1.4%	1
Yes, if the heart/spirit is divided in two	1.4%	1
Yes, if he has strong faith in God he is able to see things and pray for them	1.4%	1
Yes, some can be false prophets who hide in the church	1.4%	1
answered question		69
skipped question		2

Do you know any ngimurok who are followers of Jesus who still do the work of an emuron?

Answer Options	Response Percent	Response Count
Yes	42.3%	30
Yes, they are followers of Jesus, but no longer work as an emuron.	19.7%	14
No	26.8%	19
No, I knew one but he backslided.	1.4%	1
No Answer	9.9%	7
answered question		71
skipped question		0

Are there any ngimurok who only do evil practices (for example, akapel ka asuba)?

Answer Options	Response Percent	Response Count
Yes (Eya, eyakasi)	90.1%	64
No	1.4%	1
No Answer	8.5%	6
answered question		71
skipped question		0

What is the difference between emuron and ekapilan?

Answer Options	Response Percent	Response Count
Emuron is an ekedwaran (propecies)	14.3%	10
Emuron is one who irujae (dreams)	14.3%	10
Emuron uses ngikito	1.4%	1
Emuron does emurae	7.1%	5
Emuron deceives people (ekelaman)	4.3%	3
Emuron is ekaaran (killer)	4.3%	3
Emuron has power from ngikaram (ancestors)	2.9%	2
Emuron does things that make a person go against God's will	1.4%	1
Emuron goes against God's command	1.4%	1
Emuron worships gods	1.4%	1
Emuron makes people sick	4.3%	3
Emuron helps sick people	2.9%	2
Emuron eats people's goats	1.4%	1
Emuron is an ekasuban	8.6%	6
Emuron can make something happen	1.4%	1
Emuron lives among people	1.4%	1
Emuron becomes angry because of etau	1.4%	1
Emuron wishes people both good and bad	2.9%	2
Emuron has demon power to kill and to bless	2.9%	2
Emuron can solve problems	1.4%	1
Emuron is a diviner (English)	2.9%	2
Emuron is good- God gifted	1.4%	1
Refuses the words of God, wants own word to be true	1.4%	1

G.B: Complete Survey Responses

What is the difference between emuron and ekapilan?

Answer Options	Response Percent	Response Count
Ekaplian is a witch (English)	2.9%	2
Ekapilan only does evil (bad, evil gifted)	4.3%	3
Ekapilan is a witchdoctor (English)	1.4%	1
Ekapilan does akiyeng, ekayangan ngitunga lukatoak (cuts up dead people, skins dead people)	30.0%	21
Ekapilan has devil eye, evil eye	1.4%	1
Ekapilan does akirakar, ekaaran (killing)	21.4%	15
Ekapilan does ngilam (bewitcher)	2.9%	2
Ekapilan does asuba, ekasuban (witchcraft)	4.3%	3
Ekapilan anyam ngitunga (eats people)	5.7%	4
Ekapilan is ekirimrimon (comes around at death, smells death, wants elos a itwaan)	5.7%	4
Ekapilan wants sick people to die	2.9%	2
Ekapilan walks naked at night (also, nightrunner)	4.3%	3
Ekapilan lives alomoding (in the wilderness)	1.4%	1
There is no difference between them.	18.6%	13
I'm not sure.	1.4%	1
No Answer	8.6%	6
answered question		70
skipped question		1

G.C

Graphs of Key Survey Responses

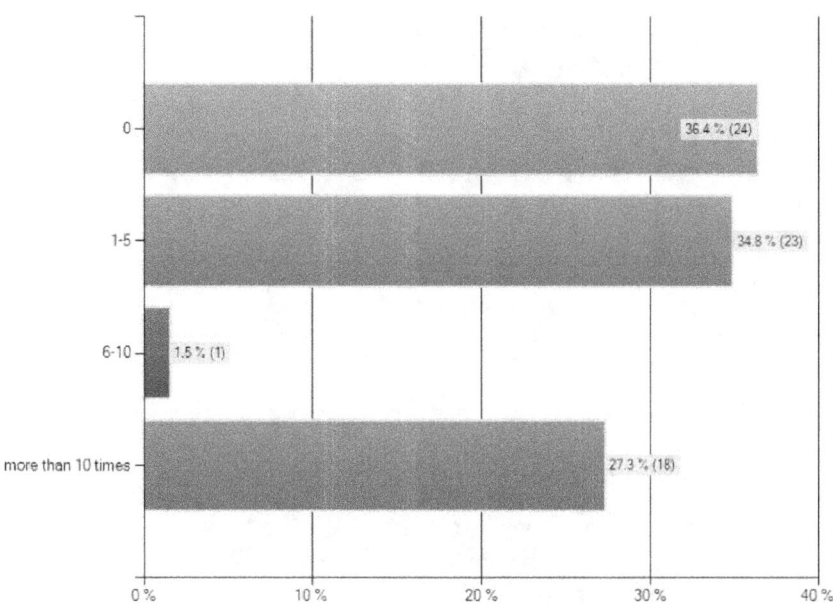

G.C: Graphs of Key Survey Responses

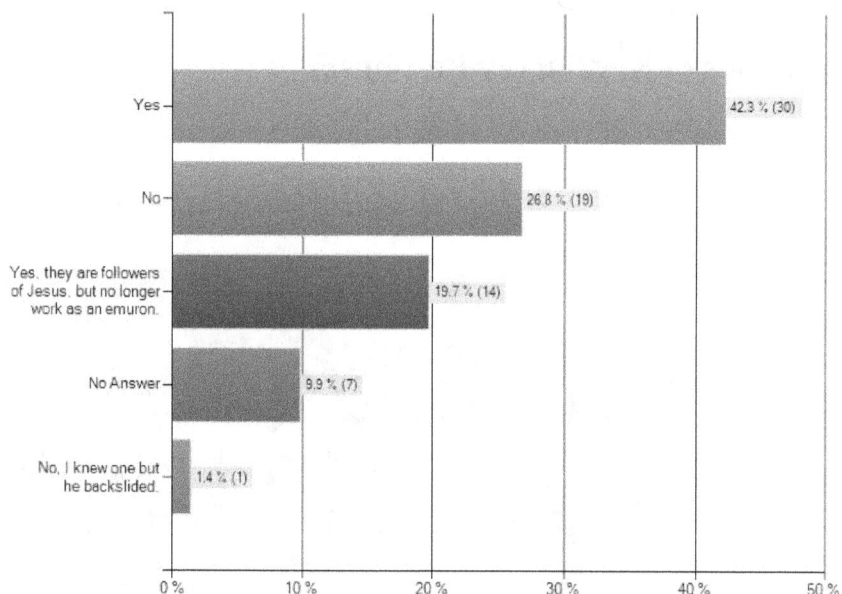

Do you know any ngimurok who are followers of Jesus who still do the work of an emuron?

- Yes — 42.3 % (30)
- No — 26.8 % (19)
- Yes, they are followers of Jesus, but no longer work as an emuron — 19.7 % (14)
- No Answer — 9.9 % (7)
- No, I knew one but he backslided — 1.4 % (1)

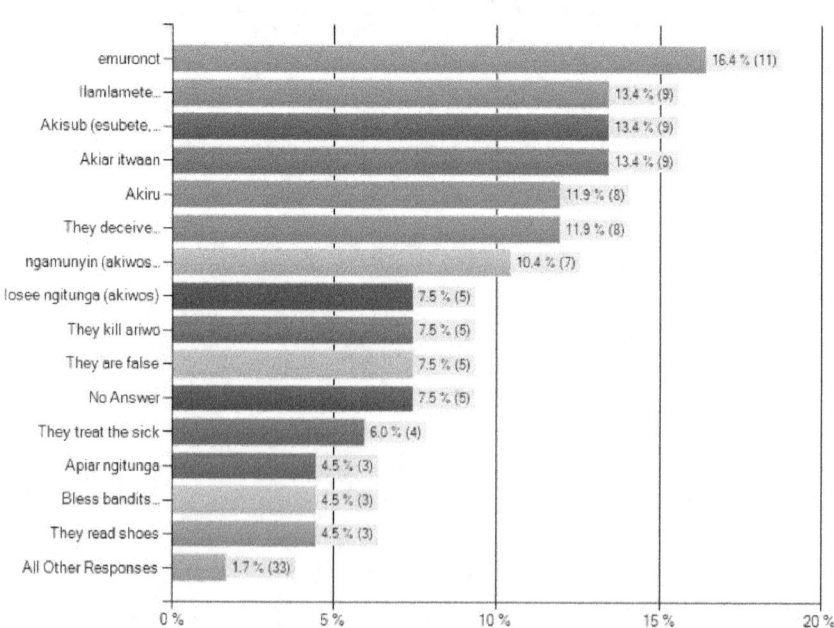

From your understanding, what are the specific practices that ngimurok do?

- emuronot — 16.4 % (11)
- Ilamlamete — 13.4 % (9)
- Akisub (esubete) — 13.4 % (9)
- Akiar itwaan — 13.4 % (9)
- Akiru — 11.9 % (8)
- They deceive — 11.9 % (8)
- ngamunyin (akiwos) — 10.4 % (7)
- Iosee ngitunga (akiwos) — 7.5 % (5)
- They kill ariwo — 7.5 % (5)
- They are false — 7.5 % (5)
- No Answer — 7.5 % (5)
- They treat the sick — 6.0 % (4)
- Apiar ngitunga — 4.5 % (3)
- Bless bandits — 4.5 % (3)
- They read shoes — 4.5 % (3)
- All Other Responses — 1.7 % (33)

G.C: Graphs of Key Survey Responses 251

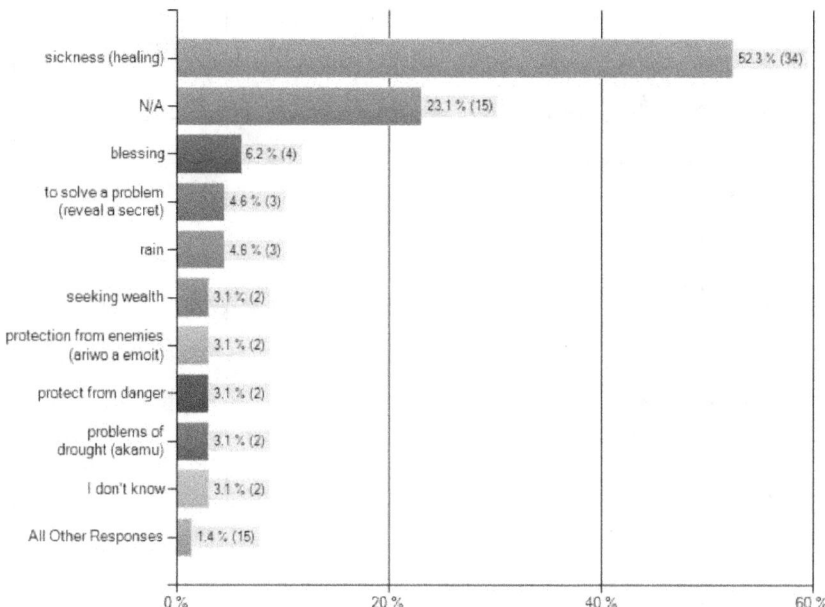

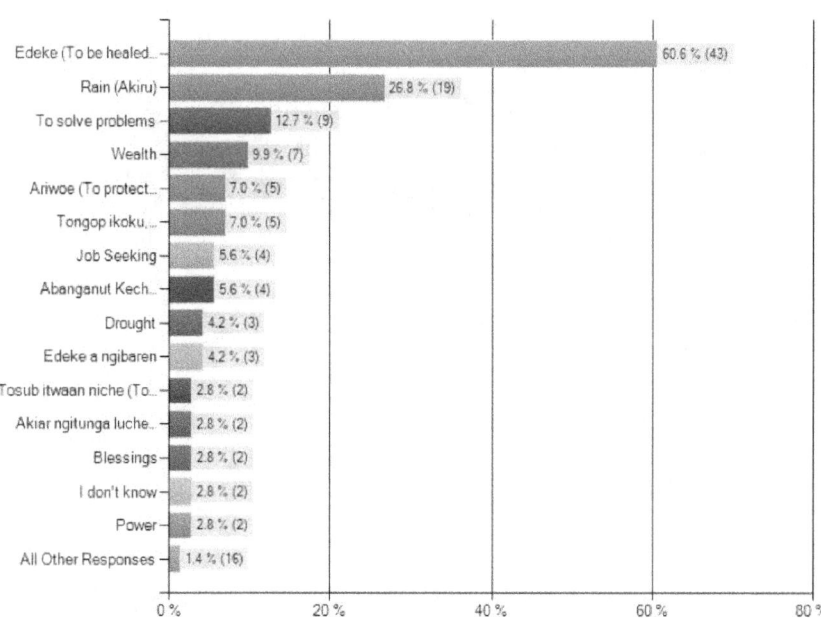

G.C: Graphs of Key Survey Responses

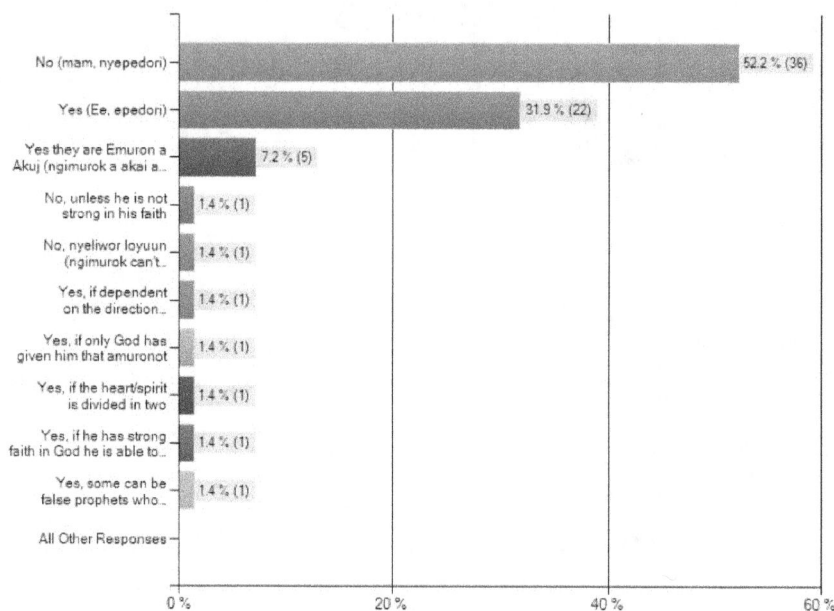

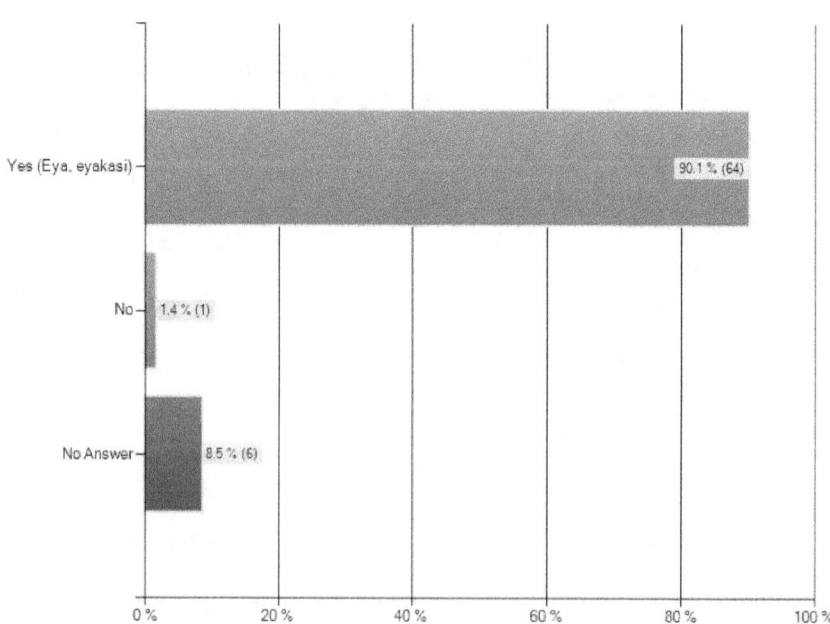

G.C: *Graphs of Key Survey Responses* 253

Do you know of anyone in your church who still visits the ngimurok?

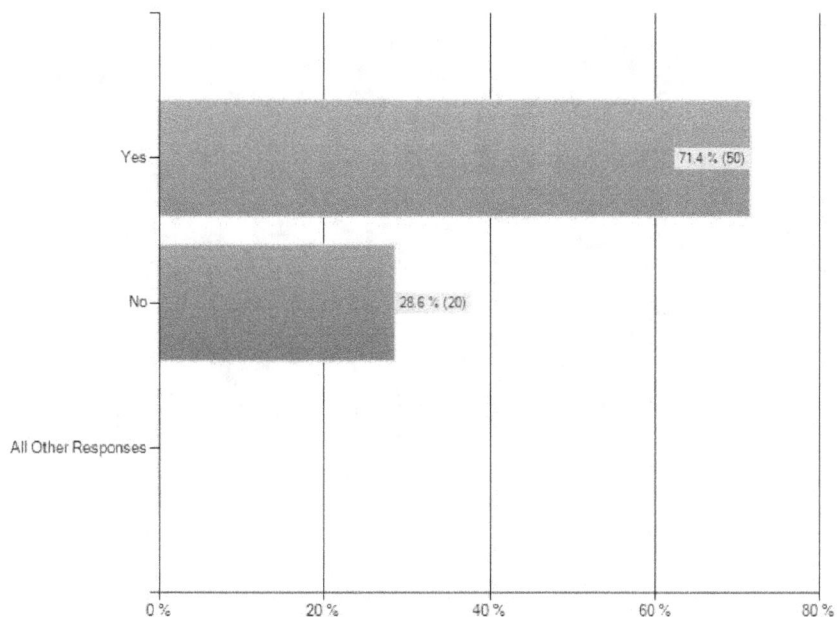

Are there any ngimurok in your home area?

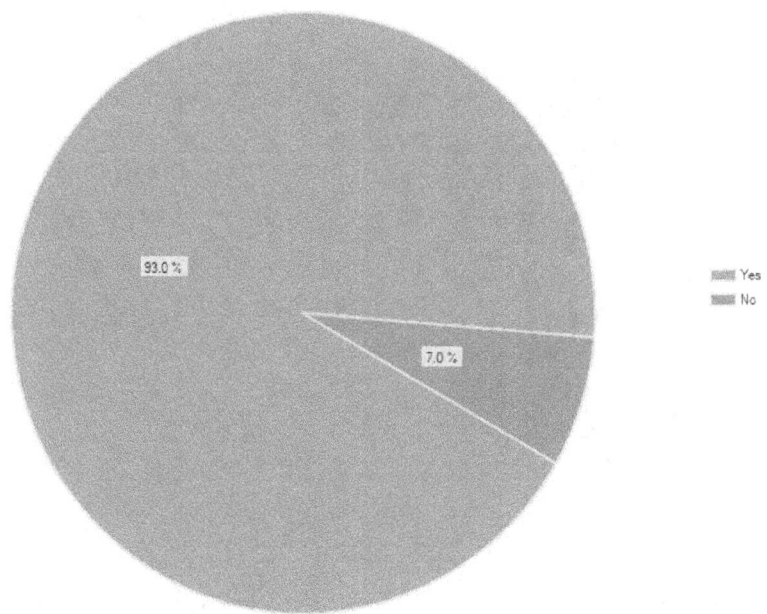

254   G.C: *Graphs of Key Survey Responses*

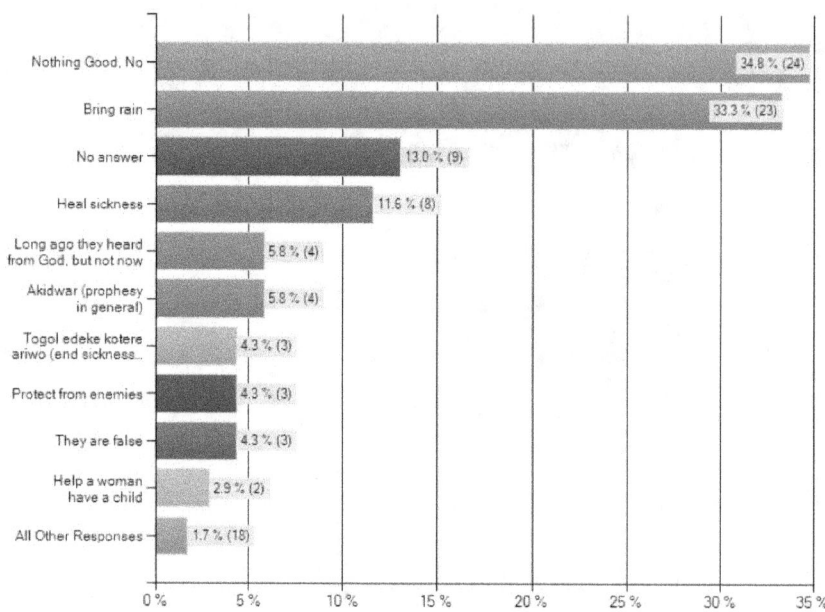

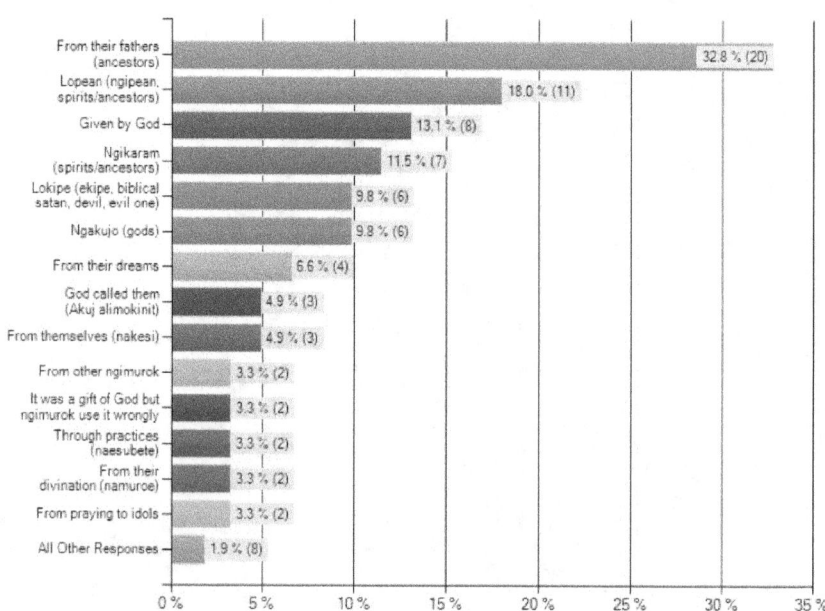

G.C: *Graphs of Key Survey Responses* 255

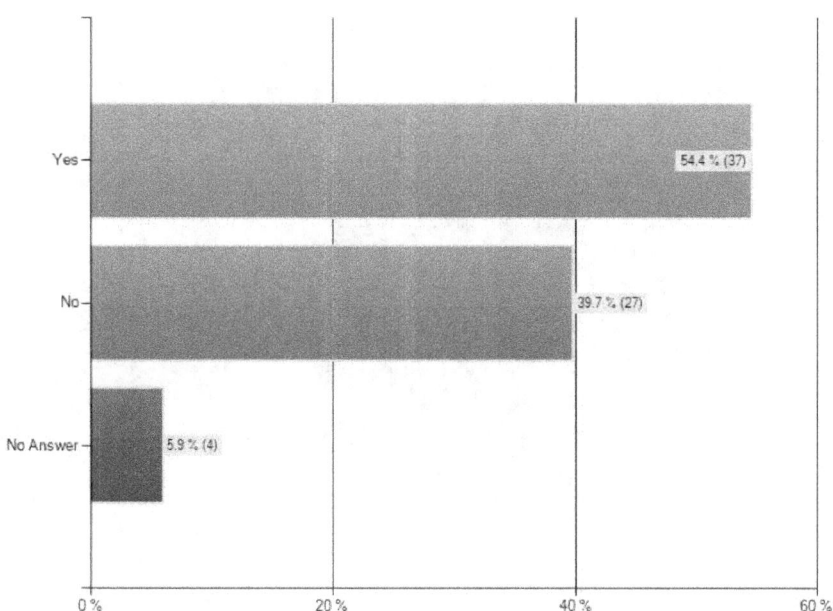

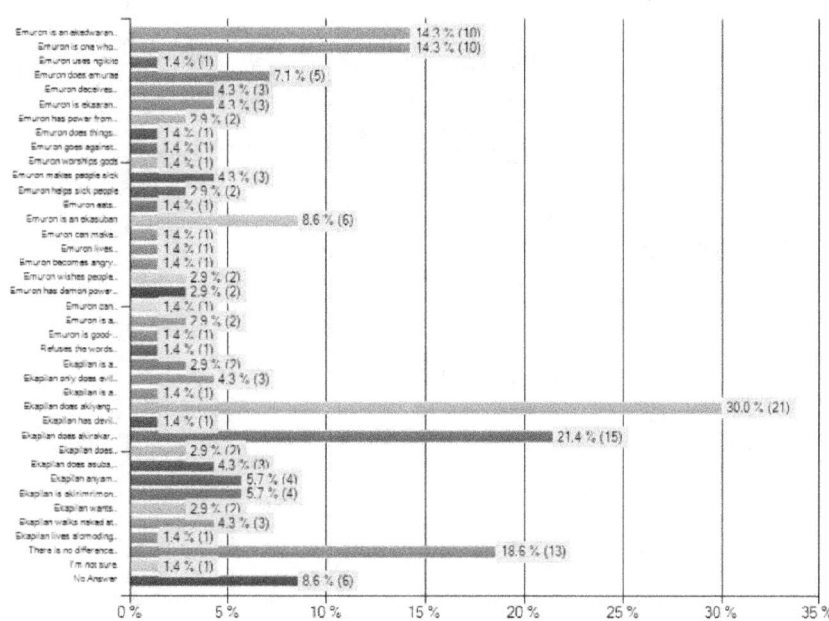

G.C: Graphs of Key Survey Responses

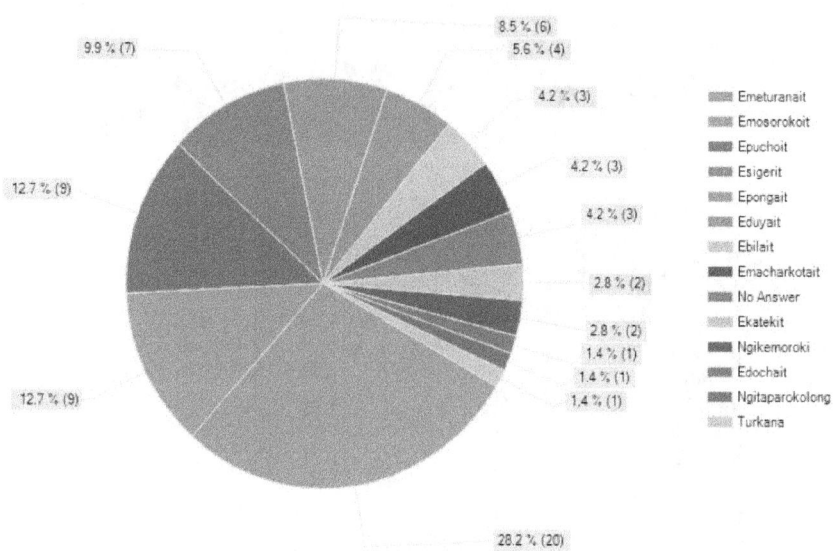

What is your clan (emachar) name?

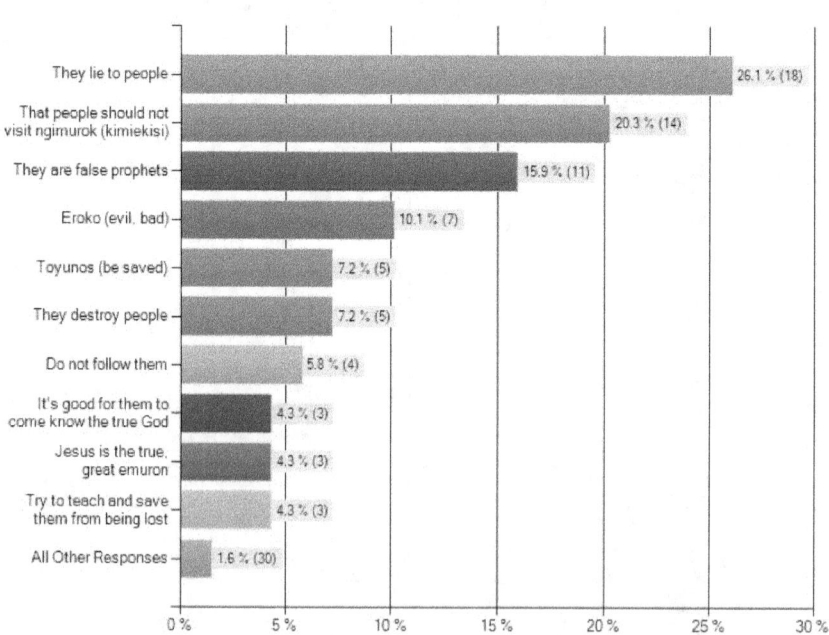

What does your church teach about the ngimurok?

G.C: *Graphs of Key Survey Responses* 257

What are the BAD things the ngimurok have done in your area in the past and now?

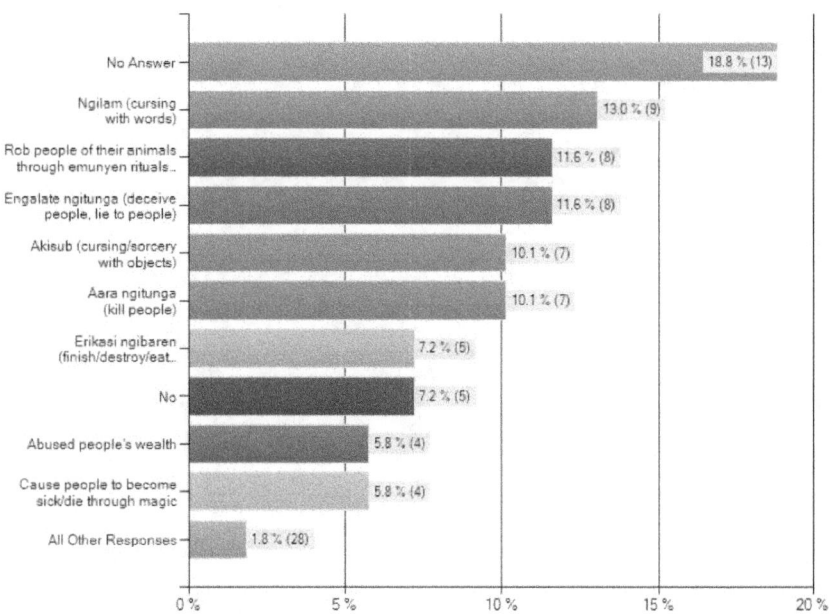

After becoming a Christian, how many times did you visit an emuron on your own or with family members?

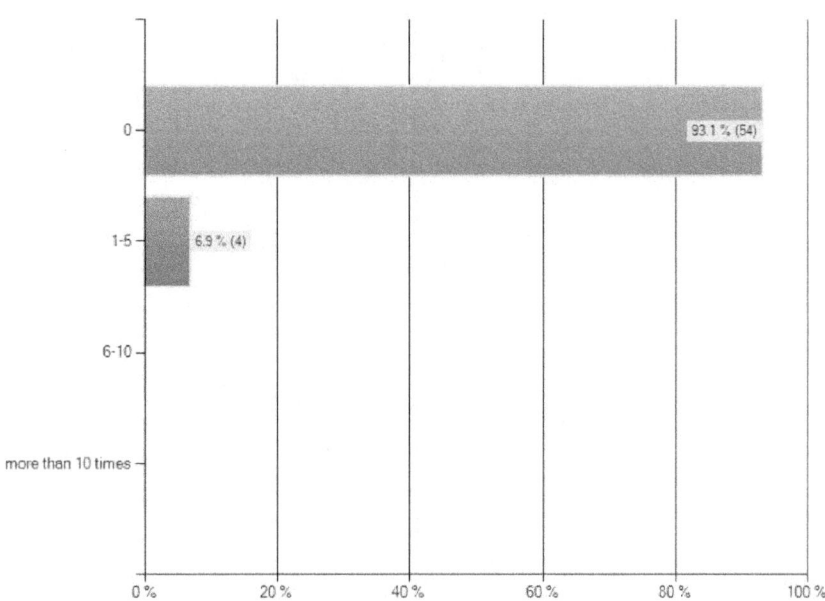

Bibliography

Amach, Daniel. "An Evaluation of Churches and Church Based Organizations Roles in Enhancing Food Security in Turkana District." MA thesis, Africa Nazarene University, 2009.
Anderson, David. *The Poor Are Not Us: Poverty & Pastoralism in Eastern Africa.* Eastern African Studies. Athens: Ohio University Press, 1999.
Anderson, David, and Douglas Johnson, eds. *Revealing Prophets: Prophecy in Eastern African History.* Eastern African Studies. Athens: Ohio University Press, 1995.
Anderson, Dick, and Betty McKay. *Team for Turkana.* London: Africa Inland Mission, 1967.
Arid Lands Resource Management Project II. "Drought Monitoring Bulletin, April 2011: Turkana County." Government of Kenya, 2011.
Balzer, Marjorie Mandelstam. *Shamans, Spirituality, and Cultural Revitalization: Explorations in Siberia and Beyond.* New York: Palgrave Macmillan, 2011.
Barrett, Anthony J. *Dying and Death among the Turkana: Part I.* Spearhead 97. Eldoret, Kenya: Gaba, 1987.
———. *Dying and Death Among the Turkana: Part 2.* Spearhead 97. Eldoret, Kenya: Gaba, 1987.
———. *English-Turkana Dictionary.* London: Macmillan Kenya, 1988.
———. *Incarnating the Church in Turkana.* Eldoret, Kenya: Gaba, 1978.
———. *Sacrifice and Prophecy in Turkana Cosmology.* Nairobi: Paulines Africa, 1998.
———. *Turkana-English Dictionary.* London: Macmillan, 1990.
———. *Turkana Iconography: Desert Nomads and Their Symbols.* Kijabe, Kenya: Kijabe, 1998.
Barua, Archana. *Phenomenology of Religion.* Lanham, MD: Lexington, 2009.
Bediako, Kwame. *Christianity in Africa: The Renewal of a Non-Western Religion.* Maryknoll, NY: Orbis, 1995.
Bernard, H. *Research Methods in Anthropology: Qualitative and Quantitative Approaches.* 4th ed. Lanham, MD: AltaMira, 2006.
Best, Günter. *Culture and Language of the Turkana, NW Kenya.* Heidelberg: Winter Universitätsverlag, 1983.
Bevans, Stephen B. *Models of Contextual Theology.* Faith and Cultures. Maryknoll, NY: Orbis, 2004.

Bianco, Barbara. "Songs of Mobility in West Pokot." *American Ethnologist* 23, no. 1 (1996) 25–42.

Bible Society of Kenya. *Abibilia: Ngakiro Naajokak [Bible: Good News]*. Nairobi: Bible Society of Kenya, 2001.

Biko, Steve. "Towards True Humanity in South Africa." *Ecumenical Review* 30, no. 4 (1978) 355–68.

Boogaard, Rudolf. "Food Insecurity and Entitlements Among Turkana Pastoralists, Northern Kenya." PhD thesis, University of Sussex, 2003.

Bosch, David Jacobus. *Transforming Mission: Paradigm Shifts in Theology of Mission*. American Society of Missiology 16. Maryknoll, NY: Orbis, 1991.

Broch-Due, Vigdis. "The Fertility of Houses and Herds: Producing Kinship and Gender Among Turkana Pastoralists." In *Rethinking Pastoralism in Africa : Gender, Culture & the Myth of the Patriarchal Pastoralist*, by Dorothy Hodgson. Athens: Ohio University Press, 2000.

Bruen, Richard. "*Akipeyos Nachamunet*: A Model for Contextualizing the Lord's Supper Among the Turkana?" MDiv thesis, Emmanuel School of Religion, 2002.

Burnett, David. *World of the Spirits: A Christian Perspective on Traditional and Folk Religions*. Oxford: Monarch, 2005.

Callaway, Henry. *The Religious System of the Amazulu in the Zulu Language with Translation into English and Notes in Four Parts: Part I Unkulunkul; or the Tradition of Creation, Part II Amatonga; or Ancestor Worship, Part III Izinyanga Zokubula; or Divination, Part IV Abatakato; or Medical Magic and Witchcraft*. Cape Town: C. Struik, 1970.

Cannell, Fenella. *The Anthropology of Christianity*. Durham, NC: Duke University Press, 2006.

Caukwell, R. A. "The South Turkana Expedition: Scientific Papers VI Field Survey in South Turkana." *The Geographical Journal* 137, no. 2 (1971) 157–64.

Cavendish, H. S. H. "Through Somaliland and around and South of Lake Rudolf." *The Geographical Journal* 11, no. 4 (1898) 372–93.

Cavendish, Richard. *A History of Magic*. New York: Taplinger, 1977.

Chalk, Frank Robert, and Kurt Jonassohn. *The History and Sociology of Genocide: Analyses and Case Studies*. New Haven: Yale University Press, 1990.

Collins, Robert O. "The Turkana Patrol of 1918 Reconsidered." *Ethnohistory* 53, no. 1 (2006) 95–119.

Cragg, Kenneth. *The Call of the Minaret*. New York: Oxford University Press, 1956.

Crane, Julia, and Michael Angrosino. *Field Projects in Anthropology: A Student Handbook*. 3rd ed. Prospects Heights, IL: Waveland, 1992.

Creswell, John. *Qualitative Inquiry & Research Design: Choosing Among Five Approaches*. 2nd ed. Thousand Oaks, CA: Sage, 2007.

Curry, Patrick. *Divination: Perspectives for a New Millennium*. Burlington, VT: Ashgate, 2010.

Dahl, Espen. *Phenomenology and the Holy: Religious Experience After Husserl*. London: SCM, 2010.

Davis, Raymond. "Church Growth and Culture Change in Turkana: A Study of the African Inland Church among Kenya's Turkana People." MA thesis, Fuller Theological Seminary, 1978.

DeLuca, Shauna. "Fluid Intake among the Turkana Pastoralists in a Semi-Arid Environment." MA thesis Colorado State University, 2006.

Devisch, René. "Yaka Divination: Acting Out He Memory of Society's Life-Spring." In *Divination and Healing: Potent Vision*, edited by Philip M Peek and Michael Winkelman, 243–63. Tucson: University of Arizona Press, 2004.
Dimmendaal, Gerrit. *The Turkana Language*. Dordrecht: Foris, 1983.
Douglas, Mary. *Natural Symbols: Explorations in Cosmology*. New York: Pantheon, 1970.
Dyer, Caroline. *The Education of Nomadic Peoples: Current Issues, Future Prospects*. New York: Berghahn, 2006.
Dyrness, William. *Learning About Theology from the Third World*. Grand Rapids: Academie, 1990.
Eliade, Mircea. *Myth and Reality*. New York: Harper & Row, 1963.
———. *Occultism, Witchcraft, and Cultural Fashions: Essays in Comparative Religions*. Chicago: University of Chicago Press, 1976.
Eliade, Mircea, Ioan P Culianu, and Hillary S Wiesner. *The Eliade Guide to World Religions*. San Francisco: Harper, 1991.
Eliade, Mircea, and Willard R Trask. *Shamanism: Archaic Techniques of Ecstasy*. New York: Pantheon, 1964.
Emanikor, Isaya. *Abibilia Ngakiro Naajokak*. Nairobi: Bible Society of Kenya, 2001.
Eriksen, Thomas Hylland. *Ethnicity and Nationalism: Anthropological Perspectives*. 2nd ed. London: Pluto, 2002.
Evans-Pritchard, E. *The Nuer, a Description of the Modes of Livelihood and Political Institutions of a Nilotic People*. Oxford: Clarendon, 1940.
———. *Theories of Primitive Religion*. Oxford: Clarendon, 1987.
———. *Witchcraft, Oracles and Magic among the Azande*. Oxford: Clarendon, 1937.
Farquhar, J. N. *The Crown of Hinduism*. Oxford: Oxford University Press, 1930.
Feldmeier, Peter. *Encounters in Faith: Christianity in Interreligious Dialogue*. Winona, MN: Anselm Academic, 2011.
Fratkin, Elliot M. Roth. *African Pastoralist Systems: An Integrated Approach*. Boulder, CO: Rienner, 1994.
Frazer, James. *The Golden Bough*. London: Macmillan, 1890.
Friesen, J. Stanley. *Missionary Responses to Tribal Religions at Edinburgh, 1910*. New York: Lang, 1996.
Geertz, Clifford. *Available Light: Anthropological Reflections on Philosophical Topics*. Princeton, NJ: Princeton University Press, 2000.
———. "'From the Native's Point of View': On the Nature of Anthropological Understanding." In *Local Knowledge: Further Essays in Interpretive Anthropology*, 28:55–70. New York: Basic, 1983.
———. *The Interpretation of Cultures: Selected Essays*. New York: Basic, 1973.
———. "Shifting Aims, Moving Targets: On the Anthropology of Religion." *Journal of the Royal Anthropological Institute* 11, no. 1 (2005) 1–15.
Giles, David. "The Folk Religion of the Turkana." Unpublished paper. Fuller Theological Seminary, 1985.
Githieya, Francis Kimani. *The Freedom of the Spirit: African Indigenous Churches in Kenya*. Atlanta: Scholars, 1997.
Gray, Sandra, et al. "Cattle Raiding, Cultural Survival, and Adaptability of East African Pastoralists." *Current Anthropology* 44 (2003) S3–S30.
Grenham, Thomas. *The Unknown God: Religious and Theological Interculturation*. Religions and Discourse 25. New York: Lang, 2005.

Gulliver, P. H. *The Family Herds; a Study of Two Pastoral Tribes in East Africa, the Jie and Turkana*. International Library of Sociology and Social Reconstruction. London: Routledge, 1955.

———. *A Preliminary Survey of the Turkana, a Report Compiled for the Government of Kenya*. Cape Town: University of Cape Town, School of African Studies, 1951.

———. "The Turkana Age Organization." *American Anthropologist* NS 60, no. 5 (1958) 900–922.

Gulliver, Pamela, and P. H. Gulliver. *The Central Nilo-Hamites*. Ethnographic Survey of Africa: East Central Africa 7. London: International African Institute, 1968.

Gwynne, M. D., and W. T. W. Morgan. *A Bibliography of Turkana*. Nairobi: Royal Geographical Society South Turkana Expedition, 1969.

Harvey, Graham. *Animism: Respecting the Living World*. New York: Columbia University Press, 2006.

———. *Indigenous Religions: A Companion*. New York: Cassell, 2000.

———. *Religions in Focus: New Approaches to Tradition and Contemporary Practices*. Oakville, CT: Equinox, 2009.

Harvey, Graham, ed. *Shamanism: A Reader*. Routledge, 2003.

Hedges, Paul. *Preparation and Fulfilment: A History and Study of Fulfilment Theology in Modern British Thought in the Indian Context*. Studies in the Intercultural History of Christianity 124. Frankfurt: Lang, 2001.

Heidegger, Martin. *The Phenomenology of Religious Life*. Translated by Matthias Fritsch and Jennifer Anna Gosetti-Ferencei. Studies in Continental Thought. Bloomington: Indiana University Press, 2004.

Heimlich, Evan. "Darwin's Fortune, Jonah's Shipmates and the Persistance of Chance." In *Divination: Perspectives for a New Millenium*, edited by Patrick Curry, 143–77. Burlington, VT: Ashgate, 2010.

Hendrickson, Dylan, Jeremy Armon, and Robin Mearns. "The Changing Nature of Conflict and Famine Vulnerability: The Case of Livestock Raiding in Turkana District, Kenya." *Disasters* 22, no. 3 (1998) 185.

Herskovits, Melville J. "The Cattle Complex in East Africa, Part 1 of 2." *American Anthropologist* NS 28, no. 1 (1926) 230–72.

Heusch, Luc de. *Sacrifice in Africa: A Structuralist Approach*. Bloomington: Indiana University Press, 1985.

Hexham, Irving. *Understanding World Religions*. Grand Rapids: Zondervan, 2011.

Hiebert, Paul G. "Critical Contextualization." *International Bulletin of Missionary Research* 11, no. 3 (1987) 104–12.

Hiebert, Paul G., and Tite Tiénou. "Missional Theology." In *The Gospel in Human Contexts*, by Paul G. Hiebert, 36–57. Grand Rapids: Baker Academic, 2009.

Hiebert, Paul G., Tite Tiénou, and R. Daniel Shaw. *Understanding Folk Religion: A Christian Response to Popular Beliefs and Practices*. Grand Rapids: Baker, 1999.

Hodgson, Dorothy. *Rethinking Pastoralism in Africa: Gender, Culture & the Myth of the Patriarchal Pastoralist*. Athens: Ohio University Press, 2000.

Höhnel, Ludwig von. *Discovery of Lakes Rudolf and Stephanie a Narrative of Count Samuel Teleki's Exploring & Hunting Expedition in Eastern Equatorial Africa in 1887 & 1888*. London: Longmans, Green, 1894.

———. "The Lake Rudolf Region Its Discovery and Subsequent Exploration, 1888-1909. Part I." *Journal of the Royal African Society* 37, no. 146 (1938) 21–45.

Homewood, Katherine. *Ecology of African Pastoralist Societies*. Athens: Ohio University Press, 2008.
Horton, Robin. *Patterns of Thought in Africa and the West: Essays on Magic, Religion, and Science*. Cambridge University Press, 1993.
Howell, Brian M. "The Repugnant Cultural Other Speaks Back: Christian Identity as Ethnographic 'Standpoint.'" *Anthropological Theory* 7, no. 4 (2007) 371–91.
Husserl, Edmund. *Ideas: General Introduction to Pure Phenomenology*. New York: Humanities, 1967.
Hutchinson, John, and Anthony D. Smith, eds. *Ethnicity*. Oxford University Press, 1996.
Idowu, E. Bolaji. *African Traditional Religion: A Definition*. Maryknoll, NY: Orbis, 1973.
Isichei, Elizabeth A. *A History of Christianity in Africa: From Antiquity to the Present*. Grand Rapids: Eerdmans, 1995.
———. *The Religious Traditions of Africa: A History*. Westport, CT: Praeger, 2004.
———. *Voices of the Poor in Africa*. Rochester, NY: University of Rochester Press, 2002.
Itaru Ohta. "Coexisting with Cultural 'Others': Social Relationships between the Turkana and the Refugees at Kakuma, Northwest Kenya." In *Pastoralists and Their Neighbors in Asia and Africa*, edited by Elliot Fratkin and Kazunobu Ikeya, 227–41. Osaka: National Museum of Ethnology, 2005.
Jagt, Krijn Adriaan van der. *Symbolic Structures in Turkana Religion*. Assen/Maastricht, the Netherlands: Van Gorcum, 1989.
Jónsson, Kjartan. "Pokot Masculinity: The Role of Rituals in Forming Men." Reykjavík, Iceland: University of Iceland, Faculty of Social Sciences, 2006.
Juma, Richard Otieno. "Turkana Livelihood Strategies and Adaptation to Drought in Kenya." PhD diss., Victoria University of Wellington, 2009.
Kalu, Ogbu, and Alaine Low, ed. *Interpreting Contemporary Christianity: Global Processes and Local Identities*. Studies in the History of Christian Missions. Grand Rapids: Eerdmans, 2008.
Kärkkäinen, Veli-Matti. *An Introduction to the Theology of Religions: Biblical, Historical, and Contemporary Perspectives*. Downers Grove, IL: InterVarsity, 2003.
Kirwen, Michael. *African Cultural Knowledge: Themes and Embedded Beliefs*. Nairobi: MIAS, 2005.
———. *The Missionary and the Diviner: Contending Theologies of Christian and African Religions*. Maryknoll, NY: Orbis, 1987.
Klauck, Hans-Josef. *Magic and Paganism in Early Christianity: The World of the Acts of the Apostles*. Minneapolis: Fortress, 2003.
Knighton, Ben. *The Vitality of Karamojong Religion: Dying Tradition or Living Faith?* Burlington, VT: Ashgate, 2003.
Knitter, Paul F. *Introducing Theologies of Religions*. Maryknoll, NY: Orbis, 2002.
Kraemer, H. Hendrik. *The Christian Message in a Non-Christian World*. 3rd ed. Grand Rapids: Kregel, 1963.
Kraft, Charles. *Appropriate Christianity*. Pasadena, CA: William Carey Library, 2005.
Kuper, A. *The Reinvention of Primitive Society: Transformations of a Myth*. 2nd ed. New York: Routledge, 2005.
Lambek, Michael. *A Reader in the Anthropology of Religion*. Malden, MA: Blackwell, 2002.
Lamphear, John. "Aspects of 'Becoming Turkana.'" In *Being Maasai: Ethnicity and Identity in East Africa*, edited by Thomas T Spear and Richard Waller, 87–104. Athens: Ohio University Press, 1993.

———. "Aspects of Turkana Leadership During the Era of Primary Resistance." *The Journal of African History* 17, no. 2 (1976) 225–43.
———. "Review: Complex Cattle." *The Journal of African History* 35, no. 1 (1994) 136–38.
———. *The Scattering Time: Turkana Responses to Colonial Rule*. Oxford Studies in African Affairs. New York: Oxford University Press, 1992.
Leslie, Paul W. *Turkana Herders of the Dry Savanna: Ecology and Biobehavioral Response of Nomads to an Uncertain Environment*. Research Monographs on Human Population Biology. New York: Oxford University Press, 1999.
Lévi-Strauss, Claude. *Structural Anthropology*. New York: Basic, 1963.
Lienhardt, R. G. *Divinity and Experience; the Religion of the Dinka*. Oxford: Clarendon, 1961.
Lines, Kevin P. "The Continued Importance of a Mission Moratorium." MAR thesis, Emmanuel Christian Seminary, 1998.
———. "Exegetical and Extispicic Readings of the Bible in Turkana, Kenya and North America." *The Asbury Journal* 66, no. 1 (2011) 65–94.
———. "Neoliberal Witches, Christian Diviners, and Neocolonial Big Men: Globalized African Interpretations of Missionary Identity." A paper presented to the EMS, Feb 26, 2011.
Lokuruka, Michael N. I., and Pauline A. Lokuruka. "Ramifications of the 1918 Turkana Patrol: Narratives by Ngturkana." *Ethnohistory* 53, no. 1 (2006) 121–41.
Lokuruka, Pauline. "Constraints Facing the Development of Girl-Child Education in the Nomadic Pastoral Communities in Kenya: A Case of Turkana of Northwestern Kenya". MPS(ID) thesis, Cornell University, 2003.
Ludwig von Höhnel. "The Lake Rudolf Region: Its Discovery and Subsequent Exploration, 1888-1909. Part II." *Journal of the Royal African Society* 37, no. 147 (1938) 206–26.
MacCabe, Robert. *Desert Nomads: A Study of the Pattern of Health and Disease of the Turkana People of North Western Kenya*. Dublin: Irish Carmelites, 2009.
MacDougall, David. *Lorang's Way a Turkana Man*. DVD. Berkeley Media, 2004.
———. *The Wedding Camels a Turkana Marriage*. DVD. Berkeley Media, 2004.
———. *A Wife Among Wives*. DVD. Berkley Media, 2004.
Magesa, Laurenti. *African Religion: The Moral Traditions of Abundant Life*. Maryknoll, NY: Orbis, 1997.
———. *What is Not Sacred? African Spirituality*. Maryknoll, NY: Orbis, 2013.
Maurice, F. D. *The Religions of the World and Their Relations to Christianity*. 3rd rev. ed. Cambridge: Macmillan, 1852.
Mbiti, John. *African Religions and Philosophy: Second Edition*. 2nd rev. and enl. ed. Portsmouth, NH: Heinemann, 1990.
Mburu, Nene. *Ilemi Triangle: Unfixed Bandit Frontier Claimed by Sudan, Kenya and Ethiopia*. Dagenham, Issex: Vita House, 2007.
Mbwambo, Zakaria, Paul Erasto, Ramadhani Nondo, Esther Innocent, and Abdul Kidukuli. "Antibacterial and Cytotoxic Activities of *Terminalia stenostachya* and *Terminalia spinosa*." *Tanzania Journal of Health Research* 13, no. 2 (2011) 1–8.
McCabe, J. Terrence. *Cattle Bring Us to Our Enemies: Turkana Ecology, Politics, and Raiding in a Disequilibrium System*. Human-Environment Interactions. Ann Arbor: University of Michigan Press, 2004.

———. "Impact of and Response to Drought Among Turkana Pastoralists: Implications for Anthropological Theory and Hazards Research." In *Catastrophe & Culture: The Anthropology of Disaster*, edited by Susanna Hoffman, 213–36. Santa Fe, NM: School of American Research Press, 2002.
McGeehan, Keri. "Understanding the Inter-Dependencies Between the Turkana and Kakuma Refugess Prospective Impaact of Repatriation." MPS(ID) thesis, Cornell University, 2007.
Middleton, John. *Magic, Witchcraft, and Curing*. Published for the American Museum of Natural History. New York: Natural History, 1967.
Mirzeler, Mustafa. *Lake Rudolf (Turkana) as Colonial Icon in East Africa*. Durham, NC: Duke University Press, 2006.
Monier-Williams, Monier. *Modern India and the Indians Being a Series of Impressions, Notes, and Essays*. 3rd ed. London: Trübner, 1879.
Moon, W. Jay. *African Proverbs Reveal Christianity in Culture: A Narrative Portrayal of Builsa Proverbs Contextualizing Christianity in Ghana*. American Society of Missiology 5. Eugene, OR: Pickwick, 2009.
Morgan, W. T. W. "Ethnobotany of the Turkana: Use of Plants by a Pastoral People and Their Livestock in Kenya." *Economic Botany* 35, no. 1 (1981) 96–130.
Morris, Brian. *Religion and Anthropology: A Critical Introduction*. New York: Cambridge University Press, 2006.
Moustakas, Clark. *Phenomenological Research Methods*. Thousand Oaks, CA: Sage, 1994.
Muck, Terry C. *How to Study Religion: A Beginning Guide to Method*. Wilmore, KY: Wood Hill, 2005.
Muck, Terry C, and Francis S. Adeney. *Christianity Encountering World Religions: The Practice of Mission in the Twenty-First Century*. Grand Rapids: Baker Academic, 2009.
Mugambi, J. N. Kanyua, and Mary N. Getui. *Religions in Eastern Africa under Globalization*. Nairobi, Kenya: Acton, 2004.
Müller, F Max. *Natural Religion*. London; New York: Longmans, Green, 1889.
Müller, Harald. *Changing Generations: Dynamics of Generation and Age-Sets in Southeastern Sudan (Toposa) and Northwestern Kenya (Turkana)*. Saarbrücken: Breitenbach, 1989.
Muriithi, Karambu. "Ethno-Botanical Uses and Phytochemical Analysis of Cyperus Articulatus." Rise AFNNET Workshop, 2012.
Narby, Jeremy, and Francis Huxley, ed. *Shamans through Time: 500 Years on the Path to Knowledge*. New York: Tarcher, 2001.
Newbigin, Lesslie. *The Open Secret: An Introduction to the Theology of Mission*. Rev. ed. Grand Rapids: Eerdmans, 1995.
Ngeiywa, Benson, and Naval Postgraduate School (U.S.). "Deterring Cross-Border Conflict in the Horn of Africa a Case Study of Kenya-Uganda Border." MS Defense Analysis, Monterey, CA: Naval Postgraduate School, 2008.
Ngugi, K., and R. Maswili. "Phenotypic Diversity in Sorghum Landraces from Kenya." *African Crop Science Journal* 18, no. 4 (2010) 165–73.
Nhema, Alfred G, and Tiyambe Zeleza. *The Roots of African Conflicts: The Causes & Costs*. Athens: Ohio University Press, 2008.

Norris, Frederick A. "God and the Gods: Expect Footprints." *Unto the Uttermost: Missions in the Christian Churches/Churches of Christ*, edited by Doug Priest, 55–69. Pasadena, CA: William Carey Library, 1984.

O'Dempsey, T. J. "Traditional Belief and Practice Among the Pokot People of Kenya with Particular Reference to Mother and Child Health." *Annals of Tropical Paediatrics* 8, no. 2 (1988) 49–60.

Ogembo, Justus. *Contemporary Witch-Hunting in Gusii, Southwestern Kenya*. Lewiston, NY: Mellen, 2006.

Ohta, Itaru. *Bridewealth Negotiations among the Turkana in Northwestern Kenya*. Kyoto: Center for African Area Studies, Kyoto University, 2007.

Ott, Craig, and Harold Netland. *Globalizing Theology: Belief and Practice in an Era of World Christianity*. Grand Rapids: Baker Academic, 2006.

Owiti, John. "Local Knowledge Of, and Responses to HIV-1 Aids Among the Turkana of Lodwar Township." PhD diss., Montréal: McGill University, 2007.

Paden, William E. *Religious Worlds: The Comparative Study of Religion*. Boston: Beacon, 1994.

Peek, Philip M. *African Divination Systems: Ways of Knowing*. African Systems of Thought. Bloomington: Indiana University Press, 1991.

Peristiany, J. G. "The Age-Set System of the Pastoral Pokot: The 'Sapana' Initiation Ceremony." *Africa: Journal of the International African Institute* 21, no. 3 (1951) 188–206.

Peterson, Eugene H. *Under the Unpredictable Plant: An Exploration in Vocational Holiness*. Grand Rapids: Eerdmans, 1994.

Pierli, Francesco. *The Pastoralists: A Challenge to Churches, State, Civil Society*. Nairobi: Paulines Africa, 2006.

Pkalya, Ruto, and Intermediate Technology Development Group. *Indigenous Democracy: Traditional Conflict Resolution Mechanisms: Pokot, Turkana, Samburu, and Marakwet*. Nairobi: Intermediate Technology Development Group, Eastern Africa, 2004.

Popelka-Filcoff, et al. "Trace Element Characterization of Ochre from Geological Sources." *Journal of Radioanalytical and Nuclear Chemistry* 272, no. 1 (2007) 17–27.

Powdermaker, Hortense. *Stranger and Friend: The Way of an Anthropologist*. New York: Norton, 1966.

Premawardhana, Shanta. "A Brief Overview of Ecumenical Engagement in Interfaith Relations." 2006. http://nccinterfaith.blogspot.com/2006_02_01_archive.html.

Price, Neil S, ed. *The Archaeology of Shamanism*. New York: Routledge, 2001.

Priest, Robert. "On the Meaning of the Words 'Witch,' 'Witchcraft,' and 'Sorcery.'" A paper presented at the annual meeting of the American Society of Missiology. Chicago, IL. June 15, 2012. http://henrycenter.tiu.edu/2012/05/meaning-of-witch-witchcraft-and-sorcery/. Accessed March 18, 2014.

Race, Alan. *Christians and Religious Pluralism: Patterns in the Christian Theology of Religions*. Maryknoll, NY: Orbis, 1983.

Rahner, Karl. "Christianity and the Non-Christian Religions." In *Christianity and Plurality: Classic and Contemporary Readings*, edited by Richard Plantinga, 288–303. Oxford: Blackwell, 1999.

Richardson, Don. *Eternity in Their Hearts*. Ventura, CA: Regal, 1984.

Robbins, Pat. *Red-Spotted Ox: A Pokot Life*. Copenhagen: International Work Group for Indigenous Affairs, 2010.

Roebroeks, Wil, et al. "Use of Red Ochre by Early Neandertals." *Proceedings of the National Academy of Sciences* 109, no. 6 (2012) 1889–94.

Roller, Dietmar. "The Turkana: Their Cosmology and the Task of Missions: A Theoretical Analysis of the Turkana's Concept of Life and the Resulting Approaches to Mission among the Nilo-Hamites." MA thesis, Columbia Graduate School of Bible and Missions, 1990.

Rosin, H. H. *Missio Dei: An Examination of the Origin, Contents and Function of the Term in Protestant Missiological Discussion*. Leiden: Interuniversity Institute for Missiological and Ecumenical Research, Dept. of Missiology, 1972.

Ruhnau, Bernhardt. "Celebrating Easter Among the Turkana Nomads." *AFER* 22, no. 6 (1980) 386–92.

Sakumichi, Shinsuke. "Coping with Illness in Turkana: A Preliminary Report." *African Study Monographs* 18, nos. 3–4 (1997) 229–40.

Schreiter, Robert J. *Constructing Local Theologies*. Maryknoll, NY: Orbis, 2007.

Schultz, Ulrike. "'One Day, We Will Return Home': Turkana Women Migration and Remigration." In *Women and Migration: Anthropological Perspectives*, edited by Jacqueline Knörr, 164–80. New York: St. Martin's, 2000.

Sharpe, Eric. *Not to Destroy but to Fulfil*. Uppsala: Swedish Institute of Missionary Research, 1965.

Shaw, R. Daniel. "Beyond Contextualization: Toward a 21st Century Model for Enabling Mission." *International Bulletin of Missionary Research* 34, no. 4 (2010) 208–15.

Shorter, Aylward. *Jesus and the Witchdoctor: An Approach to Healing and Wholeness*. Maryknoll, NY: Orbis, 1985.

Siegel, James. *Naming the Witch*. Stanford, CA: Stanford University Press, 2006.

Smith, Anthony. "Chosen Peoples." In *Ethnicity*, edited by John Hutchinson and Anthony D. Smith, 189–97. Oxford University Press, 1996.

Smith, James Howard. *Bewitching Development: Witchcraft and the Reinvention of Development in Neoliberal Kenya*. Chicago: University of Chicago Press, 2008.

Smith, Jonathan, Paul Flowers, and Michael Larkin. *Interpretative Phenomenological Analysis*. Thousand Oaks, CA: Sage, 2009.

Smith, W. C. *Towards a World Theology: Faith and the Comparative History of Religion*. London: Macmillan, 1981.

Somé, Malidoma Patrice. *The Healing Wisdom of Africa: Finding Life Purpose Through Nature, Ritual, and Community*. New York: Putnam, 1998.

———. *Of Water and the Spirit: Ritual, Magic, and Initiation in the Life of an African Shaman*. New York: Putnam, 1994.

Soper, R, and University of Nairobi. *A Socio-Cultural Profile of Turkana District : A Report of the District Socio-Cultural Profiles Project*. Nairobi: Institute of African Studies, University of Nairobi: Ministry of Finance and Planning, 1985.

Spear, Thomas T, and Richard Waller, ed. *Being Maasai: Ethnicity & Identity in East Africa*. Eastern African Studies. Athens: Ohio University Press, 1993.

Spradley, James, and David McCurdy. *The Cultural Experience: Ethnography in Complex Society*. 2nd ed. Long Grove, IL: Waveland, 2005.

Stanley, Brian. "Conversion to Christianity: The Colonization of the Mind?" *International Review of Mission* 92, no. 366 (2003) 315–31.

Stav, Jorn, Gufu Oba, Inger Nordal, and Nils Chr. Stenseth. "Traditional Ecological Knowledge of a Riverine Forest in Turkana, Kenya: Inplications for Research and Management." *Biodiversity: Journal of Life on Earth* 16, no. 5 (2007) 1471–89.

Stroeken, Koen. *Moral Power: The Magic of Witchcraft*. New York: Berghahn, 2010.

Taber, Charles R. "Contextualization." *Religious Studies Review* 13, no. 1 (1987) 33–36.

Tagliaferri, Christine. "The Impact of Nutrition and Animal Exposure on the Specific Health Complaints of Settled and Nomadic Turkana." MS Anthropology thesis, University of Wisconsin, 2008.

Taylor, John V. *The Primal Vision: Christian Presence and African Religion*. London: SCM, 1963.

Tennent, Timothy C. "The Challenge of Churchless Christianity: An Evangelical Assessment." *International Bulletin of Missionary Research* 29, no. 4 (2005) 171–77.

———. *Christianity at the Religious Roundtable: Evangelicalism in Conversation with Hinduism, Buddhism, and Islam*. Grand Rapids: Baker Academic, 2002.

———. *Invitation to World Missions: A Trinitarian Missiology for the Twenty-First Century*. Grand Rapids: Kregel, 2010.

———. *Theology in the Context of World Christianity: How the Global Church Is Influencing the Way We Think about and Discuss Theology*. Grand Rapids: Zondervan, 2007.

Thomas, M. M. "The Absoluteness of Jesus Christ and Christ-Centered Syncretism." *Ecumenical Review* 37, no. 4 (1985) 387.

Tiénou, Tite. "The Invention of the 'Primitive' and Stereotypes in Mission." *Missiology* 19, no. 3 (1991) 295–303.

Tingle, William. "The Relationship of Evangelism to Development in Working with a Tribal People, with Primary Emphasis Upon the Turkana People of Kenya." MDiv thesis, Emmanuel School of Religion, 1982.

Turner, Victor W. *The Drums of Affliction: A Study of Religious Processes among the Ndembu of Zambia*. Oxford: Clarendon, 1968.

———. *The Forest of Symbols Aspects of Ndembu Ritual*. Ithaca, NY: Cornell University Press, 1967.

———. *The Ritual Process: Structure and Anti-Structure*. The Lewis Henry Morgan Lectures 1966. New York: de Gruyter, 1995.

Twesigye, Emmanuel K. *Religion, Politics, and Cults in East Africa: God's Warriors and Mary's Saints*. New York: Lang, 2010.

Tylor, Edward. *Religion in Primitive Culture* [orig. published as chaps. 11–19 of *Primitive Culture*, 1871]. New York: Harper, 1958.

Van Engen, Charles E. *Mission On the Way: Issues in Mission Theology*. Grand Rapids: Baker Academic, 1996.

Van Rheenen, Gailyn. *Communicating Christ in Animistic Contexts*. Grand Rapids: Baker, 1991.

Vatican II. "*Lumen Gentium*: Dogmatic Constitution on the Church." 1964. http://www.vatican.va/archive/hist_councils/ii_vatican_council/documents/vat-ii_const_19641121_lumen-gentium_en.html.

Vermi, Mario. *Turkana Dictionary: Turkana-English and English-Turkana*. Mayuku, Kenya: Bosco, 2006.

Vicedom, Georg. *The Mission of God: An Introduction to a Theology of Mission*. St. Louis: Concordia, 1965.

Waller, Richard. "Kidongoi's Kin: Prophecy and Power in Maasailand." In *Revealing Prophets: Prophecy in East African History*, edited by David Anderson and Douglas Johnson. Athens: Ohio University Press, 1995.

Walls, Andrew F. *The Cross-Cultural Process in Christian History: Studies in the Transmission and Appropriation of Faith*. Maryknoll, NY: Orbis, 2002.

Ward, Keith. *Religion and Revelation: A Theology of Revelation in the World's Religions*. New York: Oxford University Press, 1994.

Watts, Ian. "Red Ochre, Body Painting, and Language: Interpreting the Blombos Ochre." In *The Cradle of Language*, edited by Rudolf Botha and Chris Knight, 62–92. New York: Oxford University Press, 2009.

Wawire, Violet. *Gender and the Social and Economic Impact of Drought on the Residents of Turkana District in Kenya*. Addis Ababa: OSSREA, 2003.

Weber, Max. *Max Weber on the Methodology of the Social Sciences*. Glencoe, IL: Free, 2011.

White, Major R. F. "Notes on the Turkana Tribe." In *Sudan Notes and Records*, 3:217–22. 1920. Repr., Liechtenstein: Kraus-Thompson, 1975.

Whitehouse, Harvey. *Religion, Anthropology, and Cognitive Science*. Durham, NC: Carolina Academic, 2007.

Wijsen, Frans Jozef Servaas. *Seeds of Conflict in a Haven of Peace: From Religious Studies to Interreligious Studies in Africa*. Studies in World Christianity and Interreligious Relations 44. New York: Rodopi, 2007.

Williams, Rowland. *A Dialogue of the Knowledge of the Supreme Lord, in Which Are Compared the Claims of Christianity and Hinduism, and Various Questions of Indian Religion and Literature Fairly Discussed*. Cambridge: Bell, 1856.

Winkelman, Michael, and Philip M Peek. *Divination and Healing: Potent Vision*. Tucson: University of Arizona Press, 2004.

Winzeler, Robert. *Anthropology and Religion: What We Know, Think, and Question*. Lanham, MD: AltaMira, 2008.

Wolcott, Harry. *Ethnography: A Way of Seeing*. 2nd ed. Lanham, MD: Altamira, 2008.

World Council of Churches. "Ecumenical Considerations for Dialogue and Relations with People of Other Religions." *World Council of Churches*. 2004. http://www.oikoumene.org/en/resources/documents/wcc-programmes/interreligious-dialogue-and-cooperation/interreligious-trust-and-respect/ecumenical-considerations-for-dialogue-and-relations-with-people-of-other-religions.html.

Zahniser, A. H. Mathias. *Symbol and Ceremony: Making Disciples across Cultures*. Monrovia, CA: MARC, 1997.

Znamenski, Andrei A. *Shamanism: Critical Concepts in Sociology*. Vol. 2. New York: Routledge, 2004.

www.ingramcontent.com/pod-product-compliance
Lightning Source LLC
Chambersburg PA
CBHW070241230426
43664CB00014B/2374